About the author

Egyptian novelist, doctor and militant writer on Arab women's problems and their struggle for liberation, Nawal el Saadawi was born in the village of Kafr Tahla. Refusing to accept the limitations imposed by both religious and colonial oppression on most women of rural origin, she qualified as a doctor in 1955 and rose to become Egypt's Director of Public Health. Since she began to write over 30 years ago, her books have concentrated on women. In 1972, her first work of non fiction, *Women and Sex*, evoked the antagonism of highly placed political and theological authorities, and the Ministry of Health was pressurised into dismissing her. Under similar pressures she lost her post as Chief Editor of a health journal and as Assistant General Secretary in the Medical Association in Egypt. From 1973 to 1976 she worked on researching women and neurosis in the Ain Shams University's Faculty of Medicine; and from 1979 to 1980 she was the United Nations Advisor for the Women's Programme in Africa (ECA) and Middle East (ECWA). Later in 1980, as a culmination of the long war she had fought for Egyptian women's social and intellectual freedom, an activity that had closed all avenues of official jobs to her, she was imprisoned under the Sadat regime. She has since founded the Arab Women's Solidarity Association and devoted her time to being a writer, journalist and worldwide speaker on women's issues.

With the publication by Zed Books in 1980 of *The Hidden Face of Eve: Women in the Arab World*, English language readers were first introduced to the work of this major writer. Zed Books has also published four of her previous novels, *Woman at Point Zero* (1983), *God Dies by the Nile* (1985), *The Circling Song* (1989) and *Searching* (1991). Nawal El Saadawi has received three literary awards.

The Nawal El Saadawi Reader

Zed Books
LONDON AND NEW YORK

The Nawal El Saadawi Reader was first published by Zed Books
Ltd, 7 Cynthia Street, London N1 9JF, UK, and Room 400,
175 Fifth Avenue, New York, NY 10010, USA, in 1997.

Distributed exclusively in the USA by St Martin's Press, Inc.,
175 Fifth Avenue, New York, NY 10010, USA.

Cover designed by Andrew Corbett
Set in Monotype Dante by Ewan Smith
Printed and bound in the United Kingdom
by Biddles Ltd, Guildford and King's Lynn

Library of Congress Cataloging-in-Publication Data

Saʿdāwī, Nawāl.
    The Nawal El Saadawi reader / Nawal El Saadawi
        p. cm.
    Includes bibliographical references and index.
    ISBN 1-85649-513-2 (hb). — ISBN 1-85649-514-0 (pb)
      1. Women—Arab countries—Social conditions. 2. Women
in Islam.   3. Women in politics—Developing countries.
4. Women in politics—Arab countries.   5. Women in
politics.   6. Women—Social conditions.   I. Title.
HQ1784.S19   1997
305.42'0917'4927—dc21   97–25250
                                      CIP

A catalogue record for this work is available from the British
Library

ISBN 1 85649 513 2 hb
ISBN 1 85649 514 0 pb

To women and men who choose to pay the price and be free rather than continue to pay the price of slavery

Contents

Acknowledgements

'Women and Islam' is reprinted from *Women's Studies International Forum*, Vol. 5, No. 2, pp. 193–206, 1982, by permission of Elsevier Science Ltd, Oxford, England. Copyright © Nawal El Saadawi, 1982.

'Dissidence and Creativity' is reprinted from *Women: A Cultural Review*, Vol. 6, No. 1, pp. 1–17, by permission of Oxford University Press. Copyright © Oxford University Press, 1995.

'The Bitter Lot of Women' is reprinted from 'The Bitter Lot of Women' by Nawal El Saadawi, *Freedom Review*, Vol. 25, Issue 3, pp. 22–4, by permission of Transaction Publishers. Copyright © Nawal El Saadawi, 1994.

Introduction

My mother told me that I was a quiet child, that I spent hours alone humming tunes to myself before I could even speak. Once I learned to speak, I started asking those questions that parents do not answer, such as 'Where did I come from?' or 'Where did my dead grandfather go?' and 'Why does my older brother enjoy more freedom and privileges than I do?'

Once I learned to read and write, I started writing stories for myself in which the protagonists were my mother, my father, and my eight brothers and sisters. I used to take a pencil and sketch the faces of the members of my family. I felt a strong desire to draw portraits of people around me. I also had a strong urge to express my moods through my writings, and to register the events I witnessed in a way that reflected my thinking and my views of them.

My mother was a woman of great intellectual ambition, which was aborted when her father took her out of school at the age of seventeen to marry my father. And though her married life was relatively happy, she yearned for her old dream of being a woman of importance, intellectually or scientifically.

I have probably inherited from my mother this ambition. When I was a child, I used to hear her repeat that she would have loved to visit the whole world by plane, or that she would have wanted to be a scientist like Madame Curie, or an accomplished pianist, or a poet, painter or surgeon.

I never heard my mother praise marriage as an institution even though my father was in her view an ideal husband. She was very perceptive and considered my father a rarity among men. She witnessed the life of her mother and father, and she lived the sadness and misery of her mother, whose husband imprisoned her in the house. My mother hated marriage because her own mother hated marriage and cursed marriage as a cemetery for women.

So as a child I hated marriage and I never dreamed of myself in a wedding dress. Instead I dreamed that I was a physician, a creative writer, an actress, a poet, a concert musician, or a dancer.

*

When I graduated from medical school in 1955 at the age of twenty-four, I was a very young woman, extremely idealistic, daydreaming that I would live in a poor, sick village where I would treat everybody without ever charging them, where I would never be afraid of contagion, where I would work day and night until I died of a contagious disease.

I was very influenced by these persistent dreams which were enriched by all the novels that I read. No wonder then that I started practising medicine in the country. But after a few years I realized that the diseases of the peasants could only be cured by curing poverty. From this point on, I realized that writing was a stronger weapon than medicine in the fight against poverty and ignorance.

I started by writing poetry. Then I wrote short stories, novels and plays. Writing was a release for my anger. What angered me most was oppression: oppression of women and oppression of the poor. I used to write about love. Love that was nonexistent in the relations between men and women. I used to praise freedom and justice, without which life would have no value.

Then I discovered the relation between love and politics. Between poverty and politics. Between sex and politics. I realized that the political regime imposed the will of men upon women and imposed poverty and slavery upon the poor and the destitute. Later I discovered the relationship between the local rulers and the international rulers. And I understood what constitutes global imperialism, class exploitation, and patriarchal oppression of the family.

I realized the connection between the liberation of women and the liberation of the country from subordination or occupation by any form of new or old colonialism. I understood the connections between sex, politics, economics, history, religion and morality. This might be why my writings led me to the loss of my position in the government and to prison, to the confiscation of my books and to my being black-listed.

The boldest of my writings were hidden in the drawers of my desk since no publisher could dare to publish them. They dealt with the taboos (sex, politics, religion).

Despite the actions of the government, my writings spread among the Arab people from Morocco and Algeria to Egypt, Sudan, Iraq, Syria and Yemen. They even penetrated Saudi Arabia. This triggered the enmity of the Arab governments towards me, enmity that became stronger as the numbers of people (women, men and the young) reading my writings increased.

The same authorities tried to alienate me from my readers. I became a target of attack of the political forces that dominated the Arab countries, including Egypt. Among the means of attack was what we call the propaganda war. The authorities claimed that I was inciting women to absolute sexual freedom and immorality, even though in everything I wrote I tried to combat the reduction of women to sex objects fit only for seduction or consumption. I was even opposed to women wearing makeup. I encouraged women to be intelligent human beings and not mere bodies to satisfy men, to produce children, to work as slaves.

The authorities also claimed that I was a communist because I wrote about the subjugation of the poor and the causes of poverty and hunger. They claimed that I was against religion because I discussed rationally matters pertaining to religion and because my faith was not like theirs, inherited blindly as one inherits land or camels.

During the eighties, when my books were being translated into English, French, German and other languages, the authorities claimed I was writing for Western consumption. They made this claim even though I always wrote in Arabic, and all first editions of my books were published in Cairo. Only when my books were confiscated did I move publication to Beirut, Lebanon.

If my books met the approval of readers in Europe, America, or Japan, they met a greater degree of approval in the Arab countries, including Egypt.

The authorities in Egypt and the Arab world tried to prevent my message from getting to the people, and they largely succeeded, since they dominated all media of information and propaganda.

The most dangerous medium of information in our country is television, which explains why I have been banned from speaking on television in Egypt and in most of the Arab countries to this day. I still remember my last visit to Tunisia, in 1983. I was invited by a television director to talk onscreen about Tunisian women. We talked for about half an hour and the conversation was broadcast on television. As a result of the programme, the director was fired by a decree signed by President Bourguiba. Why? Because in our conversation about Tunisian women, I failed to mention that Bourguiba had liberated them.

I have numerous memories of my travels in the Arab countries; I always met with hospitality and love on the part of the people, but with hatred and enmity on the part of the rulers. This was natural, since everything I wrote unveiled the close connection between antiquated forms of government and all sorts of poverty, repression and discrimination based on sex, social class, religion or race.

I have met Israeli women who side with the Palestinians against the

Israeli government, which proves that a woman who praises justice transcends the artificial boundaries between countries, and sides with the truth even if that pits her against government.

The women's liberation movements have played a very important role since the 1970s in struggling against neocolonialism and the multinational companies, against wars, the arms race and nuclear armament, against racism and against discrimination based on race, colour, religion or social class.

I have always felt that the pen was an effective weapon that I could use against injustice and oppression. But writing is also a very private undertaking, which could lead to one's isolation and removal from the battles of life. In order to avoid such isolation, in 1982 I founded the Arab Women's Solidarity Association. We have been working diligently since then towards the advancement of Arab women. Our motto is: 'Power of Women – Solidarity – Unveiling of the Mind.'

Power is necessary, for what is right is lost without power. Just as power without right is tyranny.

Awareness is also necessary, since knowledge generates power. It is impossible for a woman (or a man) to know her or his rights if she or he wears a veil on the mind. What the media accomplish in the Arab countries (as in the rest of the world) is that they delude the people by placing a veil on their minds through which they cannot see what is happening to them or around them.

This delusion takes different forms depending on the country. In the industrial capitalist countries, there are modern technological means to brainwash the people. The governing bodies in our countries imported this modern technology, and television became one of the most dangerous devices for destroying the human mind.

What is the role of the book against this octopus? Millions watch television but only thousands read books. Such is the tragedy, which is compounded by the fact that the books promoted by the authorities are not the best: rather they are the ones that can best be used to mislead and delude the minds of the people. What I mean here by 'mind' is not limited to the conscious; the brainwashing also manipulates the subconscious minds of the people.

In spite of all that, I still believe in writing. I still believe in the power of the truthful word to reach the minds and souls of people in spite of the barriers erected around them.

Writing has been the most important thing in my life, more important than marriage and more important than medicine. It is no wonder that I walked away from marriage and from medicine in order to write. I did not completely quit medicine, but I never devoted much time to it. Similarly, I did not reject marriage completely, but I refused to be married to a man who would hinder my writing.

Even though my parents were relatively liberated, I sometimes clashed with them when I felt that they restricted my freedom.

For example, I married my first husband without the approval of my parents, and I assumed full responsibility for doing so. The marriage ended in divorce when I discovered that he was not the man I dreamed he was, that he was imposing restrictions on me, that he was standing in the way of my creativity. I had had a daughter with him. She was still a baby when she and I left the house. My daughter and I lived together alone for several years. Then I married my second husband, whom I later left. I remember my second husband telling me one day, 'You have to choose between me and your writings.' I answered, without hesitation, 'My writings.' Because I was pregnant, I had an abortion to get rid of the foetus. I decided never to get married again. But several years later, I met a truly liberated man who in 1964 became my third husband. I had a son with him, so I now have a daughter and a son.

I was unable to become a mother without becoming a wife, and I have always liked to experience life to the full, including motherhood and love. I am still married to my third husband, who respects the freedom and dignity of women. He too is a creative writer and artist in addition to being a physician. He knows the value of literature and creativity to human life. He encourages the rebellious and revolutionary spirit; he is also a revolutionary and a rebel. Literary writing, medicine, and the liberation of human beings – men or women – brought us together. His name is Sherif Hetata and he has a long history of struggle against the British and against oppression and exploitation. He was among the best students at medical school, but he spent thirteen years in prison because of his intellectual and political rebellion.

I also was imprisoned during the regime of Sadat, but I was luckier than my husband. After Sadat was assassinated, I was set free by Hosni Mubarak, the president who succeeded him, after having spent only three months in prison. Were it not for these circumstances, I would probably have spent thirteen years in prison as my husband did.

Imprisonment in my country is always a possibility for any person who thinks and writes freely. Most of the men and women I know have been in prison at one time in their life.

As for women generally in my country, their husbands are their permanent prisons. It is very difficult for a woman not to be married. Extramarital love and sex are forbidden to women, but men are free in this regard. I have fought this moral double standard in my writings.

The first nonfiction book I wrote about women was titled *Women and Sex*. It was published in 1970, and confiscated by the Egyptian censors. It was because of this book that in 1972 I lost my job as director general of health education at the Ministry of Health and the publication of the health journal of which I was editor-in-chief ceased.

During the Sadat regime I was blacklisted, publication of my books was forbidden in Egypt, and I therefore started publishing my books in Beirut. I wrote articles that criticized Sadat's policies and uncovered his ambivalence. He preached democracy but practised dictatorship.

Nothing proves Sadat's dictatorship more than the fact that he threw me in prison because of what I wrote, even though I had never belonged to any political party. It was well known that I was a writer, independent from political parties, who expressed her opinions freely.

That is why I write. I write everywhere and under any circumstances. Even in the prison cell I wrote. Every morning the prison guards would enter and search my cell from floor to ceiling. Their chief would shout: 'If we find a paper and a pen, that would be more dangerous for you than if we found a gun.'

They never found the paper and the pen that I hid. This was my small triumph which filled me with hope in my prison cell.

But even outside prison, life is filled every day with small triumphs over the oppression, aggression and tyranny of the authorities. Because of these small triumphs I live my life and never lose hope or optimism even in the gloomiest and darkest of circumstances.

We are going through times of decadence – not only in the Arab world but in the world in general – but such decadence will be out-weighed by a new awakening, and a new dawn.

Women pay dearly with their freedom and dignity to obey the laws of marriage and the patriarchal class system that dominates society. Women also pay dearly in order to become free and escape domination.

I have chosen to pay such a price and become free rather than pay the price and become a slave. In either case we pay a high price. Why pay it to attain slavery and not freedom?

My third husband and I have succeeded in forming a family that abides neither by the prevailing laws of marriage nor by the inherited traditions. He and I instituted our own law based on equality among us. We also succeeded in creating a new understanding of motherhood and fatherhood in relation to our daughter and our son.

All four of us joined hands in founding the Arab Women's Solidarity Association. We have all been active in its various committees. The educational and the youth committees, among the most active com-mittees in the organization, were founded by my daughter with the help of my son and other young men and women. The Arab Women's Solidarity Association was the first pan-Arab organization to be accorded international status at the United Nations.

What distinguishes the activities of our organization is that men and women are involved: we do not classify people according to their sex. Some of the male members are more zealous towards women's causes than some of the women.

On 15 June 1991 the Egyptian government closed the Egyptian branch of the Arab Women's Solidarity Association illegally, and without reason – except that we had stood out against the Gulf War. We took the government to court. Since then, the case has remained buried in the court system.

But the international Arab Women's Solidarity Association continues its work, and our fifth international conference is scheduled to take place in Cairo in October 1997.

In June 1992 the Egyptian government said that terrorist organizations had placed a number of writers, including myself, on a 'death list'. Government security guards surrounded my home and I was provided with a bodyguard to accompany me everywhere. After their arrival, I no longer felt safe in my own home. I left Egypt and went to Europe and then to the USA, where I was a visiting professor at Duke University for four years. But I decided to return, and since the end of 1996 I have lived in Egypt once again with my family.

My work as a psychiatrist has allowed me to meet many women (and men) who are victims of subjugation, oppression and fear. But I have for many years considered myself a writer rather than a physician. Today I devote most of my time to writing, and in my spare time, after I have finished writing for the day, I tend to other work that awaits me at my office. Very often I escape to my village where I spend a few days, weeks or months tending a new literary work away from the congestion and noise of Cairo.

In 1995 I published the first part of my autobiography in Arabic. I am now writing the second part. In 1993 my novel *Love in the Kingdom of Oil* was published in Arabic. The 1991 Gulf War was important in the genesis of this novel: after the war the characters of this novel started to live with me. Oil was the reason for the Gulf War. Oil has been the reason for the continuing colonial aggression against us in the Arab world for the past half-century. Arab rulers, including the Gulf kings and princes, collaborated with the neocolonizers. Millions of women and men in our region suffer poverty, ignorance and disease. My novel *Love in the Kingdom of Oil* is about that suffering. And it describes what happens when its heroine tries to escape her oppression

– in all its forms. It deals, that is, in fictional terms with the ideas and themes contained in the nonfiction writings collected in this anthology.

[Edited and updated version of 'An Overview of My Life', translated from the original Arabic by Antoinette Tuma and published in *Contemporary Authors' Biography* series, Vol.11, Gale Research Inc., 1990, and updated by the author]

PART ONE

Gendering South–North Politics

CHAPTER I

Women and the Poor: The challenge of global justice

Why do we have inequality and poverty in the world? I notice that some people still use the phrase 'Third World' to name us, that is to name the people who live in Africa, Asia and South America. This term is no longer used by many people, including myself, because we live in one world (not three) and we are dominated or governed by one global system which is now called the New World Order. However, we know that in fact it is an old world order which uses new methods of exploitation and domination, both economic and intellectual. Language and the media have become more efficient at obscuring the real aims of those international institutions or groups that speak about peace, development, justice, equality, human rights, and democracy, but whose agreements and decisions lead to the opposite, that is, to war, poverty, inequality and dictatorship.

While I was writing this, I came across a recent issue of the magazine *International Viewpoint*. On its back cover I read a letter written by the Secretary General of Oxfam in Belgium in which he explains why he resigned from the NGO World Bank Group.[1]

The remedies provided by the World Bank for development are poisoned remedies that accelerate the process [of poverty, hunger and unemployment]. For my soul and conscience I am obliged to tell you 'enough'. You have stolen the correct discourse of the NGOs [nongovernmental organizations] on development, eco-development, poverty, and people's participation. At the same time your policies of structural adjustment and your actions accelerate social dumping in the South by obliging it to enter defenseless into the World Market.... Africa is dying, but the World Bank is enriching itself. Asia and Eastern Europe are being robbed of all their riches, and the World Bank supports the initiatives of the IMF, and GATT, that authorize this pillage, which is both intellectual and material. Latin America, like other continents, watches in horror as its children serve as a reserve army of labor and, worse, a reserve of organs for the new transplantation market in North America.

These are the words of an expert who worked very close to the international institutions that speak about development, peace, social justice, democracy, human rights … and decide what should be done. These international insti tutions are often considered to be economic or social only. In fact, they are political as well and the international military machine supports them.

We all know that the United States of America is the most powerful country in military terms in the world. In 1993 the financial editor of the *Chicago Tribune* proposed that the USA should become a mercenary state using its monopoly power in the 'security market' to maintain its control over the world economic system, selling 'protection' to other wealthy powers who would pay a 'war premium'.

How can we speak about real development in Africa, Asia, or South America without knowing the real reasons for poverty and maldevelopment, and for the increasing gap between the rich and the poor not only at the international and regional levels but also within each country, at the national level? We have to make a correct diagnosis of the problem if we wish to have the right remedies. We cannot speak about global injustice without speaking about inequality between countries, inequality between classes in each country, and inequalities between the sexes. All these different levels of inequality are linked together in the patriarchal capitalist system that governs the world today.

What is development?

Countries in our region and in the South generally are subjected to what is called 'development'. Development is not something we choose. It is dictated to us through local governments dominated by the international institutions such as the World Bank, the International Monetary Fund (IMF) and the General Agreement on Tariffs and Trade (GATT). The result of development carried out in line with the policies of these institutions continues to be increasing poverty, and an increasing flow of money and riches from South to North. From 1984 to 1990 the application of structural adjustment policies (SAPs) in the South led to the transfer of $178 billion from the South to the commercial banks in the North.

'Development' is just another word for neocolonialism. We need to be very careful when we use the word 'development'. The word 'aid' is just as deceiving: we know that money and riches flow from the South to the North, not in the opposite direction. A very small portion of what was taken from us comes back to us under the name 'aid'. This creates the false idea that we receive aid from the North.

In this way, we are robbed not only of our material resources, but also of our human dignity. Human dignity is based on being independent and self-reliant, on producing what we eat rather than living on aid coming from the exterior. 'Aid' is a myth that should be demystified. Many countries in the South have started to raise the slogan 'Fair trade not aid'. What the South needs in order to fight against poverty is a *new international economic order* based on justice, and on fair trade laws between countries, not 'aid' or charity. Charity and injustice are two faces of the same coin. If we have real equality between people and between countries, there will be nothing called 'charity' or 'aid'.

Countries in the South plead for justice, equality and democracy in the global society; their plea is for a *new world order based on justice*. The title New World Order has been taken from the South by the powerful military machine in the North to continue the now undivided rule of the neocolonial order following the end of the Cold War. This New World Order was inaugurated by launching the Gulf War. The media and the international information order concealed the real economic reasons behind the Gulf War (oil) behind a false morality built on phrases such as 'human rights', 'democracy', 'liberation of Kuwait', etcetera.

This was repeated with the war in Somalia. All wars in human history have been concealed behind humane, or religious camouflage. If we reread the Old Testament we discover how the war to invade the land of Canaan was considered a holy war ordered by Jehovah (God).

Today we live in a world dominated by a unipolar power, by one superpower which is the USA. The USA dominates the United Nations (UN), the World Bank, the IMF, GATT and SAPs etcetera. Through these international agreements and institutions the North is strengthening its grip on the world economy. The USA and powerful European countries in the North have become a *de facto* board of management for the world economy, protecting their interests and imposing their will on the South.

The problems facing the South are rooted in the North, problems like increasing poverty, low commodity prices, the huge debt burden, unequal trade agreements. The trend to privatization and deregulation forced on the South has coincided with huge and rapid increase in the profits of transnational corporations (TNCs). It is known that 90 per cent of TNCs are based in the North. They control 70 per cent of world trade. Five hundred of these corporations have almost complete control of the world economy. The South is forced to open up the agricultural sector to the TNCs, endangering its ability to feed itself.

Many fertile agricultural countries in the South, such as Egypt, where the valley of the Nile is cultivated with three crops a year, are unable to feed themselves. In Egypt we import 90 per cent of our food.[2] The export of cotton from Egypt has diminished to one tenth of what it was in 1984, and the import of cotton has tripled.

The average monthly wage of the Egyptian worker in 1994 is 300 Egyptian pounds, whereas his foreign colleague in Egypt is paid 4,000 pounds per month. Some 40 per cent of the population in Egypt live below the poverty line. That is, their annual income is less than $386. The World Bank and the IMF help the TNCs to relocate their units of production to the countries of the South where social costs are low. Here labour laws are not applied or do not exist, social and health insurance is lacking, labour unions are weak and dominated by their governments, collective agreements between trade unions or workers and their employers often do not exist, and legislation is enacted to favour the employers. Governments are dominated by TNCs, women and children can be used as labour at lower wages especially in the informal sector, and the pollution of the environment is uncontrolled since the technologies used are under almost no constraints.

What is a good government in the South?

The result of this international economic and international information order is constant pressure on economies to be more competitive. The aim is more and more profit with lower and lower costs. The aim cannot be achieved except through growing pressure on governments in the South to cut spending and diminish social costs – especially those related to subsidies that reduce the prices of essential foods, and to health and educational services, energy, etcetera. In 1977 there were widespread demonstrations in Egypt, mainly composed of the poor, women and youths. These demonstrations erupted as a result of the government's decision to raise the prices of most essential foods. The decision came after continuous pressure from the World Bank.

A good government is now defined as the government that accepts the conditions of the World Bank and submits the nation's economy to the interests of TNCs and other international groups. A good government is a government that accepts what is called 'aid' in order to achieve what is called 'development'.

In Egypt two words, 'aid' and 'development' have resulted in increased poverty and increased deprivation. Between 1975 (when American aid began) and 1986, Egypt imported commodities and services from the USA to a total of $30 billion. During the same period, Egypt exported to the USA total commodities worth only $5 billion.[3] This shows the real aim of this 'aid', namely to enrich the capitalist US economy and not to help Egypt advance on the road to development.

Religion, the poor and women

In this world economic order, the indispensable sacrifices of structural adjustment are required for the globalization of the economy and of markets. They are the indispensable 'desert crossing' *en route* to the Eden of development (to use the words of the World Bank). This fatalistic, almost metaphysical conception of necessity, has recourse to religion. Religion is the ideology used by the rich to exploit the poor in the South. The majority of the poor in the world are women, youth, and children. These days a new term, 'the feminization of poverty', is often mentioned. It means that more women are becoming poor. According to UN figures, the number of rural women living in absolute poverty rose over the 1970s and 1980s by about 50 per cent (from an estimated 370 million to 565 million), and women (who are half the world's population) work two thirds of the total labour hours worked, earn one tenth of total world income, and own one hundredth of world possessions.

Gender, or women's oppression is inseparable from class, race, and religious oppression. The patriarchal class system propagates the idea that the oppression of women and the poor is a divine law and is not man-made:

> The rich man in his castle
> the poor man at his gate.
> God made them high or lowly,
> and ordained their estate.

We all know that in all religions women have an inferior position relative to men. This is especially true for the monotheistic religions. Adam is superior to Eve, and in almost all religions women should be governed by men. In human history, to exploit women and the poor was not possible without the use of religion. Slavery was considered to be a divine law by prominent philosophers in the past and even in our own days.

Now we are faced by a resurgence of religious so-called fundamentalism. Some people think it is only Islamic. This is not true. Religious fundamentalism is an international phenomenon. The international patriarchal class system is encouraging the revival of religion all over the world. Christian fundamentalism was encouraged in the USA by

Reagan and Bush. They also used, and often encouraged, Islamic fundamentalism in our region, the so-called Middle East, in order to fight
against the Soviet Union and communism. In Egypt it was Sadat who
encouraged religious fundamentalism to neutralize the socialist, the
progressive liberal, and the Nasserite political currents in the country.
In Algeria, it was the state (under Chadli) that encouraged the religious
groups to grow in power.

The term often used to describe this phenomenon is 'state fundamentalism'. State political power and religious political power are two
faces of the same coin. They feed each other. Sometimes they clash
and fight each other in their struggle to dominate the state. This is
what is now happening under Mubarak. In fact, they are old friends
and new enemies. Sadat was killed by the fundamentalists after he had
encouraged them to grow. The son killed the father. This is an oft-
repeated story with which we are familiar in history. Wherever there is
a religious revival, women are among the first victims. All fundamentalist groups, whether Christian, Jewish, or Islamic, are antagonistic to
women's liberation and women's rights. The backlash against women's
rights is thus also a universal phenomenon, and is not restricted to our
region.

Women, and population control

The capitalist patriarchal system (reframed as the New World Order)
has developed population control policies to facilitate more exploitation
of the poor and women in the so-called Third World. It is no surprise
that population control institutions (such as the Population Council,
the UN International Planned Parenthood Federation [IPPF], the multinational pharmaceutical corporations, US Aid) work in collaboration
with the neocolonial global institutions such as the World Bank and the
IMF. Population control policies are a new biological war against
women and the poor whose aim is to keep the economic and intellectual resources of the world under the control of minority power
structures in the North and their collaborators in the South.

To hide their anti-women, anti-poor policies, population controllers
have stolen the language of the women's liberation movements. Phrases
such as 'women's needs', 'free choice', 'reproductive rights', 'empower-
ment of women' and 'family planning' are used to elaborate strategies
against women and the poor. In the North, 20 per cent of the world's
people consume 80 per cent of global resources. Instead of working
towards global justice or a more egalitarian distribution of wealth and
power, the multinational corporations work to eliminate the poor

people in the so-called Third World. Women are pushed to consume unsafe contraceptive methods such as the injectable contraceptive Depo Provera, and the contraceptive implant Norplant. The basic needs of women – such as food, education, health, employment, social, economic and political participation, and a life free of violence (whether inflicted from inside the family or by the state) – are neglected.

Population control programmes started in the 1950s under the banner of 'poverty eradication'. The results have been the eradication of the poor, not poverty. Poverty is increasing year after year. More and more people in our countries are killed by hunger, more than those killed by war. Population control programmes nowadays are working under new titles, such as 'to curb environmental destruction', 'to ensure sustainable growth', etcetera. But nothing of all this is happening. The reality is that women in the South are subjected to a range of coercive technologies and drugs, which have often destroyed their health and lives. People in the South are not looked upon as people but as demographic variables or population indices.

Yet people in the South are not really poor. Our continents are rich but our riches are robbed by continuous pillage by colonial and neo-colonial powers.

The New Economic World Order and the media have consistently equated poverty in the South with population growth. This is another myth which hides the real causes of economic and political crises in our countries. After the oil crises, credit-based development was forced on the South. It resulted in the debt crisis and increasing poverty and unemployment.

Commodification and trafficking in women (in the South and in the North as well) are increasing. Women are looked upon as bodies to be exploited and used to produce more profit. They must be veiled, covered physically according to the religious fundamentalists, but should be undressed according to the postmodern capitalists, or made to buy makeup and body conditioners. Sex is a commodity, a thriving industry. Sex shops and pornography, the commerce of sex, spread like fire.

Veiling of the mind

The mass media and the international information order are working together with the international economic order to veil the minds of billions of people living on our planet. The new technology of communications transmits lies and myths all over the world in a matter of minutes or seconds.

The new international order is working to foster *globalization* or *global multinational capitalism* (the postmodern stage of capitalist development). The globalization of the economy requires the globalization of information, mass media and culture. This requires the breaking down of national and regional barriers to permit the free flow of capital, commodities, labour and information. Global capitalism requires global flexibility to ensure the so-called free market (freedom of the powerful to dominate the weak). Despite the competitive struggles between the different powerful groups in the North and between the TNCs, a global market requires the establishment of a market of consumers who develop similar needs, similar interests, similar desires, and similar habits of living in a certain way: that is, similar patterns of consumption. These patterns of consumption are constituted by a similar outlook on life, similar values and ideas. This is a postmodern culture which is similar in many ways across the globe, irrespective of regional or national location.

The beauty mentality and its material products such as makeup, perfumes, earrings, fashion, etcetera are sold globally by global media (TV, radio, newspaper, magazines, movies, videos, songs, music). The aim is to create a conception of beauty that becomes part of the culture and has its set of values, feelings and desires which are absorbed by the conscious and the subconscious mind. The cultural unconscious and the political unconscious are not separate from the conscious. The relation between culture, politics and economics is very important; this is true not only of the economic and political processes within which the cultural takes form, but also of the psychological processes that engage in its production and reception. I remember a French woman who came to me in 1993 and criticized Muslim women for wearing veils. This French woman had a thick coating of makeup on her face, but she was completely unaware that this also was a veil. The French woman's veil was considered by the global media as modern and beautiful, but the other veil was considered backward and ugly; yet the two veils were almost the same since they both hid the real face of the woman.

Unveiling of the mind

When we started the Arab Women's Solidarity Association in 1982 we had two major objectives: the unveiling of the mind, and political power through unity and solidarity. We faced strong opposition from local Arab governments (who work with the international capitalist powers) and from fanatical religious groups and from a variety of political parties. But we continued to resist. We had to fight at different levels and on different fronts, to link the psychological with the economic, the political with the historical, the cultural with the religious, the sexual with the social.

To unveil the mind necessitated exposing the contradictions of the New World Order (both economic and cultural). This order encourages globalization and unification when these serve its economic interests, but fights against globalization or unification between people if they resist its policies. To unveil the mind we had to expose the link between religion and politics, between capitalism and religious fundamentalism.

The globalization needed by the international capitalist system leads people in different countries or cultures to resist homogenization resulting from the global culture, or so-called universal values. It is a self-defence mechanism. It is an attempt to hold on to an authentic identity, or authentic culture or heritage, and these are some of the factors in the growth of religious fundamentalism, racism, and ethnic struggles. It is a protest movement (especially among the youth), but very often takes on reactionary, retrograde, anti-women, and anti-progressive characteristics thus leading to division and discord; it thus serves the purpose of capitalist globalization because it divides the people who are resisting it.

How to empower the resistance

We need unity and solidarity between men and women who resist this global injustice at the local level as well as at the international level. But we need a movement that is progressive, not backward, which seeks unity in diversity, by breaking down barriers built on discrimination (by gender, class, race, religion, etcetera), and by discovering what we have in common as human beings with common interests that may express themselves differently. People can unite and cooperate if they struggle for greater equality and against all forms of discrimination. This requires establishing a network step by step from the local up to the global level to face the international capitalist network. We can use modern technology such as videos, cassettes, public radio, TV, etcetera, and begin with local, grassroots networks to create our own mass media. For example, we all know the role the cassette played in the Iranian Revolution. Many of the religious fundamentalist groups in Algeria, Egypt and other parts of the world are using the cassette, transmitters, cellular telephones, etcetera, to reach masses of people.

Women and the poor in the South have to cooperate with the progressive forces in the North who are fighting the same battle, but resistance starts at home. We can only change the international order by each one of us, step by step, changing the system in which we live. Without genuine democracy this movement cannot succeed. Democracy as practised in the North under the patriarchal class system is just a set of institutions such as a parliament or a congress. It is a limited, formal and false democracy which excludes the majority of women and the poor from elections and other means of expression. We need real democracy. This real democracy starts at the personal level, at home, in the family. If we have men or husbands who are dictators in the family how can we have democracy in the state, since it is based on the family unit? Democracy is day-to-day practice and should be rooted in childhood, in the psyche, in beliefs, ethics, attitudes, and private life as well as public life.

It is necessary to undo the separation between the private and the public because in this separation lies the oppression of women and the poor. We need a new family, a new educational system at home and at the primary, secondary, and university levels. We have to work together at home and locally, nationally, regionally, and globally to restore our dignity, to satisfy our physical and mental needs, to achieve self-reliance and the right to choose our own way towards economic and intellectual progress.

[Keynote address to the Global '94 Congress, Tampere, Finland, 3–7 July 1994]

Notes

1. Pierre Galland, 'World Bank: "Criminal"', *International Viewpoint*, April 1994.

2. *Al-Arabi* (Cairo); 4 April 1994, p. 4.

3. Interview with Mahmoud Wahba, president of Egypt American Businessmen, *El-Shaab*, Cairo, Egypt, 26 April 1994, p. 4.

CHAPTER 2

Women in the South in Relation to Women in the North

Egypt, my home country and where I live, is part of Africa of course. Just look at the map and you will be sure of that. I mean the map of the earth, of the natural earth (our very ancient mother goddess) and the natural boundaries – not the boundaries made by the colonialists, who divided Africa into so-called 'white Africa' and 'black Africa'. I believe we should undo what the colonialists and neocolonialists did and are still doing. We should have *one* Africa.

Why one Africa? some people ask. Why one Europe? The reasons for one Europe are exactly the same as for one Africa, but the colonialists and neocolonialists accept the idea and practice of one Europe but not the idea and practice of one Africa. It is obvious that the unity of Africa (or of any oppressed continent or country or countries) will be against the colonial or neocolonial powers that exploit them. 'Divide and rule' has been the philosophy of exploitation since the evolution of slavery (or the patriarchal class–race system). Divide the earth or the universe into sky (spirit) and earth (body). Divide the country, divide the people into masters and slaves. Divide the human being into body and spirit, or soul or mind. Let the masters, the rulers, the patriarchs and their gods and their philosophers represent the mind and the soul. Let the slaves and women and the devil represent the body, the inferior body, with all its animal instincts and sins.

During the Gulf War in 1991 we saw the face of the so-called 'devil' in newspapers and magazines in Europe and the USA. Who was the devil? He was the 'enemy' of the USA and Europe – the dictator of Iraq who was oppressing the Kuwaitis and the Kurds, who was violating human rights and democracy and not respecting UN resolutions. Thirty armies from the USA and Europe gathered their high-tech military weapons to punish this devil. This same devil was their good friend when he was fighting another devil (Iran). Who is the devil in Africa now? Who is disobeying the orders of the masters in the USA?

How many times did the South African apartheid government and the Israeli government violate human rights and democracy and fail to respect UN resolutions? In 1993 Israel deported four hundred Palestinians and did not respect the UN resolution that it should return them, but there was no punishment, no war was waged against Israel, there were not even any economic sanctions. Just read the history of the struggle of the South African and Palestinian people, just read the newspapers today and you see the obvious double standard of the rulers in the so-called 'first' or 'developed' world – what is called now the North.

Can we speak about women in the North separate from men in the North? What do we mean by 'women in the North' or 'women in the South'? If we mean Western feminism versus feminism in Africa can we separate feminism from politics (international and national)? Can we separate feminism from economics or history or philosophy or religion or medicine (of the body and of the so-called psyche) or sociology or anthropology or science or art?

I am originally a medical doctor. I studied the body separate from the mind. I became a very good physician ignorant of the human being as a whole. I had to study psychology and psychiatry to know more. I had to go beyond the medical sciences to study religion, economics, politics, history, philosophy, etcetera, to understand why I was oppressed as a woman, why Egypt was colonized by the British and other foreign powers, why Africa is suffering hunger, starvation, famines and foreign debt though Africa, as I learned in primary school, is a very rich continent.

Africa is one of the richest continents in the world, rich in both material and human resources. Who made Africa so poor? Just one week ago I asked this question to one of the leading feminists in the USA. She said, 'You know, poverty in Egypt or Africa is due to the population problem: women there give birth to more children.' I told her: 'Do you think that women and children are the cause and not colonialism or neocolonialism?' She said, 'Oh my god, why do you blame others? Why blame the United States and not the local dictatorship or African governments?' I told her: 'Of course the local governments in Africa are responsible, but who keeps them in power?' She said: 'Their people, their people in Africa elected them and keep them in power.' I told her: 'But a few seconds ago you were mentioning dictatorships in Africa, which mean no democracy and no real free elections.' She could not answer the question.

Feminists in the USA (and in the North in general) are not all the same. They differ a great deal. Some of them are aware of the link between colonialism or international imperialism and poverty or other problems from which we suffer (women and men) in Africa and other parts of the so-called Third World. A feminist from the North (the USA) called Susan Griffin, who is a poet and a researcher living in California, has this to say:

> I wrote 'Hunger' [a poem] after seeing an exhibition in Paris of a series of photographs taken by Sebastião Salgado. The photographs document the starvation in a region of Africa known as the Sahel. In the United States we have told ourselves that this is a *natural calamity*. But if we look more closely at the history of colonialism, we discover a different story. Disregard for the *natural ecology* of a region goes hand in hand with disregard for the *natural rights* of people to determine their own fate and to live the way they choose. This pattern of domination and disregard has created many of the famines in Africa. Many African people in areas subject to drought used to grow *millet* and rotate it seasonally. *Millet* is an important crop because it can grow with very little water. When the white colonists came to Africa they uprooted the millet and substituted other crops such as wheat. When the weather conditions changed, as the tribal societies that had lived there for centuries understood would happen, the *wheat* could not withstand the dry spells, and hence a famine was created. Seasons of drought would not have had such a devastating effect on millet, but because of the planting of wheat, terrible starvation resulted.
>
> This pattern has been repeated over and over again and is still being repeated. Today, now not in the name of colonialism but in the name of *development.*[1]

How was such an American woman able to know some of the truth about our continent? Because Susan Griffin is not an academic but a poet. She is not a pure scientist using only her intellect to understand the world, but a real artist who does not work with her head only but with all her being. That is why I write novels more than so-called nonfiction. In art you feel whole, with no separation between body and mind, spirit or soul. With no separation between form and content, or art and politics or economics or medicine.

As a medical doctor in rural Egypt in 1956 I asked myself why poor people became more sick than rich people, and I discovered the relationship between poverty and disease. When I asked myself why people became poor I discovered colonialism and dictatorship and politics. When I asked myself why girls are mutilated by female circumcision I discovered slavery in history and the patriarchal class system. But what happened when I started to discover the original causes of physical and mental diseases? I lost my job in the Ministry of Health in Egypt in 1972 under Sadat. I was placed on the blacklist as a writer and a novelist. In September 1981 I was sent to jail, and I was not released until 25 November 1981, two months after the assassination of Sadat.

But this is a very common story in Africa and the Arab world, and indeed in most countries. The oppression of women, especially of women who start to learn, is universal, even though the degree of oppression differs from country to country. In Africa, because the political and economic systems are not as powerful as in the capitalist, military industrial North, the governments and local dictatorships are fiercer in fighting the opposition. In the North, governments do not mind opposition so long as it does not threaten the class–patriarchal–race system. This is 'Western democracy'. We in Africa call it 'Hyde Park democracy': people can talk, they can write, they can demonstrate, so long as they have no real power.[2] Real power is the police, the military, capital, and religion. Women are outside this real power in the North as well as in the South.

I do not like to divide the globe into North and South. Such a division hides the real causes of oppression and exploitation. There are many local black governments, containing both men and women, who oppress their own people, who collaborate with international colonial and neocolonial powers in the North. There are also many white women and men in the North who fight against their own governments and support people in the South who fight against colonialism and neocolonialism.

In 1982 we established our Arab Women's Solidarity Association: 30 per cent of our members are men fighting with us against the class patriarchal system internationally, nationally and in the family. In 1990 I was in Johannesburg to attend an international writers' conference and met a lot of women who were fighting against the racist apartheid government. They understand feminism in the same way we understand it in our Arab Women's Solidarity Association: there is no separation between race, gender or class oppression. There is no separation between war in the Gulf and war in South Africa or war in Bosnia or war in Palestine. The original causes are the same.

Why is it that the international powers hurried to save the Kuwaiti women who were raped by Iraqi soldiers but did not hurry to save women who were raped in Bosnia by the Serbs? I read that at least 30,000 Bosnian women were raped, versus 30 in Kuwait. Everybody now says, if Bosnia had oil ... Yes, that is the real problem of the Arab world. Since the discovery of oil, our region, the so-called Middle East, has become a target of colonial and neocolonial exploitation. Since the discovery of the rich raw materials of Africa, the diamonds and other treasures of the earth, Africa has been a target of colonialism and neocolonialism.

On 9 March 1993 an American feminist called Susan Jeffords gave a lecture in Duke University under the title 'Rape and US National Identity'. She explained how the US military patriarchal machine used the rape of women as a pretext to launch war against the 'villain' or 'devil'. She also explained how the 'devil' changed all the time according to the economic and political interests of the US government and the multinationals. On 21 February 1993 I participated in a demonstration in Washington, DC, organized by the National Organization of Women (NOW). The demonstration was against the raping of women in Bosnia. It was a very cold Sunday, and hundreds of women and men stood in rain, and sometimes snow, shouting against the oppression of women all over the world, including the USA. There were five speakers, including myself. The US media covered the event on TV and radio and in newspapers, but they censored our speeches. They covered only the descriptive parts, about rape in Bosnia. They cut the points that linked the rape of women to politics and economics.

The media in the North is part of the war against us, the people in Africa and other people in the so-called Third World. In the North it is women, mainly, who support us, and who fight with us against colonialism, whether international or national or in the family.

We are facing an economic and mental crisis in the South as well as in the North. Most countries in the South and the North are facing economic crisis, manifested by high rates of unemployment, foreign debts, inflation and increasing budget deficits. The so-called 'only superpower in the world', the USA, is on the verge of economic collapse, according to President Clinton's speech to Congress of February 1993. The former Soviet Union is collapsing economically. A young African university woman asked me, 'If the US is collapsing economically why do they send military personnel to rescue Somalia from starvation and famine?' I asked her, 'Why does the US want to rescue Somalia and not Bosnia, and why do children in Somalia throw stones at the US troops who have come to rescue them or feed them, as the media says?' It seems that those hungry children in Somalia are more aware of politics and the real reasons behind military intervention in Africa than many of our university women and men, and than many African leaders and journalists who participate in the media campaign of brainwashing, in the South as well as in the North.

[Excerpt from a paper given to the Afrikagrupperna conference, Stockholm, 13 March 1993]

Notes

1. Susan Griffin, writing in Irene Diamond and Gloria Orenstein (eds.) *Reweaving the World* (Siena Club Books, 1990), p. 95.

2. Or make open-air speeches, as people do at Speaker's Corner, in London's Hyde Park.

CHAPTER 3

Women's Voice in the North–South Dialogue

So-called foreign aid

When women of the Arab countries started to organize ourselves in the Arab Women's Solidarity Association we had no funds with which to start the projects we had formulated. So we started to seek assistance from individuals, institutions and organizations within our countries. Then we made attempts to obtain funds from foreign sources. I wrote over one hundred letters to different people and organizations. Some of the Arab petrodollar institutions agreed to assist us but posed conditions that we refused and so this source of assistance never materialized. Then some international bodies in the countries of the North sent us sums for our activities and posed no conditions except the presentation of a final report after the assistance had been expended. But after this initial phase was over, all further requests for assistance were met by complete silence. We could not understand why, but later we came to realize from various sources that this was because we had not complied with these bodies' view of what a women's organization in the South should do. We were an organization that spoke of patriarchy and class and women's oppression and tried to organize women and make them more conscious so that they would become a progressive force capable of changing their situation and developing their societies. What they wanted was a women's organization that told women they should have fewer babies, that distributed contraceptives and fixed IUDs in the orifices of women's uteri or developed the kind of 'development projects' that have failed all over the Third World and only serve to fill the pockets of those who sponsor them or to change people into instruments of certain policies. So we began to depend on ourselves and in the process found out that we had possibilities that had not been thought of. We were learning to be independent, growing up. We were learning the truth of the saying 'Instead of giving me a fish, teach me how to catch it', a principle that should apply, and rarely does, to all development aid going to the countries and institutions of the South.

I do not want to expand on a subject that is familiar to all of you. The negative impact of aid on the economies of the South is only too well known. It is one of the instruments of increased exploitation, of the linking of the economies of the South to the North, of the creation of divisions, of the depletion of resources, of the maintenance of dependence. Today we are faced with the disastrous consequences of the enormous international debt owed by the countries of the South to the North, and we feverishly seek ways to keep the economies of the countries of the South afloat. Ostensibly aid is meant to help the poorer countries of the world. In fact it is a means of linking them and exploiting their natural and human resources to the advantage of the North. And with the growing crisis in the South, its countries must seek new ways of solidarity and cooperation, new relations between themselves, and between themselves and the North in a world faced by the need to remould its economic order more equitably on a broad range of issues.

How can the countries of the South reinforce their solidarity and their strength?

We in the Arab Women's Solidarity Association know that solidarity can only grow in the light of knowledge and understanding. That is why the aims expressed in our motto are threefold: 'Power of Women – Solidarity – Unveiling of the Mind'.

How can the mind of the South be unveiled, for the South is like an African, or an Asian, or an Arab woman wearing a veil imported from abroad, who thinks that she is defying the North by returning to tradition, to what she imagines as being her identity, and by donning what is called the Muslim dress. This is one of the most widespread forms of brainwashing, and it creates the illusion that a return to the religious traditions and values practised hundreds of years ago is a solution to the economic and political dependence that holds the South in its yoke.

What we require is not a formal return to tradition and religion but a rereading, a reinterpretation, of our history that can illuminate the present and pave the way to a better future. For example, if we delve more deeply into ancient Egyptian and African civilizations we will discover the humanistic elements that were prevalent in many areas of life. Women enjoyed a high status and rights, which they later lost when class patriarchal society became the prevalent social system.

Western orientalist circles have tried to deprive us of our history just as Western capitalist circles have deprived us of our resources. We are required to be without a civilization, without a culture, without a past, and without roots. Misconceptions related to our history have been widely mooted. For example, Ancient Greek civilization has been cut off from Ancient Egyptian and Ancient African civilizations; this has paved the way for a consistently dominant school of history which considers that modern Europe is the descendant of Ancient Greek civilization and thought. According to this theory, the civilization of the North has no roots in the South. This school of thought severs the human patrimony into two, creates the dichotomy between South and North, and facilitates the ideology of domination which still prevails in the relations between the two.

One of the modern historians, however, has made an original contribution in his book *Black Athena* by tracing the Egyptian and Afroasian roots of the civilization of the Ancient Greeks.[1] Martin Bernal has tried to make the human linkages that bring us together rather than the linkages of exploitation and denial that separate us and keep pushing the world to the brink of disaster.

Technology exported by the North to the South has not served as an instrument of real development but has tended to propagate the patterns that serve the interests of the North, to integrate the periphery into the centre, and to make it wholly dependent instead of helping its countries to stand on their own feet and strengthen their agricultural, industrial and human capabilities. True, the peoples of the South produce more, grow more, and work more. But are they better off? And if not, how is it that aid and technological cooperation have led only to debts, a growing deficit, falling standards of living, inflation and unemployment? Are these the fruits of North–South cooperation? Western economists and politicians say this state of affairs has come about because we are lazy or inefficient or backward or have bad leaders. But is it not a fact that in the world of today our riches continue to be pumped out from South to North? True, there is a lot that the peoples of the South must do to change things: to depend on their own inner strength and their own resources to create solidarity among themselves in the struggle for a new economic order.

The world economic order is the witness of an important change in the relative development of economic forces, with the European Economic Community (EEC) and Japan moving abreast of the US giant. The economic potential of the EEC is enormous if note is taken of the fact that it encompasses a market of 325 million consumers as compared to 246 million in the USA and 122 million in Japan. By the end of 1988 it is expected that total production in the EEC will represent 22 per cent of total world production, that is, $4,100 million compared to the USA's $4,700 million. Statistics also show that the economic weight of the USA in total world production dropped from 32 per cent at the beginning of the seventies to 28 per cent in 1988. It also shifted from being a net creditor owed a total of $141 million, to being a debtor to the tune of $400 million.

This means that the EEC is called upon by the world economy to play an increasing role in North–South relations. To attain real equality in mutual relations and benefits between South and North countries will be a long struggle, and will require substantial changes in the direction of a new economic order. But my question is, will the EEC continue to follow policies dictated predominately by US interests, or interests linked to the USA? Is it possible to envisage a gradual trans-formation in relations between North and South built on a new vision of the world of tomorrow? If capitalist relations continue to govern the major part of our world, must it be the most aggressive and reactionary forces that hold the upper hand, those built on war, on military production, on the arms race, on racial, ethnic, sexual and religious discrimination, on destruction of the natural environment, pollution and imbalance of the ecosystem, on master–slave relations between countries and peoples of the South and countries and peoples of the North? Or is it possible to imagine that Europe can constitute an independent force that can discover new horizons for the capitalist world where peace between nations is possible, where economic development and profits are perceived as best served by a more balanced development for all, where a more prosperous South can help to create a greater prosperity for the North and to halt the vicious circle of currency depreciation, reduced production and unemployment, and face the rapidly growing problems of environmental deterioration?

That is the question asked with increasing insistence in many circles. So far the response has been negative. The years pass, congresses and meetings are held, politicians and experts exchange views, institutions are born or stagnate in boredom, yet nothing seems to change in the North–South dialogue. Yes, we agree on the need for solidarity and independence, but on what terms: mutual benefit, or the terms dictated by a powerful minority who can see no further than their profits and control?

We need a new solidarity, a new vision that can transform the present confrontation between South and North into a new dialogue. Let me cite as an example the UN conference for the promotion of Inter-national Cooperation in Peaceful Uses of Nuclear Energy (held in

Geneva, March–April 1987). The summary of the work of the conference adopted by participants includes this statement:

> exclusive efforts were made by the conference to reach agreements on principles universally acceptable for international cooperation in the peaceful uses of nuclear energy ... despite its efforts, the conference was unable to reach an agreement on principles for international cooperation in the *peaceful* uses of nuclear energy.

Failure to solve this major problem indicates a deep crisis of purpose and goals resulting from the preponderance of narrow interests. In the absence of a change in the mentality of influential sectors in the North, the dialogue between South and North will continue to go round in a circle, leading to an unnecessary gap between North and South and to rapidly growing inequities in a world where scientific and technological knowledge remains the devastating prerogative of a privileged few.

It is vital that all concerned work hard towards agreement on new purposes and new goals not only in the fields of military (defensive) and nuclear technology and material production, but also in the social, educational, cultural and informational fields. This redefinition of goals and purposes is a fundamental condition for any success in the North–South dialogue. The ideas of solidarity and interdependence must receive a new impetus, a new outlook that will change master–slave relationships into a common endeavour for a better world for all concerned. In this area, solidarity between the peoples and states of the South can be a potent lever. If this is coupled with a new outlook amongst the peoples of the North, and in particular amongst capitalist circles not primarily interested in military production and war, we may witness a new turn in the North–South dialogue.

History is bringing North closer to South and East closer to West. It is bringing different, diversified cultures closer. The globe is shrinking and we face globalization. But the concept of universality should be redefined. It should not mean central control, monopoly, and domination of one country over another. Real human universality and unity should be democratic, and respect differences, interests, and multiple systems.

Women of the South and the North

Women in the South and the North have been playing an increasingly important role through the feminist movement. You may see both negative and positive aspects in this movement, yet on the whole its general contribution in the field of human thought – of new ideas and forms of action – and in changing society has been important. Women continue to raise issues related to social justice, peace and development, and they tend to emphasize the cultural and human aspects of relationships between people rather than matters related to economic growth and military strength. They have contributed to the struggle against patriarchal class relations entrenched in state and religious institutions on a global scale: in the multinational economic and political network right down to the smallest unit constituted by the family.

The International Women's Decade (1975–1985) helped to bring women of the North and South closer together and to eliminate some misunderstandings. In the South, mistrust of the 'white woman', which often leads to over-reaction and sensitivities, is being overcome by the multiple exchanges taking place and by common action. There has been a tendency amongst some women in the North to consider the feminist movement as a Western innovation and to lay down patterns of thought and action for all women – even those in the South whose conditions and history are different and who must therefore seek original forms of organization and appropriate solutions to their problems.

For example, in the countries of the South we do not believe that the women's emancipation movement should be developed on the basis of solidarity between women against men, that the struggle is that of woman against man. Women must organize and be able to exert pressure as a political, economic and cultural force. But the aim is a concerted effort to change relations within society – and between men and women – in the direction of greater equality, a more profound understanding and a deeper humanity. This will entail struggle, but we are against animosity, hatred and enmity between the sexes which can only serve to accentuate problems and prevent men and women from being partners in building a better future.

One notable development has been the changing attitude of women in the 'socialist countries' toward the feminist movement. I quote from the opening statement made by the president of the World Federation of Democratic Women, Freda Brown, at the International Conference of Women held in Moscow during June 1987:

> We have never made an effort to understand and analyze the feminist movement, despite the deep influence it has had on events in different areas and in different parts of the world. In the 'Plan of Work' approved by the Federation one of the resolutions runs as follows:
> 'Give special attention and importance to the understanding and analysis of feminist movements, and to studying ways and means of cooperation with these movements and with different groups of women all over the world.'[2]

There is no doubt that we have learned a lot during the period through which we are living. We realize that the world is growing smaller, that peoples and nations are coming closer, that our future hangs together. Men and women all over the world must seek to change the system under which we live, a system built on exploitation and oppression, on a dualism that creates more and more divisions between higher and lower, black and white, men and women, North and South, rich and poor. We need to work towards a new world system, a new economic, political and information order built on increasing equality, mutual respect and exchange, human dignity and human rights.

In this difficult struggle women can play an increasingly important role. Not only do they constitute half the society, they suffer a double burden of oppression, and their relations with the human experiences of life, death, reproduction and child-rearing are much more intimate and concrete than those of men. They can therefore bring to the task of creating new relations between North and South a human depth that so far has been sadly lacking in the ruthless struggle for power and wealth.

[Part of a keynote address to an EEC/Council of Europe conference in Barcelona, 30–31 May 1988]

Notes

1. Martin Bernal, *Black Athena: The Afroasian Roots of Classical Civilization*, Rutgers University Press, 1987, pp. 2–27.

2. Pamphlet summarizing the Ninth Congress of the World Federation of Democratic Women (Moscow, 28–29 June 1987) pp. 10 and 33.

CHAPTER 4

The Enigmatic South: Different stages of development[1]

Countries like Egypt, Arab countries on the southern coast of the Mediterranean and countries belonging to the South in general have many characteristics in common (as well as differences of course). One of the most important is that side by side there coexist different stages of development; that is, there are economic, social and cultural characteristics that belong to the slave system (pre-feudal) and others that belong to various stages of socioeconomic development leading up to the higher levels of capitalist development with its technological achievements related to atomic energy and the information system based on computers and remote control.

This leads to an extreme complexity which is difficult to grasp for people coming from another society where capitalism and technological development have led to a high degree of homogeneity despite the fact that remnants of the past exist. As a result of this diversity, we in the South find it difficult to understand and study our own societies, where paradoxes, ambiguities, contradictions and an extreme diversity are habitual aspects of life. But is also why we are conscious of history because we see it living before our eyes. It is also why when properly educated (but not rigidified by Western educational systems) minds from the South are often extremely versatile, flexible and creative (witness fiction from the South).

This complexity is very important in the understanding of the South. It reduces the importance of established theories and abstractions and increases the importance of living, experiencing, observing, listening, learning and concretizing. Openmindedness, youth, and the capacity for listening and for learning from experience that so many women have are therefore important in those chosen to work in the South, especially as our societies are also young: 51 per cent of our people are younger than twenty-five years of age. Complexity is reflected in every area of life, economic, social, cultural, religious, psychological and sexual. People in the South are a product of different things, and difficult to understand by the Western mind accustomed to rules, measures, laws and criteria. We are a tropical forest or desert with its excitement and its dangers. This diversity, these living contradictions cohabiting side by side, these levels and stages apply to the economy, to politics, to culture and religion, to democracy, women and human rights, to good and bad government, and therefore in the end to North–South relations.

Out of this galaxy of areas we will discuss here a limited number of topics namely democracy, human rights and women, good governance, and culture in an attempt to draw a simple, and unfortunately simplified picture.

Democracy

Democracy in the Arab region is a monster with many parents. It is the product of different degrees of centralized administration handed down from the slave–agricultural era several thousand years old which led to a pervasive, autocratic, parasitic and corrupt apparatus living on the backs of the people. Colonizers, neocolonizers and those who cooperate with them have systematically reinforced this apparatus to maintain power and control. Only recently have cries arisen in the Western capitals about the need for civil society and nongovernmental organizations (NGOs) to try and escape from this all-pervasive, parasitic and corrupt administrative apparatus. But the neocolonialists and the neo-rulers are caught up in their own game, and nowhere have they been able to escape except in limited areas of the world where they have had a special stake in developing some national initiative such as in South Korea, Formosa and Singapore, and where the cultural characteristics of Asiatic Chinese people have helped. Elsewhere, democracy in the South and especially in the Arab countries is in the grip of this state apparatus. How to escape? The answer is in nongovernmental organizations. But most if not all of these are tied to government or controlled by elites linked in one way or another to the establishment and the power structure. The second question therefore becomes, How to escape the elites? How to discover new elites?

The second factor contributing to the formation of Arab democracy is the existence of feudal and tribal remnants everywhere but especially in the rural areas. This has a very important impact on democracy. It breeds autocracy: in the state, at the local administration level, in all institutions, in school education and in the university where learning is largely rote, in the family and in relations between men and women. It thus strengthens all forms of patriarchal and class oppression and all forms of autocratic rule, despite some of the positive aspects that these feudal remains may have: like certain remnants of matriarchy, the enhanced role of elder women in a village situation, informal co-operation at village level, the support of extended families, and so on. The existence of feudal and tribal remnants reduces human rights, women's rights, and the chances of good governance and it uses tradition and culture including religion as a servant to maintain outdated structures. Religion is therefore not the cause, but the mirror image and at the same time wilful instrument of fanaticism, bigotry, narrow-mindedness and reaction.

In the Arab countries an important element is the growth of Islamic (and also Christian and Jewish) political religious movements. These movements tend to support a highly autocratic form of government based on what is called *shura*. *Shura* means 'consultation', and was a situation in which the ruler or caliph used to hold open audiences with those around him to consult them on certain matters. He was free to adopt the opinions expressed in this meeting or to reject them. Within the Islamic movements most circles consider a form of *shura* obligatory, but some currents consider it a matter to be left to the ruler. At the present moment the Muslim Brotherhood and other political movements that belong to the so-called 'moderate' tendency and constitute the bulk of the Islamic political movement have opted to play the parliamentary game, and participate in elections. The probability is that if they come to power they would set up some form of limited representative participation which could vary from one country to the other. However at present it is certain that an Islamic government would institute a system that would be highly anti-democratic despite the existence of more liberal tendencies within Islamic parties and movements. All Islamic movements insist that the constitution must be built on the Qur'an and *Shari'a* (religious jurisprudence) and consider themselves the only legitimate interpreters of what this will mean in principle, in practice and in everyday life.

The third factor is bourgeois liberal economic, social and political development accompanied by some industrial development which liberalized structures in the cities and towns to some extent, and over-flowed to rural areas. It led to the introduction of the multiparty system, a constitution and a parliament after the First World War in Egypt and at various other periods in certain other Arab countries in the South Mediterranean. This liberalization is positive but has its limits, and in recent years has often degenerated into an instrument for economic and political manipulation by foreign and local centres of power. However it gives some leeway for the exercise of freedom, for women, and for human rights. Yet it is a very strictly controlled democracy from which only selected elites are able to profit, and from which women, youth and the poor are largely excluded.

The fourth factor is foreign intervention in the choice of government. This is exercised mainly by economic means, by influencing certain power groups, and by force of arms to ensure that the countries of this region do not stray too far away from the fold.

The question this situation poses is: Do the Arab countries of the South have to discover their own versions of democratic functioning which can gain from the experiences of others without trying to copy them? For many years this was the contention of the Arab Marxist left, but the so-called 'socialist' regimes themselves degenerated into highly dictatorial regimes, and the functioning of the Arab left-wing parties proved to be far from democratic in many ways. The question remains, How can we build up participation of the people at all levels in all institutions, economic, social, political, cultural, religious and educational? How do we draw women, youth and poor people into the democratic process? How can we democratize the content of education, and the structure and functioning of the family? How do we change relations between men and women to enhance the role and status of women? What can the contribution of women and youth be to the democratic process? And is it not true that democratic development in the South can in the long run help democratic development in the North and vice versa, and lead to a more peaceful, more prosperous, more stable situation for all? And what can we do to understand, to study the experiences of the past and develop more effective democratic functioning in the future?

Human rights

The movement for human rights in Arab countries grew significantly during the 1980s. Organizations for the defence of human rights exist in some Arab countries in the Mediterranean region such as Egypt, Tunisia, Algeria and Morocco. These movements are however severely restricted by government intervention and control. In some countries such as Egypt, they lack any legal status and function on a *de facto* basis subject to the graces and aims of the state.[2] They are mainly composed of intellectuals and professionals with a sprinkling of youth and few women. Their means are limited and their premises too modest to permit anything except limited organizational meetings. They concentrate their activities mainly on matters concerning political arrests, treatment in prison, legal rights of political prisoners, torture and so on. In more recent years the movement in Egypt has also taken up the issue of violence whether by terrorists or on the part of the government, which is a new and important dimension of work. One of the failings of these organizations is that they have been the seat of political struggles between parties who seek to dominate their activities instead of cooperating to reinforce the movement for human rights. However some progress has been made in this area.

The activities of human rights organizations in Arab countries have been mainly informational. Such activities have also been adopted on a limited scale by political parties in the opposition and their newspapers. Amnesty International has groups in all the Arab countries. Nevertheless, so far these groups have only interested limited elites involved in one way or another with political activity and therefore sensitive to the need for some form of protection. In countries of the South the issue of human rights raises the question, How far can we talk of human rights without a new conception which extends them to the economic, social, cultural, racial and religious fields as well as to women and youth? How far can the present limited approach go? Does it not need to expand, to interest much wider sections of the population in action for human rights?

Women

The women's movement in the Arab countries until very recently was limited to two areas. Within the political parties, women's wings and activities were considered of secondary importance and had to be placed at the service of the party, that is, at the service of a programme or platform defined by men, in the service of men, who were seeking power. Women's specific needs could go as far as creches, or matters related to employment or wages or leave (in left parties) but no further. The other area for women's activities was that of so-called nongovernmental – but in fact largely governmental – organizations dedicated to one or another form of social service or charity.

The establishment of a woman's organization of the kind of the Arab Women's Solidarity Association (AWSA), based in Egypt, in 1982 was a new and important development. AWSA had affiliate groups in a number of countries including Algeria, Tunisia, Syria, Libya, Morocco, Sudan, Lebanon and Yemen, as well as amongst emigrant Arab groups outside the Arab region. But in addition women's associations and groups were started during the same period in some of these countries, notably Tunisia, Algeria and Morocco, in the face of many obstacles which so far have severely restricted their activities and even forced some of them to close down.[3]

What was new in these organizations and especially in AWSA was the radically different conception and approach that governed their activity. AWSA with its 3,000 members insisted on the need to develop an independent organization for women. Without such an organization, they were convinced, it was impossible to create consciousness amongst women and to build up their power so that they could defend their specific interests and contribute effectively to the development and progress of society as a whole – whence the slogans 'unveiling of the mind' and 'solidarity and power of women'. AWSA made the link between gender or sexual problems (that is, relations between men and women in the family and in society) and the political, economic, social, cultural, religious and psychological aspects of life in Arab societies. In addition it insisted on the link between the local, national, regional and international levels. As a result it became the target for attack by different tendencies in society extending from the far right to the far left. The most important, of course, in this attack were the Islamic political forces most opposed to the rights of women. They were the voice of reactionary economic and social forces entrenched mainly in the countries of the Gulf headed by Saudi Arabia. Some were operating from inside the state apparatus and the government, and some from outside it. So when AWSA was closed down it was thought that this was due to the religious factor, to the increased strength of Islamic fundamentalist movements. But although these movements were the spearhead of the attack there is no doubt that the orientation of AWSA, its unveiling of the relationships between gender discrimination and the socioeconomic structure of society, was the main reason for closing it down. Such a conception inevitably meant highlighting the need for deep changes in the structures of Arab society and in all aspects of life starting from the family and extending nationally to the state and including education, culture, religion, and social and economic activity. AWSA also showed that the status of women in Arab countries, their cause, was a crucial one that could no longer be neglected by governments, institutions, the media and people. Its quarterly publication *Noon*, although published in only 5,000 copies, was both in content and form like an explosion that shattered the normal functioning of the media.[4] It created widespread interest and controversy and led *Al-Ahram*, the most important official newspaper in the Arab region, to publish a women's weekly called *Nisf Al-Dunia* (Half the World). It was because of all this that AWSA and its magazine had to be closed down, especially after the even-handed position they both took in the Gulf War which aroused the wrath of the Egyptian government and Saudi Arabia, now a very influential power in Egyptian society.[5]

Islamic fundamentalism

The words 'Islam' and 'Arab' tend to create an atmosphere of fear and panic. It would not be an exaggeration to say that the 'spectre' of Islam has replaced the 'spectre' of communism which once haunted the West, that the enemy Marx has been replaced by the enemy Muhammad.

Although we believe that some of the developments in the Arab region have been conducive to the creation of this mood, we do not feel that these developments are the basic reason. For us the basic reason is oil. The North depends largely on the oil in the Arab countries and particularly in the Gulf region. A cutoff in the supplies of oil would spell chaos and death. A rise in oil prices can spell economic disaster to many sectors of people unless a prior restructuring and replanning of production have been implemented. It would mean at least a substantial reduction in the power, influence and profits of many giant multinationals controlling the world. According to them, the status quo built on exploitation, oppression and control of the Arab countries must be maintained and wherever possible increased. Any attempt to change it or to rebel against it must be crushed mercilessly. This is something we understand, would like to change, but must accept. The question is, How do you change it without upsetting the economy of the whole world even more than it is already upset? How do you change it by a combination of struggle, cooperation, dialogue, understanding and controversy within a peaceful democratic framework? And how do we gradually overcome those forces that see in Islam and the Arabs an enemy which must be painted black, which people must hate all over the world and especially in the North, but also in the South in order to sow discord and division?

We could be accused of making a sweeping statement. But for us this statement is obvious, is proved by our history, by the present, by the Gulf War, by everyday life. How else can we explain the fact that Saudi Arabia, the most conservative, reactionary, dictatorial Arab regime, is supported by the United States which professes to dislike what is now commonly called 'fundamentalist terrorist Islam'? How can we explain that the West has always supported the most reactionary, tribal, Islamic states in the Gulf region even if from time to time some voices in the US government are raised to reclaim some modernizing or liberalizing changes which give a better face to regimes that are known to be exploitative, oppressive and corrupt?

For those who believe in change, in the need for cooperation and for improving relations between the North and the South, for those who believe in progress, a proper understanding of Islam as it manifests itself in the region today is essential. This is true not only for people in the North but also for people who like us live in the South and who cannot pretend that it is easy to deal with all the complex consequences of the gaining of power by fundamentalist Islamic groups, in society and in our daily life. For example, the Islamic movement Hamas is struggling against the Israeli occupation of Palestine. Progressive people like ourselves support this struggle and yet oppose Hamas on other issues. Another example is the Islamic newspaper *El-Shaab* (People) which is the official newspaper of the Labour Socialist Party, one of the Islamic parties infiltrated by the Muslim Brotherhood; this is opposing IMF and World Bank policies in Egypt, which are considered by most progressives in Egypt to be antagonistic in many ways to the vital interests of the majority of women and men in Egypt.

In so far as dealing with the Islamic phenomenon and so-called Islamic fundamentalism is concerned we would like to make the following remarks.

The growth of fundamentalist movements during the 1980s and into the 1990s is a world phenomenon. It is visible not only in the Arab and Islamic countries but also in Christian countries like the USA and South Africa, or in Hindu majorities in India, or in Judaism in Israel. It is, in the analysis of some, a reaction to the economic and social crisis sweeping over our world, and is encouraged by powerful financial and military circles in the North. Some of these circles have no objection to fundamentalist regimes, or a fundamentalist takeover of power in certain countries. At different stages in the past and even today these circles, and others, have encouraged and supported fundamentalist movements to serve their ends. Witness Sadat's encouragement to these movements in his struggle against Nasserites, socialists, communists, democrats, and more radical liberals. Or support to Saudi Arabian, or to Kuwaiti regimes known to be autocratic, unpopular, corrupt and very oppressive to women and the poor, or British support of the Muslim Brotherhood movement since its establishment in 1928. If the fundamentalist phenomenon is particularly visible in the Arab countries this is due to the depth of the crisis in this area, the virulence of the struggle for oil, the revolt against 'Western policies' of important sectors of the population who see in Islam a way to struggle against the evils of Westernization and the corruption and oppression it has often brought with it despite whatever benefits colonialism and neocolonialism have bestowed as a part of integration into the world market in the economic and social fields. And another cause of the growth of fundamentalism in the Arab countries is some of the dynamic (good or bad) characteristics of the Arab people, their history and the history of

Islam. We should not forget that Islam and the Arab people at one time built up an empire that extended from Indonesia to Spain and constituted an important stage in the development of the world.

Although certain cultural aspects of a nation or a people, including cultural aspects of religion, play a role in the shaping of society and its characteristics, these are rarely a deciding factor in its development except at certain specific moments of history. In other words Islam is not the deciding factor in the so-called 'backwardness' or 'underdevelopment' of the Arab countries on the south coast of the Mediterranean, even though it could be helping in maintaining some elements of this 'backwardness'. To us the most important factors are of a socio-economic and political nature related to the history of the countries in the region, to the Turkish invasion and later colonialism and neo-colonialism, to the aborted industrial and agricultural development of these countries, to corrupt governments and dictatorship; they have also influenced culture and the degree of economic and social separation between the state and religion. This is shown by the fact that Islam has been interpreted and applied in different ways in different socioeconomic contexts. The situation and legal provisions governing the lives of women and their relations with men are much more liberal in Tunisia than in Saudi Arabia or Egypt for that matter, and were even more liberal and progressive in South Yemen when it was governed by a so-called Marxist regime. This understanding is important in dealing with the Arab countries of the South Mediterranean. It is vital to realize that Islam is not the main obstacle to progress, but rather the oppressive, reactionary and backward regimes which are often on good terms with certain centres of power in the North. This understanding is also essential if good and friendly relations are to be set up with Muslim Arab countries and cooperation is to be improved between the North and the South. Islam is an integral part of people living in this region, and cannot be ignored, or brushed aside, or dealt with by a purely secular approach. It is necessary to realize that it can be a liberalizing as well as an enslaving force depending on how it is interpreted and utilized in governance, culture, human rights and women's emancipation. In Islam as in all religions or ideologies there has been a rigid, dogmatic and fanatical approach and a more liberal, open-minded and progressive approach. In all the stages of Islamic history the struggle between different tendencies has gone on, and the role of progressive movements attached to the cause of cooperation between people is to study Islam objectively, and encourage the forces that have an interest in a liberal, enlightened approach. In view of the mounting problems related to the Islamic political movements, such a study is imperative for all proponents of North–South cooperation in the Mediterranean region.

The Islamic political movements as a whole should be understood as a product of a deep crisis, of economic difficulties, of the failure of other solutions and regimes to solve people's problems, as a return to what is familiar and reassuring including God, as a protest movement against corruption, oppression, and exploitation, whether national or international (especially by the West), as a struggle to maintain a certain identity and independence from others and not be absorbed, as a search for a moral and spiritual code that other political and social movements have failed to provide. This is what the masses of recruits to the Islamic movement see in it no matter what current they belong to.

At the leadership level of this popular protest movement, however, are the different power circles that lead and orient the various tendencies, groups and parties to serve ends that are often not necessarily those of the common people. There is establishment Islam institutionalized in Al-Azhar University which is the official religious centre of Egypt and the Arab region. It largely serves and supports government policies and competes with other more radical movements that oppose it in the struggle for government and power. The Gulf regimes, especially Saudi Arabia, are representative of establishment Islam, and belong to the Sunna sects which are largely supporters of official *shari'a* teachings.[6] There are also the more recent Islamic political movements that are against establishment Islam, and vie with it for power. They tend to be more radical, and anti-Western, but this may be partly related to the fact that so far they have never wielded power. These political movements include the more moderate Muslim Brotherhood and all the grades of more radical, often fanatical movements using terrorist methods and ostensibly opposing the Muslim Brotherhood, who seek to reach power at the present stage by parliamentary means, and who the more radical groups consider to be partly linked to the establishment, with considerable economic and financial means at their disposal. The Muslim Brotherhood have used these means to provide a network of services, and to control different professional unions, clubs, associations, etcetera. However it is now clear that some degree of co-ordination exists between these different oppositional movements, and that the Muslim Brotherhood, which traditionally had a military wing, prefers to reap the benefits of terrorist action without being directly implicated – whence the growth of autonomous, radical, fanatical terrorist organizations.

There remain the Shi'ite Islamic movement of Iran and the Islamic regime of Sudan, which has vacillated between cooperation with Iran and with Saudi Arabia. Not much can be said about them here as they need separate examination, except that the Shi'ite sect grew up traditionally as anti-Sunna, anti-establishment-Islam, but later on, and especially now, has built up its own establishment in the state of Iran and competes, as a more radical force, with Saudi Arabia.

With the present equilibrium of forces it is unlikely that the more liberal, progressive tendencies in Islam will be able to gain the upper hand. This would require a strong popular democratic movement or front to tip the balance and exercise pressure on the Islamic political movement. Ideas without considerable power would find it difficult to influence the rather narrow-minded and rigid mentality prevailing in these movements.

[Excerpt from 'East/West: A Different View of Cooperation', report to Swiss Development Cooperation, 1992]

Notes

1. Co-written with Sherif Hetata.

2. In 1987 the Egyptian Organization for Human Rights initiated legal proceedings against the government in the state Council Court. The case is still pending. Sherif Hetata was secretary general of the organization at that time and raised the case with the aim of obtaining legal recognition for it. [*Author's note, 1997*: The court still has not announced a decision, and we may have to wait twenty years for a judgement.]

3. In June 1991 the Ministry of Social Affairs in Egypt issued a decree to close down the Egyptian branch of AWSA. AWSA began legal proceedings against the government in the state Council Court. The case is still [1997] bogged down in the courts.

4. Noon was the ancient goddess of the universe.

5. AWSA condemned both Sadaam's invasion of Kuwait and US military intervention.

6. The schools and systems of religious jurisprudence have historically been in the service of establishment Islam.

CHAPTER 5

Cairo '94 and the Dignity of Feeding Oneself

Pro-life or pro-death?

The Pope (and the Vatican) heads an international religious movement calling itself 'pro-life', whose principal role is to confront those women's liberation movements that support abortion and call themselves 'pro-choice', in the sense that it is a woman's right to choose between continuing a pregnancy or aborting it.

Former United States presidents, such as Ronald Reagan and George Bush, encourage religious movements both at home and abroad in order to undermine their main enemy at the time – the Soviet Union and communism. But the current US president, Bill Clinton, no longer needs these fundamentalist groups. He needs to win the votes of American women, most of whom belong to the 'pro-choice' movement. Clinton announced that he was 'pro-choice', saying that abortion must be legal, sanitary and also rare. In 1994 the US health administration agreed to produce the abortion pill known as RU486, and Clinton prohibited demonstrations against medical abortion centres. The religious fundamentalist or 'pro-life' movement had attacked abortion centres with bombs and fired bullets at doctors. They even attacked pregnant women within these centres in the name of protecting the life of the foetus, or fighting the 'pro-death' movement.

In March 1994 the Pope sent an angry letter to heads of states participating in the United Nations population conference Cairo '94, including the US president, Bill Clinton. The Pope wrote that Cairo '94 would be a dangerous point of decline for humanity, and that the United Nations was trying to destroy the family and promote the organized killing of foetuses in the womb. The Vatican published a sixty-six-page report in which it condemned the UN's preparatory reports for the conference, in which abortion was approved as one means of birth control. The Vatican report said that this was 'the imperialism of birth control' and that the population explosion or what is called the 'population bomb' is nothing more than a false slogan. Some Vatican clergymen have been asking how it is possible for a US president to be 'pro-death' and against 'life'. Naturally the Vatican did not direct such a question at George Bush in 1991, when he killed half a million people in the Gulf War.

The divide between women in the world

At all the international conferences I have experienced since the 1970s, there have been two groups of women (and men) and they were invariably at loggerheads. These were the governmental group (including officials, both men and women, from the United Nations), and the nongovernmental group (including delegations from popular liberation movements).

At the first UN population conference held in Bucharest in 1974, the nongovernmental group's voice was strong and the group was led by women's liberation movements from Africa, Asia and South America, supported by socialist and national liberation movements, the youth movement, the black movement and movements opposed to war and colonialism. At the 1980 International Women's Conference in Copenhagen such women's voices were strong in confronting the control the governmental group was trying to impose. At the second UN population conference held in Mexico in 1984, the progressive women's forces were still present and the women from the nongovernmental group were able to surround the conference hall and raise their voices in protest.

And at the Third World Conference on Women held in Nairobi in 1985, women from nongovernmental bodies formed a large demonstration which walked to the official (governmental organizations') conference hall. The Kenyan government almost arrested some of them. However these progressive feminist and political movements have suffered severe setbacks since the defeat of liberation forces in a number of countries in Asia, Africa and South America and the inception of what has been called the New World Order, the disastrous Gulf War and subsequent wars and crises, and the subjection of the world to one capitalist, classist, patriarchal and militarist superpower, which strikes whomever it wishes whenever it wishes to achieve its own economic gain. Progressive movements in general have been dismantled and new racist forces which believe in tyranny have appeared, attempting to discriminate between people on the basis of religion, belief, colour, ethnic origin, gender or nationality. These racist movements flourish at times (when governments encourage them) and wane and almost die out at other times (when governments attack them).

This is the political climate of Cairo '94. There will as usual be two meetings within the conference: one for the governmental group and one for the nongovernmental group. But the disagreement between the two groups is no longer so great, and some governmental bodies now disguise themselves beneath nongovernmental banners.

The logic of the governmental group

Why are the United Nations, the United States and governments supporting Cairo '94 concerned with the 'population problem'? Why the huge crowds and heavy media coverage at the conference?

The logic of the governmental group and the United Nations is based on the fixed idea that global resources are limited and that these limited resources cannot be sufficient for the world's population by the year 2050, if the population increases at its present rate. The world population now stands at 5.7 billion and it should not exceed 7.8 billion by the year 2050, according to this group's logic. But the rate of population growth (especially in the Third World) indicates strongly that the world population will reach 12.5 billion by 2050 (a surplus of 4.7 billion people).

How can those 4.7 billion people be gotten rid of? The governmental and United Nations group believes that these billions of people should not be born in the first place, that their ignorant mothers, who are unaware of this problem, should not become pregnant with them. That is why Cairo '94 was convened, and with two main goals: raising the awareness of families and women who are unaware of the problem, and the supervised distribution of birth control drugs and loops to 350 million families in the so-called Third World.

Feminist nongovernmental logic

Right from the start feminists of the nongovernmental group have proclaimed their wish not to be placed in the same category as the Pope, the Vatican, and those with racist or fundamentalist tendencies and others who consider that the only sacrosanct life is that of the foetus in the womb whilst people killed by the thousand (in Africa, Asia or South America) in consequence of war, famine or poverty are not worth defending.

The logic of these women is based on the following:

1. World resources are not limited. Huge tracts of land in Africa, Asia and South America have never been made use of. Parts of the world's

resources are being wasted, including surplus produce which is being disposed of by being thrown into the oceans.

2. Development projects imposed on peoples (through the World Bank and other international institutions) are projects that retard true development and increase poverty. These projects led to the transfer of $178 billion from the Third World to North American and European banks between 1984 and 1990 alone.

3. Global resources are not distributed to citizens of the world in equal measure. Eighty per cent of those resources are consumed by 20 per cent of the world's population in the USA and Europe. The real problem is not the population increase, but the increase in consumerism among the world's rich minority.

4. Ninety per cent of international companies (including multinational corporations) are owned by the USA and Europe and control 70 per cent of world trade. Five hundred of these companies possess total control over the world economy, and impose unfair trading regulations on Third World countries, forcing them to open up their markets unconditionally to these same companies. Hence most Third World countries have become unable to meet the food needs of their populations, and are living on what has been called 'aid'.

Between 1975, when US aid to Egypt started, and 1986, the United States received $30 billion in return for US goods and services imported by Egypt. During the same period, Egypt received only $5 billion from the USA (for exports). Only a very small proportion of what is taken from us is returned to us in the form of 'aid'; we are not only being divested of our material resources, but also of our dignity. Dignity stems from the ability to feed oneself. This applies to the state as much as it does to the individual, man or woman.

A dose of dignity

There is an erroneous idea prevalent within the United Nations and among population experts that women are incapable of practising birth control without their help, or without resorting to contraceptive medicines. History, ancient and modern, nevertheless proves that women have always been able to determine the number of children they need without United Nations interference, even before the United Nations was set up, and before the discovery of contraceptive pills. At the beginning of the twentieth century, during the severe economic crisis that swept through the world, women in rural and urban areas, in both East and West, were able to reduce the number of children they had by means of natural contraception. Over the past thirty years the world's population has increased by something like a billion people. This increase has not occurred through Third World women's ignorance of contraceptives (as the UN experts say). This increase occurred because of the world's need for it. Every country in the world has its own specific need to increase or decrease its population.

At times of war and crisis when more people die or are killed, women's fertility rises to compensate for the deficiency or to meet a new need in society or the extended family. In occupied Palestine for example, women's fertility rose above the customary average. Without this demographic increase there would have been no Intifada or stone-throwing revolution, whose heroes are the children of mothers who gave birth to them during the war. In the Occupied Territories, this population increase posed a greater threat to the Israeli government than the guns of the PLO, forcing Israel to solutions, including peace.

When I was a child I was always filled with wonder to see my peasant grandmother walk through the village with her head held high, defiant of the mayor, working all day long in the fields then returning home, never ceasing to work or to be cheerful. She produced precisely the number of boys and girls she needed. It has been scientifically proved that productive women (even peasant women who cannot read) are just as capable of producing the children they need as they are of feeding themselves and their children. What is more, it has been proved that idle women who remain at home (even if they are the educated wives of rich men) are just as incapable of determining the number of children they need as they are of providing for themselves. This is because productive women (even if they are peasants, poor and illiterate) feel dignity as productive members of the family and society, and it is this dignity that enables them to determine precisely what they do or do not want, that makes them capable of making their own decisions, without being in need of the external intervention of a local or foreign authority imposing contraceptives on them.

[Edited version of an article first published in Arabic in *Al-Ahram*, 31 August 1994 and translated by David Aldridge]

PART TWO

Women's Health

CHAPTER 6

Women and Health in the Arab World

This is the first time in long years that I have returned to the subject of women and health, though I am a medical doctor and practised medicine for many years. My medical career, unlike that of my colleagues, was not limited to a single specialized branch of medicine. For several years I worked as a general practitioner in rural areas, when I had to treat a variety of maladies, in particular epidemic and endemic diseases in children and adults, diseases and infections of the reproductive system, especially in women, and malnutrition.

In a rural situation there were almost no limits to the variety of cases with which I had to deal personally, or diagnose and refer to a specialized institution. Later I moved over to a number of new areas in the city. First I worked as a physician in a specialized hospital, where I dealt with cases of tuberculosis and other chest diseases. Then I spent two years in the area of obstetrics, gynaecology and paediatrics. But as my interests widened both professionally and as a writer, I abandoned clinical work, and concentrated on preventive medicine, hygiene and health education. Eventually I became director general of health education in the Ministry of Health. This was the period that permitted me not only to observe how health programmes are carried out in a developing country, but also to witness the inner functionings of the bureaucratic system. The last stage in this rather unusual medical journey led me to psychiatry and mental health. I did graduate studies in 1974 at Ain Shams University in Cairo, and after that carried out a limited number of consultations, especially with women. My interest in psychiatry and mental health was a direct result of my experience as a woman observing and treating other women in rural and urban areas, of my increasing involvement in feminist studies, feminist writings, and women's problems, and of my increasing involvement too in struggle in Egypt and the Arab world. It was not a bid to discover a lucrative career in a luxurious private clinic, where I could climb the social ladder from the class that labours in order to live to a class that lives on the labour of others. For in Egypt today, the higher levels of the medical profession extract exorbitant fees from their patients, and then invest this money in land, buildings, shares and bank deposits. But perhaps this is the price of the things I learnt on the way.

Nevertheless I often dream of one day belonging to the rich class, and of being able to hire the labour of others, especially domestic servants and cooks. For my greatest suffering is the hours wasted in buying vegetables and meat, cooking for the family, cleaning the house, washing clothes and hanging them out to dry, and a host of other small things that are linked to everyday life. For despite the fact that all of us (my husband, my daughter, my son and myself) share in bearing the daily responsibilities of work inside and outside the house, much of what we are obliged to do is, for us, a waste of time.

Throughout my life I have always felt some anxiety whenever I compare my earnings and the rapid rate at which prices are rising. This anxiety reached its peak in the period after 1974 when the 'open door' economic policies of the Sadat regime started to come into play. For these policies quickly transformed the lives of the majority of Egyptians into a breathless race for their daily needs. To ask an Egyptian the size of his income is often considered an awkward question. For the rich are ashamed or wary (because of possible taxation) to speak of their enormous wealth, whereas the poor are immediately reminded of what they would like to forget.[1] The difference between classes was already great under the old colonial system. It has grown even greater under the modernized colonial system, where direct methods of oppression have been replaced by an alliance between the multinationals and new economic, political and cultural elites.

My journey through medicine: the roots of disease

Two years after I graduated from medical school my mother died. My father followed her six months later. We were nine in the family, six sisters and three brothers. Four of my sisters were still at various stages of schooling, and since none of my brothers was in a position to take over responsibility for them they were left in my charge. In addition I had already been through my first marriage and divorce, and was left with an infant daughter to care for. I needed money badly and decided to open a clinic in the provincial city of Benha, then later moved to Cairo. My patients were numerous, my earnings so limited that after four years I abandoned the attempt. I had found it impossible to take money from men and women who were almost destitute, in other words from the rural and urban poor who constituted the majority of my patients. This was one of my problems and still is, so I have never opened a private clinic since then. (The consultations I do as a psychiatrist are for young people, men and women, who have read my books or heard of me, either in Egypt or in one of the Arab countries. They come to my home and I help them as much as I can, but there is no fee.) But I had learned from this experience that poverty is synonymous with death and disease.

In my clinic days a large number of patients used to be suffering from bilharziosis (schistosomiasis)[2] which penetrates the skin as a cercaria (a kind of larva from the water), lodges in the urinary or digestive system, and grows into a worm. Its complications are manifold, including cirrhosis of the liver, and kidney swellings (like hydronephrosis) ending in renal failure, and cancer. But even before the final stage it saps the body with pain, anaemia and toxicosis, causing prolonged suffering. I used to treat these patients when they came, and if they came early enough they were cured. But once back at work irrigating their fields they would catch bilharziosis again. Each time they were supposed to pay.

Later, when I worked in the hospital for chest diseases and dealt with tuberculous patients, I found that the overwhelming majority were poor labourers, from slum areas living in crowded rooms, with no sun or fresh air, who were underfed and overworked. I used to screen over a hundred patients in a single morning starting at nine o'clock and finishing around one, seated in a small room, exposed to infection and radiation with no protection of any kind except perhaps my own sturdy build. Each time I asked a patient to take a deep breath, out of ignorance or fear he or she would instead breathe out into my face. As time went by I noticed that most of the patients were either not cured or improved temporarily, only to relapse because there was no change in their environment, or in their conditions of work and life. So once again I felt myself facing a dead end, helpless, almost useless. My rural patients had continued to be reinfected through working in the fields with their feet in water. My tuberculous patients were too weak, too exposed to resist the onslaught of the vicious little drumsticks living in their lungs and lymphatic tissues. Some died in their homes never to return. Others died before my eyes, consumed by a terrible inner combustion or bleeding to death.

I now realized that I was not treating these patients. That the only real, radical treatment was prevention. I had moved forward to another stage in my medical journey. For I had to find the answer to a crucial question: How can we prevent disease?

In medical school the fields of preventive medicine and public health were at my time and remain to this day of little importance. The least talented professors are appointed in these departments, and only very mediocre students thought of specializing in these areas. Since I had passed my examinations with merit, it was natural that I chose a clinical career. But the experiences I had been through made me think differently as the years went by. Perhaps also deep down inside me, I was running away from living amidst disease and death all the time. For in 1957 I had published my first novel *Memoirs of a Woman Doctor*, and I needed more time to meditate on things, to understand, more time to live and to read, more time to explore the society in which I lived. I needed to break through the confines of hospital or clinic life.

During the same period I began to publish articles in newspapers and magazines dealing with issues related to preventive medicine, drawn from my observation of endemic diseases such as bilharziosis and tuberculosis, but also from observing rural and urban populations, then social relations, values and problems. Running through all this was a special emphasis on women, which I had carried with me from my life as a girl, and which kept developing all the time, nourished by the difficulties I faced as a woman and by more general discrimination against the female sex, in all areas, including that of health, and by a growing consciousness. But gradually artistic writing (novels and short stories) was beginning to occupy a central position in my career. And artistic writing required culture. So I started to delve into new areas: into literature, and history, and sociology, and philosophy and religion. I developed a deeper understanding of the real causes underlying poverty and hunger, destitution, disease and even death in our country. My interest in social problems grew with every step, and with this growth I moved to a new stage of understanding, a stage where social structures and problems could no longer be separated from the economics, the politics and the culture of the country, and of the world in which I lived, a stage where I began to seek for common roots and the common causes that underlie the problems we face in all areas of life, work and activity.

And so as I had once made the link between curative and preventive medicine, then moved on to make the link between preventive medicine and social conditions, I now started to make the link between the social, the economic, the political and the cultural in society. To see the human body as a whole, to see society as a whole, to see knowledge as a whole. To break down and analyse only to build up, and synthesize. This was my progression from the particular to the general, from the personal to the political, from my life to all life, from one woman to all women, from the individual to the collective.

From medicine to collective action

So the logic of things led me to politics. Nevertheless at no time did I affiliate myself to a political party, whether during Nasser's regime or subsequently when Sadat became president. My artistic temperament made me rebel against much of the hypocrisy, compromise, organizational restrictions, pressure groups, and lobbying that have remained intrinsic parts of our short-sighted politics, which are still prevalent today. Yet I know that the economic exploitation and political oppression exercised against Third World countries like mine is collective, and organized, and therefore can only be met by collective organized resistance against the alliance between foreign domination and internal forces of economic, political and cultural exploitation.

I looked around, searching for some place where I could join my efforts with others. My first attempt was with the Medical Syndicate, a professional grouping for doctors, which is in some ways like a trade union. I thought I could play a role in a limited area, that of remoulding medical practice, and of abolishing the contradictions inherent in the present system between curative and preventive practice, and between the interests of the patient and those of his doctor. I joined a group of doctors which we constituted under the name the Committee for Social Medicine. It was successful in preparing a number of studies and mobilizing efforts to execute certain reforms, but later broke up under government pressures.

After this attempt we established a new group called the Association for Culture and Health, which started to publish a monthly magazine called *Health*. I was appointed chief editor. At the same time I decided to stand for elections. I won a seat on the board of the Medical Syndicate by an overwhelming majority of votes, and was appointed assistant secretary-general. My medical and cultural activities had evoked resentment among the more privileged elites seeking undivided power. The content of the magazine *Health* – which emphasized the social aspects of health; the importance of reorganizing the health system so as to provide better and cheaper medical services and redress the unfavourable bias against preventive medicine; and the need to deal with women's problems and sex – was met with bitter opposition, from religious traditionalist circles and also from the privileged pseudo-modernistic levels of society, but received enthusiastic support from a rapidly expanding reading public.

The concept of health we tried to propagate in our magazine was multidimensional. Health involved the body and the mind. And a healthy body and mind could only be achieved in a healthy society. Women constituted half the society, in fact the half that suffered most, and faced the worst problems. Women were victims of a double exploitation: they shared class exploitation with men, but in turn they were subject to exploitation by men, to sex discrimination, to patriarchy. My writings had drawn the attention of young women. Perhaps we were all in a sense reflecting the changes that were taking place in society, a new awareness of women's status and problems. Ever since my early years the situation of women as I lived it had continued to occupy a central place in my thoughts and writings, but now I started to address myself in a more systematic way to this area. In March 1972 a new edition was published of my first book on women, entitled *Women and Sex*. In this book I dealt with the relations between men and women, the status of women, and the problems they faced as a reflection of physical, mental and social oppression in Egypt and the Arab world. I also devoted parts of the book to marriage, sex, virginity, clitoridectomy and other practices related to the life of women. This book, added to my previous writings and lectures, brought matters to a peak. In August 1972, by order of the Minister of Health, *Health* was closed down and I was ordered to leave my job as director general of health education in the ministry. I also lost my seat on the board of the Medical Syndicate, and my book was banned. Other writings were censored. I stayed home for six years, writing and publishing outside Egypt.

In 1978, feeling that the net was closing in, I accepted a job with the United Nations as an expert on women's development, first in the Economic Commission for Africa, then in the Economic Commission for Western Asia. Both were interesting. They permitted me to travel extensively in Africa and in the Arab world. They familiarized me with the inner workings of the UN system and of some aspects of inter-national politics. They also permitted me to see for myself that the UN was not seriously interested either in development or in women. It was time to go home, to resume my writings, to oppose the policies that had made of Egypt once more a dependent state in the world multi-national system. I resigned from the UN in October 1980 and flew back to Cairo.

On 6 September 1981, Sadat put me in jail. I spent three months in the Barrage Prison for Women.

Health and women in the Arab world

I have recounted this story at some length as an illustration of how I envisage the crucial problem of health, and to tell you something about medicine, health and women in a dependent Arab country. I think that in many ways what I have described is typical of all Third World countries.

The problem of health and women in Egypt begins with our system of medical education which we have inherited from the era of British colonial rule. This system of medical education meant that when I graduated as a young doctor from college in 1955 I knew something about the anatomy, physiology, pathology and diseased functioning of the separate parts of the body, but knew almost nothing of these aspects in the body as a whole. I knew even less about the relationship of body and mind, and nothing about the relationship between health, disease, environment and society. I despised preventive medicine as a branch meant for unsuccessful medical doctors and bureaucrats sitting behind desks, or even sweepers, collectors of refuse, and inspectors of food-stuffs.

In so far as women are concerned, the academicians and specialists in charge of our education taught us that a woman is a pair of ovaries, two Fallopian tubes, a uterus, a vagina, and a vulva, all paving the way to childbirth, plus breasts for lactating and rather inclined to develop cancer and abscesses. The uterus too could be the unfortunate seat of cancerous growth, especially at the cervix, perhaps as a result of pre-disposing chronic inflammation. For us medical students these things added up to make a woman. But maybe the fault was not that of our professors. For, after all, what could we expect in a society that considered women to be instruments of human reproduction?

Despite the fact that reproduction can only take place through sex, to this very day sexology is not considered to be a science worthy of respect and therefore to be taught side by side with obstetrics and gynaecology, or with venereal diseases for that matter. Society has ordained removal of the clitoris from the bodies of women, for the clitoris is no more than an appendage to be discarded, useless or even dangerous, since it is a source of pleasure for women, and pleasure for women means sin. The medical profession, which is male in its immense majority, has kept mute over this amputation, for our men happily are the greatest enemies of Satan, and so of sin. In the same way they have amputated sexology from the body of medical knowledge.

Since women are no more than an apparatus for reproduction, a species made to depend on men, to be married to them and to live in a state of 'penis envy', psychiatry continues to live in darkness where women are concerned, or at least to practise either the tenets of the Freudian school, established over half a century ago, or the teachings of the great religions in the Old and New Testaments and the Qur'an, which say that woman is an incomplete being without a mind.

Women of course continue to be victims of the whole range of endemic and epidemic diseases which still run rampant as a result of delayed socioeconomic development, despite the important advances made in medicine as a result of vaccination and new drugs, especially antibiotics. Many of the health problems that faced women in the colonial era continue to be serious problems today. Nutrition is a prime factor. Maternal mortality and morbidity have dropped, but only to a limited extent.

But grafted on to the old problems are a new range of health hazards and risks which have been aggravated to a striking degree by what we may call the new colonial era, characterized by the 'open door' economic policies launched by the Sadat regime in 1974. These policies have thrown the doors of Egypt wide open to the multinationals which operate in close cooperation with the ruling elites. The result has been the establishment of a money economy rather than an economy based on increased industrial and agricultural production, a literal invasion by international banking interests, speculation in land and currencies, black-marketeering, dependency on imports for essential and nonessential goods, the encouraging of consumerism, and large-scale corruption.

I would like to cite a few examples of how these changes have been reflected in health. In 1982 and 1983 a series of scandals hitherto carefully hidden were brought to light. Huge shipments of chickens, frozen and tinned meat, tomato sauce, cheese and wheat in various stages of toxic decay or putrefaction running into tens of millions of pounds were discovered. In many cases they were not found until people had been poisoned or died as a result of eating such foods. Well-known examples are those of 22 children who died from eating imported cheese, and 124 hospital patients poisoned by bad frozen meat. In rural areas peasants and their family members as well as cattle have died from the toxic effects of certain insecticides used in spraying crops, and cases of paralysis have been recorded. Pharmaceuticals spotted on the market have proved to be drugs that have dropped out of use because of their toxic effects, or have not yet been sufficiently tested, or are still under trial in the industrial countries. Our markets are being used as laboratories and our people as human guinea pigs. The problem is not so much that such incidents occur – even though this remains a problem in itself – but that they started to occur on such a vast scale and specifically after the 'open door' policies came into operation.[3] All these consumer goods are being imported by intermediaries working in close collaboration with foreign companies.

A case in point is the widespread use of contraceptive pills. The family planning campaign in Egypt is a notable phenomenon closely linked to US policies and US aid. These pills are sold without prescription, which is strictly forbidden in the rich, industrial countries. They are used on a very wide scale without medical supervision. Their side effects have not been sufficiently studied. The types used in Egypt have been surpassed by medical advances. Contraindications to their use are manifold but medical control is insufficient and often non-existent. This inconsiderate and irresponsible use of contraceptives is legitimized by the objective of controlling an even more dangerous population explosion.[4] In the cynical terms of the 'family planning' enthusiasts, 'it is a choice between two evils'. Yet nowhere have such irresponsible campaigns cut down birth rates in a developing country. We are not against family planning or contraception as a considered choice practised with care and due medical attention. We are against the multinational drug companies selling their wares to women, even if they have to maim them, or bleed them, or even kill them. We are also against the contraceptive pill as an alternative to health development and real women's emancipation. We also do not know enough about what hormones can do to women's bodies and minds, to embryos and offspring.

The strains and stresses of inflation, of escalating prices, of unemployment, of consumerism, affect all people but especially women who buy in the markets, and are supposed to make ends meet, and due to their inferior position are supposed to eat less than their men and to combine work outside and inside the home. The rising costs of education and medical care, the disappearance of free or even cheap social services, have added to the burdens of women especially working women in rural and urban areas. The incidence of circulatory disturbances and mental disorders is increasing among women. The absence of men when they emigrate seeking jobs has added new stresses to women's lives. Women too are forced to emigrate to search for the means of life. The number of Egyptians, men and women, working in the Arab countries alone is estimated at 3 million. Only one third have their families with them.

Pollution is reaching alarming proportions. Cairo is now the most highly polluted city in the world. We have the singular honour of coming first before Tokyo. Industrial wastes disposed of without safeguards into the air, or into the waters of the Nile or the Mediterranean Sea, and the indiscriminate, uncontrolled import of motor cars are the main causes. The first thing that strikes foreigners when they come to Cairo is the odour of petrol fumes. Pollution of the air in houses, and of human chests by cigarette smoke, is rising rapidly. In response to the curtailing of smoking in the industrial countries, the multinationals have increased their efforts to sell more cigarettes in the developing countries, where people below twenty-five years of age constitute 50 per cent of the population. Advertisements showing naked or semi-naked women entice youths to practise more masturbation, to hustle girls on the streets, and to smoke Rothman's cigarettes as a mark of virility and a guarantee of a future of social, business and sexual success. Smoking is rising rapidly in developing countries.

Health standards remain low

Standards of health are a reflection of socioeconomic development even if the relationship is not a rigid one, for as in all human activities there is latitude for human endeavour and creative thinking. Health hazards tend to affect the weakest sectors of society, that is, women and children, unless special systems of prophylaxis and protection are set up for them; this has hardly been the case so far in Egypt and similar countries, despite a relatively more developed structure of health services than in other Arab countries. Gastrointestinal and infectious diseases still take their toll of children's lives, and infant mortality hovers around 80 per thousand live births. Maternal mortality is high and has never dropped below 8 per thousand.[5]

Even in oil-rich countries like Kuwait, these diseases remain a problem which shows that the oil riches have not made a really radical change in the lives of ordinary people. Gastrointestinal infections, especially in infants and children, still cause 14.5 per cent of total deaths.[6] In Tunisia, pulmonary tuberculosis remains a major health problem. In recent years the rate of infection has increased by 50 per cent in some of the provinces such as Al-Menestair, Al-Mahdia and Soussa.[7] In Syria, out of every 1,000 children born, 15.3 die, and maternal mortality is 10 per thousand.[8] If we examine the evolution of the figures for Egypt, we discover changes of special significance. In 1952 infant mortality rates were 127 per thousand. They dropped to 74 per thousand in 1978, but rose again to 80 per thousand in 1980.[9] This indicates a deterioration in health standards and environmental sanitation linked to the collapse of many of the social services as a result of a worsening economic situation and a rapid increase in population. The natural rate of population increase is 2.97 per cent per year, that is around 1,100,000 new inhabitants (crude birth rate of 40.5 per thousand minus crude death rate of 10.8 per thousand). Gastrointestinal disease remains the primary cause of death in children, and represents 23.5 per cent of total deaths in males, and 25.5 per cent of total deaths in females.[10] As regards patients in the central hospitals administered by the Ministry of Health,

34.9 per cent were females admitted due to complications of pregnancy and labour.[11]

If we sketch a few comparative figures indicative of the difference in health standards between a Third World country like Egypt and the USA, the gap that separates these two countries will become evident. Life expectancy at birth for women in Egypt is 56.8 years.[12] For women in the USA the corresponding figure is 77.2.[13] The American mother has a ten times greater chance of escaping death from childbirth than the Egyptian mother (maternal mortality rate in Egypt 8 per thousand, in the USA 0.8 per thousand).

In Egypt, abortion still remains a major cause of death in pregnant mothers, but because of the secrecy attached to what is an illegal procedure, precise figures are not available. Rough estimates indicate that out of every four cases of pregnancy one of them ends in an illegal abortion.[14] The result is a host of very serious complications of which the poorer women are much more liable to be victims. The situation of an unmarried mother is very serious, not only from the medical point of view but also from the social and moral aspects. The most frequent cases are poor domestic servant girls, who have been subjected to sexual assaults by males in upper- and middle-class families. The legalization of abortion in Egypt may not have a noticeable effect on the number of abortions, which is increasing, but it will have the advantage of overcoming the black market and the exploitation practised by some doctors against pregnant women.

For the millions of ordinary women, everyday life in a poor developing country is a long road fraught with risks. The growing numbers of women who are struggling for a better life also must face the risks of standing up to oppression in all its forms, from the sexual and psychological to the political, national and international.

Sometimes we feel despair. There seems so much that remains to be done, and still so few to do it. But everywhere new forces are coming up. Everywhere young women are on the move. But freedom has a price, a price that a free woman pays in terms of her peace, her health, her security, when facing the opposition and aggression of society against her. Be that as it may, a woman always pays a heavy price, even if she chooses to submit. Therefore, since a price must be paid, why not the price of freedom rather than the price of slavery?[15]

[Paper presented at a memorial day for Fredrika Schweers, place unknown, 1983]

Notes

1. The number of estimated millionaires increased from about 500 at the time of Nasser's death (September 1970) to 17,000 today [1983]. The wealth of some is probably around £E400–500 million, which is very high by our standards. On the other hand about 30 per cent of the population live below the poverty line of $375 per year.
2. Eighty per cent or more of Egyptian peasants are infected by bilharziosis (both the urinary and the intestinal types).
3. It was only after the death of Sadat (on 6 October 1981) that the facts related to food poisoning (and corruption) and other trafficking of a similar nature came to light. During 1982 and 1983, almost all the newspapers in Egypt wrote extensively about these matters.
4. Young female university graduates spend one year in civic service which is equivalent to the recruitment of male youth for the army. They are supposed to carry out various civic duties. But these duties have been mainly reduced to the distribution of contraceptive pills. They are obliged to pay for the pills in advance and then recoup the money by distributing the pills to female clients in the popular districts or rural areas. But since this task is extremely difficult and embarrassing for young girls in the Egyptian situation they end up by selling these pills to the pharmacies for cheaper prices than they paid.
5. Report of the Ministry of Health, General Department of Statistics and Evaluation, Cairo, July 1980, p. 2.
6. The Sixth Report of the WHO Concerning Health Conditions in the World, Vol. 2, Geneva, 1980, p. 84.
7. Ibid., p. 104.
8. Ibid., p. 25.
9. Report of the Ministry of Health, Cairo, 1982, p. 2.
10. Ibid., p. 3.
11. Ibid., p. 4.
12. Ibid., p. 2.
13. Public Health Reports Supplement, *Women and Health*, US Government Public Health Service, Washington DC, 1980.
14. Nawal El Saadawi, *The Hidden Face of Eve*, Zed Books, London, 1980, p. 72.
15. Ibid., p. 209.

CHAPTER 7

The Bitter Lot of Women:
An interview

Hanny Lightfoot-Klein (HL-K): Nawal El Saadawi, as a novelist, doctor, and human rights activist, and as a woman, you have been concerned with female genital mutilation (FGM), often referred to as female circumcision, for quite a number of years. Indeed I think you were one of the first women in the world to discuss this issue openly, in your writing. This is a subject that once was thought of as belonging to strange primitive practices 'in darkest Africa'. But your work challenges some of the assumptions about FGM.

Nawal El Saadawi (NES): Well, in *Women and Sex*, which appeared in Arabic in 1971, I discussed, as a medical doctor, such issues as virginity and other matters considered taboo then, or even now. I offered an analysis of why women are circumcised. In *The Hidden Face of Eve* (Zed Books, 1980), there is a chapter which includes material on female circumcision and its relation to patriarchy. I argued that it bears a relation to the ancient, pre-monotheistic practices of monogamy for women and polygamy for men, the evolution of slavery and class systems. I took a sociohistorical perspective. The patriarchal system is, of course, historically based on a double standard, and the practice of female circumcision grew out of this double standard. Because the whole idea was, and still is, to diminish the sexuality of women, forcing monogamy upon them.

HL-K: It was thus a way of telling women they did not own their bodies.

NES: No doubt domination – by the man – is essential to this practice. To keep women monogamous, to attenuate the woman's sexuality, to control reproduction too, which after all did have, still has, an economic–political function, this practice was needed.

HL-K: But men are not much, if at all, involved in FGM.

NES: At the technical level, women are more involved, but men are too. It is a very ancient practice which very long ago came under the domain of midwives, 'grandmothers', etcetera. In the West, as people become aware of this practice, they may fail to see this foundation, which allows them to see that it is a form of the same system of domination that most societies have experienced, still experience. It is not, essentially, a 'bizarre African' practice.

HL-K: It is one form of a nearly universal system of patriarchy?

NES: Patriarchy itself is an expression of socioeconomic oppression.

HL-K: It sounds quaint, after the much-heralded 'end of history' to hear one of the most famous feminists in the world speak in almost Marxist terms. However, it is true that in your work you have put feminist issues in a broad historical perspective.

NES: Western feminists simply refused to listen to the problems of so-called Third World women, and paid little attention to our analyses. In a sense, therefore, I have had to insist more than I otherwise might have on what you may describe as a 'Marxist' analysis, but which is really putting the oppression of women in the broader context of history and global politics. But I am a doctor and I started from the personal experiences of my patients. I know very well how much women have suffered. Yet I would insist that there is a danger that in the West an issue like FGM, barbaric as it is – and I know what I am talking about – is going to be sensationalized. Sexual mutilation, battered women, all that.

HL-K: It is that.

NES: We have to see the patriarchal roots, the historical roots – long before Judaism, Christianity and Islam – of this phenomenon. This is not an Arab issue or a black African issue only. Arab women and African women are no different from others. If you want to help them, you have to understand this historically.

It is related to the slave systems that have appeared in *all* continents *everywhere* in history. It's a universal phenomenon. It has nothing to do with any religion or any ethnic group or any continent.

But also, and this is important, FGM is related to contemporary international politics in a manner that is, forgive me for saying, somewhat more urgent and interesting than the politics of middle-class Western feminists. There is a connection between the revival of fundamentalism in certain parts of the world and the increasing demands that women be excluded from public life, secluded and kept at home, that they be subjugated to men and – why not? – mutilated. Well this fundamentalism is not unrelated to colonialism and neocolonialism.

HL-K: What is the connection with international affairs?

NES: The political backlash against the progress women have made in recent decades, which you see in Western societies as well as in a country like Egypt, is related to neocolonialism. The domination by the West of a country like Egypt or Somalia – through the 'restructuring' programmes of banks and international financial institutions in one case, the contemporary version of 'gunboat diplomacy' in the other – is related to religious fundamentalism. The West will not get the 'order' it wants unless the people in these countries behave themselves – tighten their belts, remain orderly. And the West, in its contempt for these people, seems to have banked on the fundamentalists to get that internal order. And so, if you want to be provocative, you could say that there is a connection between George Bush and female circumcision. ...

HL-K: You view Western feminism as too 'personal', ahistorical, and apolitical?

NES: Sometimes, not always. This Western preoccupation with sex is due to an unliberated personality, and liberation has personal (sexual) components, to be sure, but political ones as well. Twelve years ago, I put it this way: 'The most liberated and free of girls is the one least preoccupied with sexual questions since these no longer represent any problem. Girls who suffer sexual suppression however are greatly preoccupied with men and sex. It is a common observation that an intelligent and cultured woman is much less engrossed in matters related to sex and to men than is the case of ordinary women who have not got much else with which to fill their lives. At the same time such a woman takes much more initiative to ensure that she will enjoy sex and experience pleasure and acts with a greater degree of boldness than others. Once sexual satisfaction is obtained she is able to turn herself fully to other aspects of life. In the life of a liberated and intelligent woman sex does not occupy a disproportionate position but rather tends to maintain itself within normal limits. Ignorance, suppression, fear and all sorts of limitations exaggerate the role of sex in the lives of girls and women and cause it to swell out of all proportion and to end up occupying the whole or almost the whole of their entire lives.' (WHO/EMRO Technical Publication: Seminar on Traditional Practices Affecting the Health of Women and Children in Africa, 1982.) That was written when I was thinking about the relation between religion and circumcision. ... I remember writing that during the sixties and seventies when I was writing *The Hidden Face of Eve*, I was also fighting politically in order to get away from those sexual oppressions. You can't separate sex from politics or religion.

HL-K: Did you encounter discrimination as a woman in medicine?

NES: ... If I were in America I could not have been a medical doctor because when I went to medical school in 1949 medical colleges were very discriminatory against women, Jews and blacks. But it's different now of course. I remember they had quotas then. In Egypt I was lucky because in 1948 when I graduated from high school I had the highest grades in my class. And at the time Egyptian medical schools accepted only those with the very highest grades. There was no discrimination whatsoever. ... Then working as a physician in the villages and seeing women dying of illegal abortions and female circumcision, I wrote *Women and Sex*. I started as a fiction writer; my first novel was called *Memoirs of a Woman Doctor*.

But then I really became fed up with what I saw as a medical doctor in the village, and I started writing *Women and Sex*. And then I started facing problems in the Ministry of Health.

My husband, Dr Sherif Hetata [and I] established the Health Education Association during the sixties and also established a magazine called *Health*. The magazine and the association were banned by the government.

HL-K: How did the government rationalize banning a magazine about health?

NES: It was banned in 1972 when I lost my job in the Ministry of Health. The Health Minister closed the health association and the magazine because we made the connection between health and politics; between sexual operations – clitoridectomy and virginity – and politics; between poverty and disease, and poverty and politics. We were un-covering the connection between health and poverty; colonialism and poverty; disease and poverty. And also between female circumcision, all virginity problems, all oppression of women and politics and religion etcetera. They didn't like that. So I lost my job. ...

HL-K: [In relation] to female mutilation, what do you think we should do now?

NES: Recognize the scope of the issue. Recognize its historical and political causes. Admit that women in our countries have been dealing with it for a long, long time. Instead of making a sensational fashion out of something that some Western feminists discovered yesterday and will forget tomorrow.

[Edited version of 'The Bitter Lot of Women', an interview with Hanny Lightfoot-Klein, *Freedom Review*, 25(3), 1994]

PART THREE

Women / Islam / Fundamentalisms

CHAPTER 8

Women and Islam

The oppression of women is not essentially due to particular religious ideologies. The great religions of the world (of both East and West) uphold similar principles as far as the submission of women to men is concerned. They also agree in the attribution of masculine characteristics to God.

For thousands of years most of the philosophers and thinkers, all of whom were men, have been so blinded, by their 'patriarchal cataract' and class optics, that their sight and their insight could not penetrate the time significance of the myth of Adam and Eve. Eve took the first step towards the tree of knowledge. She was therefore a dynamic force lifting Adam up to new heights for which she had paved the way. Yet she was the 'sin' or the 'fall' depicted in the Old Testament, from which Christianity and Islam inherited the myth which made Eve the origin of all sin.

The concept of religion developed in the human mind long before the monotheistic religions came to be known. Primitive human beings created the idea of 'gods' in the world, or at least of some obscure forces beyond their understanding endowed with capacities that they did not possess.

Historical studies indicate that the most ancient of all gods were female. In pharaonic Egypt goddesses ruled over many areas, and participated with gods in deciding human destinies. The evaluation of women to the heights occupied by goddesses was a reflection of their status within society before the systems characterized by the patriarchal family, land ownership and division into social classes came into being. With the advent of these systems the status of women gradually dropped over a period of time. Female goddesses started to disappear and women lost many of their rights and freedoms.

The monotheistic religions, in enunciating the principles related to the role and position of women, drew inspiration and guidance from the values of the patriarchal and class societies prevalent at the time. These societies were based on the division into landowners and slaves.

In essence, the messages that were carried to their peoples by the prophets Moses, Jesus and Muhammad were a call to revolt against the injustices of the slave system. Nevertheless the position of women remained inferior to that of men in all three religions.

The active role of women in the pre-Islamic and early Islamic eras

Pre-Islamic society was composed of numerous tribes which lived in the desert and in towns under varying economic circumstances. Some tribes were more or less matriarchal in structure like those of Khandak and Jadila (Afifi, 1921: p. 1950). Kings before Islam were sometimes named after their mothers as in the case of 'Umar Ibn Hind. Muhammad the Prophet was proud of his descendancy from the women of his tribe and was wont to say of himself: 'I am the son of the 'Awateks from the tribe of Sulaym' ('Atika Bint Hilal, 'Atika Bint Murra and 'Atika Bint El-Awkass were all women of this tribe).

Women in the desert areas and oases enjoyed a greater degree of liberty and independence than women in towns because they were involved in obtaining the means of livelihood. These desert women mixed freely with men and did not wear the veil.

Both male and female goddesses were known in the pre-Islamic era, and the Arabs believed that the god or goddess of each tribe played an active role in war, and fought to ensure victory for its people. Al-Lat and Uzzah were both goddesses of Abu Sufian's tribe, and together with his active and strong wife Hind constituted a female force which brought victory over the Muslims in the battle of Uhud.

The important position occupied by some goddesses[1] was symbolic of the relatively higher prestige enjoyed by women in Arab tribal society, and a reflection of the vestiges of matriarchal society that still lived on in some of the tribes. These aspects of matriarchalism might possibly explain the relatively important role played by women in both pre-Islamic and Islamic society. As a result of women's participation in economic activity then, side by side with men, they acquired independent personalities both inside and outside the home and were often free to choose their husbands. Before Islam it even happened that a woman could practise polyandry, that is, marry more than one man. When she became pregnant she would send for all her husbands, and no one could refuse to come. Gathering them around her she would name the man she wished to be father to her child. And the man could not refuse (Al-Isfahani, *Al-Aghan* 16: p. 2).

When a bedouin woman wished to divorce her husband she simply turned around the door of her tent. Once she made this change divorce was immediate (Al-Isfahani, *Al-Aghani*, 16: p. 102).

Islam abolished all polyandric practices, but women in the early phases of Islam continued to exercise their right to choose their husbands and to divorce. One of the well-known stories concerns Khadija, first wife of the Prophet. She exercised her freedom in choosing to marry Muhammad who was fifteen years younger than her. She sent him a woman called Nefissa and instructed her to propose that the Prophet marry Khadija. And he did (Ibn Sa'ad, 1970: Vol. 8, p. 9).

Another story in this connection is that of Laila Bint El-Khatim who went to Prophet Muhammad and said to him, 'I am Laila Bint El-Khatim, I have come to show myself to you. Marry me.' And Muhammad said, 'I hereby marry you.' But Laila was of a jealous nature and would not have been able to stand the other wives of Muhammad. So she asked him to divorce her, saying, 'I am a woman with a sharp tongue and cannot bear your other wives. So let me free.' So he said to her, 'I have let you free' (Ibn Sa'ad, 1970: Vol. 8, p. 107). In fact Prophet Muhammad was more emancipated with respect to women than most men of his time, and even most Muslim men nowadays. He gave his women the right to stand up to him, rebuke him, or tell him where he had gone wrong.

'Umar Ibn El-Khattab, who became the second caliph (*khalifa*) of Islam, was known for his puritanism. He told this story:

> We the people of Quraish were accustomed to ruling our women. But when we moved over to the Ansar [the earliest believers and followers of Muhammad in Islam] we found that among them it seemed to be the women that ruled. Our women started learning a new way of behaving from them. When I raised my voice against my wife she stood up in opposition to me. I did not accept this from her so she said, 'Why do you refuse me the right to oppose you? I swear to Allah that the wives of the Prophet Muhammad tell him frankly when he is wrong, without hesitation or fear, and one of them turns away from him for a whole day and night.' I was taken aback when she said this to me, and answered, 'Whosoever does so has committed a grievous wrong.' Then I drew my clothes around me and left the house. I went straight to Hafsa Bint 'Umar [one of the Prophet's wives] and asked her, 'Is it true that one of you turns away from the Prophet in anger for a whole day and night?' She answered, 'Yes.' I said, 'You do wrong, and you will be lost. Are you not afraid that God will feel anger at the anger of his Prophet, and destroy you? Do not oppose the Prophet, and do not rebuke him or turn away from him.' (Ibn Sa'ad, 1970: Vol. 8, p. 131)

From 'Umar's story it is clear that he was proud of the fact that he belonged to a tribe that ruled over their women with an iron hand and found unacceptable a situation where a woman could have her say, as was the case of the Ansar and other tribes.

Women, in early Islam, fought the tendencies of male authority with fortitude and patience. In putting up this resistance neither timidity nor shame held them back from voicing their real thoughts. Early Muslim women preceded the women of the world in resisting a religious system based on male domination. Fourteen centuries ago these women succeeded in opposing the unilateral use of the male gender in the Qur'an when referring to both men and women. Their outspoken objection was couched in terms that have remained famous. 'We have proclaimed our belief in Islam, and done as you have done. How is it then that you men should be mentioned in the Qur'an while we are ignored!'

At the time both men and women were referred to as 'Muslimin' (masculine for Muslims) but, in response to the objection voiced by women, Allah henceforward said in the Qur'an 'Inna Al-Muslimina (masculine for Muslims), Wal-Muslimat (feminine), Wal-Mu'minina (masculine for believers), Wal-Mu'minat (feminine)' (Ibn Sa'ad 1970: Vol. 8, p. 145).[2]

Even in matters as sensitive as the right to sexual pleasure Um Salma (one of the Prophet's wives) was bold and positive enough to defend her rights without the slightest hesitation, to refuse any interference between herself and her husband by other men, and to insist on the marital obligations of the man she had married even if he was a prophet and a leader whose mind was occupied with the problems of the earth and the heavens. When 'Umar Ibn al-Khattab and Abu Bakr al-Siddiq (later first caliph of Islam) intervened in this matter she told them boldly, 'Who else beside Him [her husband Muhammad] can we ask to satisfy our need [she was referring to their sexual need]. Does any one intervene between you and your women? We have not asked for your help.' Upon which the two men turned their backs and went out. And the wives of the Prophet said to Um Salma, 'May Allah bestow many good things upon you for what you said. We would not have been able to utter one word in answer to them' (Ibn Sa'ad, 1970: Vol. 8, p. 129).

Another woman even more striking than Um Salma was al-'Amiria (Ibn Sa'ad, 1970: Vol. 8, p. 130) whom Prophet Muhammad divorced because she adamantly refused to accept a situation where her husband neglected to give her the sexual attention which was her due. Muhammad never insisted that a woman continue to live with her husband if she wished to be separated. He gave his wives the full option of choosing between living with him or asking for divorce when his age and heavy responsibilities prevented him from affording them the marital attention and satisfaction which it was natural for them to expect.

However those who came after Muhammad did not follow in his steps where attitudes to women and their problems were concerned. Instead of their previous freedom in marriage and divorce, women were subjected to new laws imposing upon them marriage against their will, if necessary by brute force, and depriving them of their right to divorce. It is not difficult to see that the greater recognition accorded by the Prophet and early Islam to the rights of women was the direct result of the comparatively higher position occupied by the Arab woman in the pre-Islamic era, her more active participation in various aspects of life whether within or outside the precincts of the home, and the prominent role played by a number of outstanding Arab women.

Prominent Muslim women

The history of the Arabs is studded with women personalities who played an important role in the tribal society of the pre-Islamic and early Islamic eras. These women occupied a prominent place in the social and economic life of their people. There were even women who became famous for their active and noteworthy participation in political struggles, wars and well-known battles.

Some of the Prophet's wives were very prominent among the Arabs at that time. His first wife, Khadija, was known for her imposing personality, her independence both socially and economically since she earned her own living through trade, and the freedom which she insisted upon in the choice of her husband. Khadija for some years had employed Muhammad to take care of her trading interests and manage her affairs. During the twenty years of their marriage, Muhammad did not marry any other woman, he was monogamous. Only after her death did he practise polygamy.

Another very prominent woman was 'Aisha, the youngest wife of the Prophet. Despite her young age, 'Aisha was a living example of how women stood firm on many issues in those days. She was well known for her strong will, versatile and incisive logic, and eloquence. She wielded a powerful intelligence which sometimes was a match even for the inspired and gifted Prophet of Allah. She had no hesitation in opposing or contradicting him, he whose word was all-powerful among the Muslims. Not only did 'Aisha stand up to the Prophet sometimes, but she was wont to do the same thing with other men. She expressed her thoughts with a forthright and cutting logic, and one day Muhammad while seated in the midst of other men pointed towards her and said to them, 'Draw half of your religion from this ruddy-faced woman' (Khairat, 1975: p. 64).

'Aisha fought in several wars and battles, and was actively involved in politics and cultural and literary activities to a degree that led the theologian of the Muslims, 'Urwa Ibn El-Zuheir, to say, 'I have not seen any one who is more knowledgeable in theology, in medicine and in poetry than 'Aisha' (Afifi, 1921: Vol. 2, p. 139). This, despite the fact that she reached the age of eighteen only after Muhammad's death.

In fact 'Aisha was capable of discussing any subject with Muhammad. She would differ with him and give vent to her anger whenever he married another wife. She would rebel against him and sometimes even incite his other wives to rebellion. She even went so far as to challenge Muhammad in relation to some of the Qur'anic verses that descended upon him from heaven. When in one of these verses Allah permitted Muhammad to marry as many women as he wished she hotly commented, 'Allah always responds immediately to your needs' (Ibn Sa'ad, 1970: pp. 140–41).

There were many other prominent women like Khadija and 'Aisha. To mention only one, Nessiba Bint Ka'ab who fought with her sword by the side of Muhammad in the battle of Uhud, and did not abandon the fight until she had been wounded thirteen times. Muhammad held her in great respect and said, 'The position due to her is higher than that of men' (Ibn Sa'ad, 1970: p. 302). Another woman was Um Sulaym Bint Malhan who tied a dagger around her waist above her pregnant belly and fought in the ranks of Muhammad and his followers. On the other side too, prominent women took part in the fighting. Among them was Hind Bint Rabi'a. She wore armour and a warrior's mask in the battle of Uhud and brandished her sword before plunging it with a mortal thrust into enemy after enemy (Sharkawi, 1967: p. 217). Hind was a woman who insisted on her freedom, and on making her own decisions in personal life. She said to her father, 'I am a woman who holds her life in her own hands and knows what she wants.' And her father answered, 'So it shall be' (Ibn Sa'ad, 1970: p. 171). Hind was well known for her logic and quick-wittedness even in answering the Prophet. Together with other women she stood before him and proclaimed their conversion to Islam. Muhammad spent some time going over the principles of Islam for their benefit. When he came to God's directive 'Do not kill your children' she said, 'It is you who have killed our children' (Ibn Sa'ad, 1970: p. 172). In the battle of Badr fought between the Muslims and the Quraishites (members of the tribe of Quraish who for a long time bitterly opposed Muhammad, Hind had lost three men from her family: her father, her brother and her uncle. After this battle

Hind had sworn to avenge them and had taken an oath not to perfume herself or to go near her husband until this was done. She kept her promise during the battle of Uhud in which the Quraishites were victorious over the Muslims.

Arab women did not lose their independence and positivity suddenly. It was a gradual, slow process related to socioeconomic changes taking place in society, and they struggled hard not to lose their ancient rights. Sometimes they were successful but mostly it was a losing battle since the fundamental principles of social justice, freedom and equality were buried under the growing authority of men over women, and the growing prosperity of the new ruling classes over the poor majority. So a struggle within Islam began, and was never to end, between those who fought for equality, freedom, and social and economic justice, and those who stood for class privilege, male domination and feudal oppression. The descendants of this latter group were later to side with the Turkish domination, with French, British, Italian and German colonialism and later with the international imperialism headed by the USA.

Thus it came about that, from the time of 'Usman Ibn 'Affan (the third caliph of the Muslims) in the eighth century AD, history was to plunge the Arab women into a long night of feudal oppression and foreign domination in which women were condemned to toil, to hide behind the veil, to quiver in the prison of a harem fenced in by high walls, iron bars, windowless rooms and the ever-present eunuchs on guard with their swords.

The Qur'anic view of women

The Qur'an is considered to be the primary source of Islamic jurisprudence and theological orientation. Next in order comes the sayings and teachings of the Prophet, followed by the consensus of religious thinkers and leaders, and last of all the methods of inference and analogy. These are the three valid sources used as complementary to the Qur'an when it is desired to take a position on women's status or any other question.

The verses of the Qur'an and the sayings of the Prophet do not relate to a single period of time, but are spread over many years. Since each verse or saying was linked to a particular circumstance or incident, and to a particular setting in terms of place and time, the verses often tended to embody conflicting directives or ambiguous instructions. This is especially true in relation to the life of women.

If we take the question of polygamy as dealt with in the Qur'an we find that it is so ambiguous that the opinions of religious thinkers differ widely. A group of them believes that polygamy is not allowed and bases its position on what was mentioned in the Qur'an under sura al-Nissa': 'Marry as many women as you wish, two or three or four. If you fear not to treat them equally, marry only one. Indeed you will not be able to be just between your wives even if you try' (Qur'an, sura al-Nissa', verse 3). This group of religious thinkers insists that the Qur'an has forbidden polygamy, since a man is not permitted to marry more than one woman unless he can treat his wives equally and not differentiate in the slightest degree between them. And the Qur'an goes on to say that this is impossible no matter how hard a man tries. Logic suggests that to marry several wives implies a preference, a preference for the new wife over the preceding one. This preference in itself is sufficient to make equality and justice impossible even if the man were to be the Prophet himself. As a matter of fact, the Prophet was not able to treat his wives with absolute equality. He used to prefer 'Aisha to his other wives and loved her more deeply.

The other group of religious thinkers insists that the Qur'an does allow polygamy and bases its position on the fact that Muhammad the Prophet married several wives and that justice or equality between wives is possible.

Early Islamic society was characterized by a patriarchal system built on private property and a class structure composed of a minority who owned the herds of sheep, camels and horses, and who as traders travelled far and wide over the commercial routes of the Arab peninsula, and a majority of slaves interspersed with a few independent plebeians. Authority in Islam belonged to the man as head of the family, to the supreme ruler, or the *khalifa* (caliph) or imam (political and religious leader), or the wali (governor of a province), or the judge, or the witness. All these were positions that could only be occupied by men.

Islam inherited from Judaism the penalty meted out to adulterous women, namely that of being stoned to death. The Qur'an stipulates that both partners in adultery, the man and the woman, should be stoned to death. However the fact that a man could have many wives and concubines and women slaves at his beck and call meant that the richer or more powerful men did not need to have recourse to illegal adultery, since the avenues of legal multiple sexual relations were open to them. Such religious laws therefore were meant to be applied only to women and to the poor men who owned only a few sheep, were small artisans and traders, hired labourers or slaves, who often found it difficult to marry or whose limited resources imposed a fidelity that lacked conviction and prevented them from changing wives or marrying up to four wives or owning slaves and concubines.

In the Qur'an monogamy remained a moral code only for women, lest the patriarchal system be eroded and collapse. This system was strongly entrenched in most of the tribes, except for a very few that still exhibited some form of matriarchal relations, and the structure built around the unquestioned predominance of men therefore remained firm and unshaken. The continuous tribal wars, in which many men were killed, the need to build up the new Islamic order, the large numbers of women war prisoners and slaves – all tended to make out of polygamy a common practice.

Al-Jahiliya or pre-Islamic society was a tribal structure built upon slavery. Prisoners of war were considered the property of the victors, and each man would take into his household a number that corresponded to his power and means. Islam brought no changes in this area and permitted a man to share his home and bed with such women prisoners, and yet be under no obligation to marry them. This system of concubinage also did not oblige the man to recognize the children that were born of these relations. However if the man did agree to this recognition the child was immediately considered free, that is, no longer a slave, and the woman was set free, in her turn, after the death of her master.

Islam does not permit adoption and a child cannot even give proof of its parentage by referring to adoption. Islam insists that every child must be attributed to its father and states that those whom you only declare to be your children cannot be considered so, for that is only word of mouth. The Qur'an says, 'Allah speaks the truth and shows you the right path, relate them to their fathers, however if you do not know their fathers relate them to your brothers in religion' (Qur'an, sura al-Ahzab, verses 4–5).

There is nothing in the Qur'an that supports or opposes birth control or contraception. But some Muslim thinkers hold firmly that Islam opposes abortion and the use of contraception. They base their views on the verses of the Qur'an that say: 'Do not kill your children for fear of heresy. He will provide for both you and them. Your needs depend on Allah and he will provide them. He who avoids Allah's wrath, Allah will find a way out for him, and will provide for him in a way he had not expected' (Qur'an, sura al-Isra'a, verse 31); 'Just as a camel does not carry in itself the wherewithal to live, Allah provides for you and it' (Qur'an, sura al-'Ankabout, verse 60); 'Allah provides generously for those among His worshippers whom he sees fit to pick out' (Qur'an, sura al-'Ankabout, verse 62); 'Your God provides generously for whom he desires, for He is all powerful' (Qur'an, sura al-Isra'a, verse 30).

However, other schools of Muslim thinkers believe that Islam does not forbid the use of contraception or even abortion within the first 120 days of pregnancy. They support their views by arguing that it will make things easier for people, and prevent any feeling of shame, especially if there is fear of excessive pregnancies in the woman, or weakness as a result of repeated pregnancies. They base their views on some of the Prophet's sayings, on the writings of the Hanafi school, and on the verse in the Qur'an: 'Allah wishes to ease your burdens not to make things more difficult' (Qur'an, sura El-Baqara, verse 185).

Many verses of the Qur'an refer to the fact that all people are equal before Allah, and that he created males and females so that there could be mercy and love between them. 'He it is who created out of you couples, so that you may live together, and have mercy and love for one another' (Qur'an, sura al-Rum, verse 21). This verse is interpreted as bestowing upon a woman the right to choose her husband, and to be separated from him if she no longer wishes to live with him, since love, mercy and cohabitation presuppose free choice rather than compulsion. On the basis of this verse Muhammad gave women the right to choose their husbands, as well as the right to be separated from them. However women were stripped of these rights at a later stage through the statutes and laws promulgated on the basis of so-called Islamic jurisprudence. This proves that some of the laws and statutes pertaining to women are at variance with Islamic teachings and are a reflection of what men of religion believed at different periods of Muslim history. Nevertheless the phrase 'created out of you' (which is addressed to men here) indicates that woman was created out of man. This is a repetition of the original conception derived from the Old Testament in which Eve is created out of Adam.

The Qur'an abjures both men and women to 'look downwards' (that is, not to raise their eyes to one another's faces) but it singles out women when it mentions that 'makeup' and other forms of embellishment are allowed exclusively before the men of the family, or other men with whom women are permitted to mix. 'Thou must say unto the believers that their eyes should look down, and that their genitals must be protected, for this is to their good, since Allah knows well what each one is doing. And say unto the women that believe that their eyes should look down, and that their genitals must be protected. Thou wilt also explain to them that their ornaments should be uncovered only by accident, their shawls should reach down to the pockets of their gowns, their makeup be shown only to husbands, fathers, fathers in law, sons, sons in law, brothers, nephews, and their wives, as well as slaves, servants to whom they cannot be married, and children who have not yet had contact with women. They should not allow their ornaments to jingle by stamping their feet on the ground so as to hint at what they are wearing. Seek the forgiveness of Allah, O believers, so that you may escape his punishment' (Qur'an, sura al-Nour, verses 31–32).

Islamic teachings differentiate between men and women in matters related to marriage with non-Muslims. A man can marry a Christian or a Jewish woman who belongs to the peoples of the Book (the sacred writings which descended from heaven). This is according to the Qur'anic *aya* (verse) which says, 'Today I declare that you are free to partake of the good things of life, of the food prepared by the peoples of the Book. And they too can partake of your food. You may also marry women who are believers, and thus protected, as well as women protected by the sacred "Books" which descended upon them before your times' (Qur'an, sura al-Ma'da). A woman however is not permitted to marry a man who is not a Muslim. There is no stipulation in the Qur'an referring to this matter but Islamic jurisprudence insists on the fact that Muslim women must marry Muslim men. This is due to the fact that Islam is a patriarchal religion in which children are named after their fathers and inherit from them. Therefore if a Muslim man marries a Christian woman the children will be named after him and will take his religion, and thus will help Islam to spread and become more powerful. But if a Muslim woman marries a Christian man, their children will take the name of the father and will be born Christians.

In Islam the dowry belongs to the woman. It is a part of her property and the man has no right to force her to use it in any particular way. For example he cannot insist that she use a part of her dowry to buy things for the household. The dowry is considered a form of security against the vicissitudes of the future (divorce or separation or death of the husband in war, which was frequent in those days). It is the duty of the husband to buy whatever is needed in the form of household goods, and to cater for all the expenses of his wife and children. The woman is not obliged to spend any of her money on the house but she can opt freely to do so if she wishes. The Islamic precepts in these matters are based on the Qur'anic *aya* which says, 'Bestow upon your women the dowry which is their right. If they freely agree to give you a part of it, you may partake of it with joy and appetite.'

Islam does not set limits on the freedom of man in the practice of sex with his wife, and does not insist on any particular method of sexual intercourse. This is based on the Qur'anic *aya* which says, 'Women are the land which is yours to plough.... You may therefore plough them wherever you wish.' However Islamic teachings permit only vaginal intercourse (anal intercourse is forbidden) and refer to the sayings of Muhammad, and the interpretation by the Imam Malik of the Qur'anic *aya* mentioned above. According to the imam, 'Land is ploughed in order to be sown, and anal intercourse can only be a grievous offence because it is contrary to wisdom, antagonistic to child bearing, uses an outlet as an inlet and leads to corruption in health and other aspects of life' (Kakhi'a, 1977: p. 139). Such teachings probably derive from the fact that sodomy and homosexuality were common practices in the Arab region before Islam and as a result anal intercourse was a widespread habit. A numerous progeny was considered a virtue especially in a situation where Islam was expanding and needed warriors to fight the numerous wars.

Muslim women enjoy the right to inheritance. In this connection the Qur'anic *aya* states that 'Men have a share in what parents and relatives leave behind, and women also have the right to a share, irrespective of whether what is left behind by the parents or relatives is small or large.' The share of the woman was later defined as being half that of the man since the Qur'an says, 'Man is entitled to the fortune of two women.' In some pre-Islamic tribes woman herself constituted a part of the inheritance which men left behind after death (Al-Hamid, 1978: pp. 16–17) on the assumption that she is a part of his property bought for a dowry, and should therefore be handed down to his sons. The men of his family had a priority right over her. If one of them wished, he could marry her. If not they could marry her off to a man of their choice. Otherwise she remained without husband as a member of their family since they had more right over her than her original family members (father and mother, etcetera). But the Qur'an abolished this practice categorically in the *aya* that states, 'O you believers, it is not your right to inherit women against their will.'

The Qur'an enjoins men to live with their wives in harmony and to treat them well. 'Live with your wives in kindness. If you hate them, remember that Allah may bring much good to you through that which you hate.' Most of the teachings that insist on the rights and responsibilities that men exercise over women are based on the following *aya*: 'Women must be treated with kindness just as they are enjoined to treat their men with kindness. Men are one step above them. Allah is Almighty and full of wisdom.' Religious teachers explain this verse to mean that women should expect men to accord them the same treatment as they themselves bestow upon their men. But men are in a position of responsibility with regard to women because of the qualities and specific characteristics that Allah has given them and through which he has differentiated them from women (Al-Hamid, 1978: p. 49).

However the Qur'an warns men not to be conceited and condescending towards women because of the responsibilities and privileges bestowed upon the male sex by Allah. In this context the Qur'an advises men in these words: 'Do not be condescending and talk much of your kindness because Allah has preferred you to others.... Men have the right to what they can earn by their efforts, and women have the right to what they earn also.' This *aya* indicates that the Qur'an allows women to work and to earn their living, since it has given them the same right as men to what they earn. Those who in the Muslim world favour a woman's right to work for her living and to earn money base themselves on this quotation from the Qur'an.

On the other hand, people who insist that Islam confines women to the home and prevents them from going outside its precincts except under duress are prone to quote another verse in the Qur'an which says, 'Settle down in your homes and do not make up as did the women of early Jahiliya times.'

It is commonly thought that the Qur'an imposed wearing of the veil on women. However one may search in vain through its many verses for such an imposition. The Qur'an nevertheless enjoins women not to use makeup and ornaments which are a source of seduction and temptation to men, and teaches that women's garments should be respectable and devoid of exhibitionism. This requires that they cover all parts of the body except the face and the palms of the hand. Even the soles of the feet are not to be exposed (Sha'arawi, 1979: p. 35). But there are still many Muslim men of religion who believe in the veil as a necessary element in Islamic practice and abjure women to cover their faces also.

A historical study of how the veil arose shows that it began with the rise of Judaism as a religion and the myth of Adam and Eve. It originates with the fact that Eve is looked upon as the source of evil and sin, and must feel shame for her corrupt nature. She must therefore cover her body including the head and face, and refrain from exhibiting any part of it. It is also inspired by the idea that Eve (woman) is a body without head and that Adam (her spouse and man) is her head.

Some problems of contemporary Arab women

Most people tend to depict the problems faced by contemporary Arab women (including attempts to force the veil upon them, polygamy and other problems) as stemming from Islam. To their minds, underdevelopment is not related to economic and political factors at the root of which lies foreign exploitation of resources, and the plunder of national riches. Instead, they still consider Islam as the main or sole cause of all these problems.

Islam is not exceptional in having transformed women into slaves of their men. Judaism and Christianity subjected women to exactly the same fate. As a matter of fact, the oppression of women exercised by the temple and the church has been even more ferocious than that in the case of Islam. For thousands of years women continued to be dominated by men, no matter to what faith they belonged. The Arab woman is no exception. She has been imprisoned within her role as a servant to men, children and the family. Her services were free of charge, except for her food, clothes and a roof over her head. Such a role does not mean that she has to stay within the four walls of her home. If the men of her family are poor and need her work outside the home, she must go out to work in the fields, in factories, in shops, in the desert, in schools, in hospitals or wherever necessity leads her. Her work outside the home does not relieve her of the burdens at home. She has to combine both. As a woman peasant she receives no payment. She works for her husband and the family.

If the husband is not poor and does not need her work outside the home, then she has to stay within the four walls of her home, and be a full-time servant of the family. If the husband is well off, she is relieved of part or all of the housework by hiring domestic help.

The majority of Arab women work full-time in the fields, shops, homes and other places. Most of them are Muslims, yet they never knew what it was to wear a veil. A poor peasant man will not envisage buying a veil to cover his wife's face. He needs his money for the purchase of bread to eat. A peasant woman is a productive worker and feels the importance of her role in the family. Yet she is dominated by men.

A woman who is constrained to live within the confines of the home is considered by peasant women to be fortunate since she avoids hard work in the fields under a burning sun. A man who can provide economically for his wife and so protect her from the need to work outside the home is considered to be more of a man than others. Women's work outside the home is regarded as a sort of humiliation, and held in low esteem. It is the product of economic necessity amongst poorer classes and is looked down upon by higher classes of society. At the beginning of the twentieth century most Arab women from the middle and upper classes were imprisoned within the walls of the home, and never went out unless there was an overpowering reason to do so (for example severe illness requiring visits to a hospital). On such visits the woman would hide her body and face behind a heavy veil and be accompanied by a male member of her family. Sometimes a woman would be lying on her deathbed, yet the husband would refuse to allow her to be examined by a male doctor.

I remember my mother saying that my grandmother had moved through the streets on only two occasions. The first was when she left her father's house and went to her husband's after marriage. The second was when she was carried out of her husband's house to be buried. Both times no part of her body was uncovered. My maternal grandmother lived in Cairo (1898–1948). She spent her whole life doing chores at home and looking after her husband and children. Some servants helped her. She belonged to a middle- or upper-middle-class family. On the other hand my paternal grandmother, who lived almost during the same period in our village (Kafr Tahla), never knew what it was to wear a veil. She used to go out to work in the field or buy and sell in the marketplace every day, just as poor peasant women would do. At that time, rich families who possessed larger areas of land did not seek to educate their children to the same extent poorer families did. My paternal grandfather owned only a small piece of land; after his death it was divided between his nine sons and daughters. Threatened by the spectre of poverty my father was sent to school in Cairo while his sisters stayed in the village.

The majority of females in the Arab countries live in rural areas, especially in predominantly agricultural countries like Egypt, Iraq, Syria, the Sudan and others. Capital cities and big towns continue to live on the exploitation of the countryside, despite numerous projects ostensibly aimed at developing rural areas in countries of the so-called Third World. However, in-depth studies of most so-called developmental projects show that they do not lead to true development but are aimed at acting either as a cover-up for the true situation or lead to further distortions and imbalances either within the rural areas themselves or in the relationship between rural and urban areas. This is mainly due to the fact that most of these projects still emphasize different forms of urbanization at the expense of true rural development. They still end up emphasizing the economic and social differences between the rich and the poor in rural areas rather than bridging the gap between them. Just as is the case with the emancipation of women, real rural development will never take place in a patriarchal class system, and will remain a chimera as long as the world remains divided into countries that belong to the First World and a majority of peoples that live in the Third World.

We can therefore state without hesitation that poor peasant women represent the lowest and most exploited stratum in underdeveloped countries, and that they are worse off than their sisters in cities and urban areas. It is easy to observe the inhuman and backward situation of rural women in the Arab countries by just moving around in the countryside and spending some time in the villages. One cannot miss the pallor, exhaustion and emaciated bodies of young peasant women as they move around in their dusty black garments. For undernourishment, hard labour and repeated pregnancies are the triple burden of such women, which strikes at the very roots of their life substance. If we add to this the inhumane treatment suffered at the hands of men belonging to exploiting classes, or men and mothers-in-law in the family, it is surprising that women survive the usual average life span of fifty-four years.

Most young girls in our villages are deprived of a chance to go to school or be educated. The brother may go to school if the family can scrape together enough money to cater to his needs. But a girl more often than not will be kept at home to work in the field, help with household chores and look after the younger children or the aged. As soon as she reaches puberty her family will seek to give her away in marriage, and very often such marriages are consummated with girls whose age lies between twelve and fourteen years. Laws fixing the minimum age of marriage for girls at sixteen are not respected. This is due to a variety of reasons, chief among which is extreme poverty. It induces the family to get rid of the economic burden represented by a female child. Another reason is fear of dishonour which is brought upon the family if a girl allows herself to be seduced by a man. For the concept of premarital virginity remains strong in both Muslim and Coptic (Christian) communities. Dire economic straits may often lead to the girl being 'sold' in marriage to a relatively richer man. A dowry can help temporarily in postponing hunger or destitution, in paying off debts, or even in solving problems with the economic and social powers in the village (such as the headman, the chief guard, the rich peasants, or even the police and administrative authorities).

A girl in the village, whether Muslim or Copt, has no right to love a man or choose her husband, contrary to what is now the case with urban female university students. Many of my female colleagues, and I myself, married men of our choice for whom we had affection. This is becoming more and more common in the big cities of Egypt and other Arab countries where girls can receive a university education and then work, thus gaining a certain degree of independence as a result of the money they earn. But in rural areas a girl cannot permit herself to act in this way. She may secretly fall in love with the neighbour's son but she keeps this fact to herself and knows that she will be married off against her will by the men and elder women of the family.

Before puberty most, if not all, girls undergo circumcision. Although this operation is mainly practised in Egypt, the Sudan and Yemen, and is almost unknown in other Arab countries, in Egypt both Muslim and Coptic families continue to practise the circumcision of girls. The tradition has nothing to do with being a Muslim or Arab, and has come down from pre-Islamic and non-Arab societies.

After marriage a rural young woman moves over to live in her husband's family, and to become a servant at the disposal of all the family members, especially the mother-in-law. She works in the field, procures water, looks after the cows and sheep, and does numerous household chores. Her husband will beat her if he feels she is being lazy or disobedient towards him or his mother. He may divorce her if she falls ill, grows older, does not bear him children, gives birth to females only, disobeys his orders, answers back or rebels in any way. She soon loses her youthfulness due to exhausting labour, undernourishment and oft-repeated pregnancies. Infant mortality in Egypt still hovers around the level of 10 per cent of live births (Central Administration for Public Mobilization and Statistics, 1979) as a result mainly of ill-health and unfavourable sanitary conditions.

Maternal mortality as a result of labour complications also remains very high; it is calculated to be around 1 per cent of cases of labour (Ministry of Health, 1980). Partial studies made by the Department of Gynaecology and Obstetrics in Cairo and Ain Shams Faculty of Medicine estimate that out of every four pregnancies one ends in abortion, which is usually induced. It is therefore not surprising that most village women around the age of thirty already look as though they are fifty years old. A peasant woman labours in the field and at home, but receives no earnings. Her productive contribution is substantial since she rarely stops working to rest; but her consumption is low, because she does not own the proceeds of her labour. She is therefore a source of the cheapest labour in existence. She is the last to eat and has the least to eat, living on the leftovers of the men, children and elder women of the family.

Sometimes she may rebel against this cruel treatment and envisage returning to her family. But almost every time, the men of her family will bring her back in order to avoid the shame of divorce, and the need to provide for her if she settles down with her family once more. She may find any way out, including that of psychic disturbance. Then she is regarded as mad and treated with all sorts of magic or traditional rituals, including a form of exorcism in which the 'devils' or 'evil spirits' are driven away by a violent collective dance carried on until all the participants reach a trance-like state.[3]

Many are the pressures and injustices to which a young peasant woman is exposed at the hands of her large family. Nevertheless, the extended family system has some advantages when compared to the nuclear family system, now common in urban areas. The advantages are clearest where children are concerned. With the extended family children can be cared for by other members of the family while the mother works; they have space and sunshine and the freedom to play and learn. But in cities children are cooped up in slum houses, deprived of sunshine and let loose in narrow streets full of refuse and stagnant water. Often they are not allowed to go out, especially in families that are slightly well-off. Women in the village help one another in the fields and at the home. They meet and talk when fetching water, or in the marketplace or at night outside their homes.

Women who migrate to the cities suffer great physical and mental hardship. If they have a family then problems are complicated by the lack of facilities for children. If obliged to work, the solidarity and help characteristic of village life will not be forthcoming to the same extent. With the increasing hardships in urban areas, higher cost of living, breakdown in services and a multitude of other problems, a female city dweller may be deprived of some of the advantages that her sister in rural areas enjoys. Women who migrate on their own will more often than not end up as domestic servants,[4] or as prostitutes in a blatant or more disguised form.

As a result of rapid population increase not accompanied by a parallel increase in agricultural productivity, land reclamation or comprehensive rural development, migration from rural to urban areas is attaining alarming proportions. This is particularly true of women.[5] Women migrate to escape the hardships of life in the countryside. They seek jobs, education, or are willing to provide services or be part of a migrant family. A female migrant will suffer much more than a male because she is much more vulnerable. She is a victim of tradition, of male exploitation and sexism, of concepts related to honour and virginity which clash with the changing moral fabric in urban societies and the development of different social and cultural patterns. Nevertheless a woman in an urban area will enjoy a greater degree of freedom than her sister in rural areas even if she lives within the framework of a nuclear family. In the nuclear family she is no longer exposed to the pressures of many men and elder women, and will usually have to submit only to her husband. In addition urban families live in greater isolation than in a village, where the pressures of relatives and neighbours are much more tangible and immediate. If she works outside the home and earns a wage, this will afford the woman a greater or lesser degree of economic and therefore social and cultural independence, and enhance her status within the family.

The number of working women, as well as that of educated women in the Arab countries has increased since the sixties.[6] In addition social services are slowly progressing, and organizations or institutions dealing with problems of women and children are on the increase.

Nevertheless Arab women still remain politically weak despite the fact that in many countries they have been accorded the right to vote.[7] It is clear that the crucial issue is not that of obtaining political rights such as the vote, but what is done with such rights. Within patriarchal class societies women are prevented from becoming an active political force by a multitude of barriers and pressures exercised by the ruling classes and by men.

Conclusion

Arab women are still exposed to different forms of oppression (national, class and sexual). The original cause of their triple oppression is not Islam but the patriarchal class system which manifests itself internationally as world capitalism and imperialism, and nationally in the feudal and capitalist classes of the Third World countries. Most women of this Third World, including Arab women, are exposed to many problems (where Palestinian women are concerned the problem is greater: the loss of their land has multiplied the burdens to which they are exposed).

Arab women have started to realize that emancipation can only be the result of their own struggle. Their only hope lies in political organization and a patient, long-enduring struggle to become an effective political power which will force society to change and abolish the structures that keep women victims of the crudest, most cruel and sometimes most sophisticated forms of oppression and exploitation.

[Edited version of a paper published in *Women's Studies International Forum*, Vol. 5, No. 2, pp. 193–206, 1982]

Notes

1. For the meaning of the word *untha* see *Lisan Al-Arab*, Vol. 2, p. 416.
2. See also the Qur'an, sura al-Ahzab, verse 35.
3. This form of exorcism is called *al-zar* in Arabic.
4. Domestic servants account for 89.3 per cent of women working in services (*Al-Mar'a al-Misria fi-'Ishrin Amin* (1952–1972). The Central Administration for Public Mobilization and Statistics in Cairo).

5. Migration from rural to urban Egypt is steadily increasing. In 1979 the number of female migrants represented 16.1 per cent of the total number of women in urban areas whereas males represented only 12.31 per cent of the total number of males in urban areas. Report entitled *Al-Nataig Al-Awalia Likhtilafat Al-Higra Al-Dakhilia Bil Aina* (Cairo, 1979; CAPMAS).

6. According to the 1976 census, employed women (apart from peasant women and housewives) represented 9.2 per cent of the total active labour force in Egypt. The number of women holding higher degrees were 1.2 per cent of the total population. In Syria the female labour force represents 16.1 per cent of the total female population (88 per cent of these are agricultural workers). The corresponding figure for the Gulf countries drops to 3 per cent, despite the fact that the number of female university students in some Gulf countries, such as Kuwait, is higher than that of males.

7. Arab women are now permitted to vote in most Arab countries. Exceptions are to be found especially in the Gulf countries: Kuwait, Saudi Arabia, etcetera. Egyptian women began to vote in 1956 but politically they do not constitute an important force. In 1972 only 12 per cent of eligible women cast their votes. The number of women in the People's Assembly is thirty-five and this represents around 7.5 per cent of the total number of members.

References

Afifi, Abdallah. 1921. *Al-Mar'a l-Arabia fi Jahiliyatiha wa-Islamiha*. Dar Ihya' Al-Kutub el-Arabiyya Publishing House, Egypt.

Central Administration for Public Mobilization and Statistics. 1979. *Census Report*. Central Administration for Public Mobilization and Statistics, Cairo.

Al-Hamid, Muhammad. 1978. *Rahmat-Ul-Islam Lil-Nisa'*. Dar al-Ansar, Cairo.

Kakhia, Tarik Ismail. 1977. *Al-Zawaj al-Islami*. Moassassat al-Zughby, Homs, Syria.

Khairat, Ahmed. 1975. *The Status of Women in Islam*. Dar El-Ma'arif, Egypt.

Ministry of Health. 1980. *Annual Statistical Report*. Ministry of Health, Cairo.

Ibn Sa'ad, Muhammad. 1970. *Al-Tabakat al-Kubra*. Dar El-Tahrir Publishing House, Cairo.

Sha'arawi, Al-Sheikh Muhammad Metwalli. 1979. *Al-Mar'a '-Muslima Wal-Tarik Ila-llah*. Maktabat al-Qur'an, Cairo.

Al-Sharkawi, Abdel-Rahman. 1967. *Muhammad the Prophet of Freedom*. Kitab El-Hilal, Cairo.

CHAPTER 9

Islamic Fundamentalism and Women

Fundamentalism is universal

Recent events have given rise to an intense debate on fundamentalism. But this debate has focused mainly on Islamic fundamentalism, failing to see that the phenomenon is universal. Thus the debate acquired racist overtones.

US governments since Ronald Reagan have subscribed fully to the fundamentalist world view. Emanating from what is known as the Bible Belt, the fundamentalists enjoy support throughout the USA. Some groups own their own TV stations. They have a clear political agenda. They totally support US imperialist interests all over the world. They have set up missions throughout Latin America, Asia, Africa and Europe to push the US agenda.

Among the issues the US fundamentalists have been actively campaigning for are measures that will increase the oppression of women, such as a segregated school system, prayer in the public schools, and a ban on Darwin's *Origin of the Species*. One of the major issues for fundamentalists now in the USA is the repeal of US laws legalizing abortion. It is just a part of a broader fundamentalist and fascist agenda which targets many different issues, groups and countries, including our Arab countries.

All fundamentalists – whether Christian, Jewish, Muslim or otherwise – are partners in the attempt to breed division, strife, racism and sexism; they help international imperialism to maintain its control and to overcome popular resistance to policies that lead to war and increased exploitation. It is known that the Mafia of today in Italy and the USA and Canada has close connections with some international fundamentalist groups, some of which are Islamic. The economic resources of such groups are, like those of the Mafia, drawn from the sale of arms, trafficking in drugs, and speculation in foreign exchange; these activities make huge profits, the money from which is 'laundered' by the so-called Islamic banks.

Islamic fundamentalism

Fundamentalist movements and other fanatic Islamic groups in Arab countries acquire political power through governments that help them secretly or openly to fight against left-wing or socialist groups. These governments give the fundamentalists access to TV and media, and under the name of democracy they are allowed to issue their own newspapers and magazines.

In Egypt today, many Islamic fundamentalist newspapers and magazines have gained licences, but the women's magazine *Noon* which we issued from the Arab Women's Solidarity Association did not gain such a licence. The fundamentalists acquire political power by organizing large numbers of young men and women under the guise of reforming society, fighting corruption, by a return to the values of Islam. They provide services and economic help to poor migrants from the villages and to students. They receive financial contributions from oil-rich circles and invest them in Islamic banks, using profiteering practices including speculation. An example of this was presented in the legal case taken recently against a number of Islamic investment companies in Egypt such as Al-Rayan, Al-Huda, Al-Badr and others.

The fundamentalist groups use revolutionary slogans against the West but they have economic connections and interests in the West. They try to show that their enemy is Christians who have never forgotten the medieval crusaders against Islam, and in some cases Islamic fundamentalist movements have constituted fanatical military groups like Al-Gihad, Al-Takfir wa al-Higra, Al-Nagoon min al-Nar, and others. They use many national liberation slogans, but they divide national unity by religion, sex, and creed, etcetera. During March 1990 some Islamic fanatic groups attacked Coptic families and properties in Upper Egypt (Minia Province).

A major factor in creating fanatic fundamentalist movements in our region is the existence of the Israeli fundamentalist Jewish state. Fundamentalist Jewish tendencies and policies cannot be maintained unless religious fanaticism continues to flourish in the surrounding states.

The power of the fundamentalist groups increased rapidly during the seventies. Sadat supported them in his fight against the Nasserite groups and other socialist parties. On 6 October 1981 Sadat was killed by those fundamentalists whom he created – the son killed the father.

The government of Egypt is trying now to stop the malignant

growth of these fanatic groups, but most of these efforts fail. Many Egyptian professionals (doctors, engineers, etcetera) who migrated to Saudi Arabia and the Gulf region during the sixties and seventies came back with reactionary ideas and a lot of petrodollars. On 13 April 1990 the Islamic groups won the election in the Medical Syndicate in Egypt against all other political groups, including the government and the left.

Islamic fundamentalism and women

When fundamentalist movements become powerful, it is women, especially poor women, who suffer most. These movements direct their attack against women and minority groups.

Like Jewish fundamentalists, Islamic fundamentalist groups are trying to push women back to the veil, back home, back under the domination of their husbands. In the name of 'protection', 'honour', 'sacred motherhood', women are degraded and exploited inside and outside the home.

Today, as a result of campaigns by conservative Islamic groups, the family code in Egypt and most Arabic countries deprives mothers and wives of basic human rights. They are governed by the law of obedience which reduces them to the status of slaves to their husbands, who have absolute right to divorce and polygamy. Theoretically the Islamic fundamentalists raise motherhood to the level of heaven, but in the legal code an Egyptian mother cannot give her nationality to her children.

Like Christian fundamentalists, Islamic fundamentalist groups are preaching segregation, and trying to ban Darwin and other scientific books. Under the name of Islamization they try to ban music parties and omit spiritual love stories or romantic pieces of poetry from school books.[1] Islamic fundamentalists shout and shriek verses of the Qur'an and prayers all day and night into microphones and loudspeakers. They can insult anybody who complains or who differs in opinion with them, and accuse him or her of heresy.[2]

The veil

The veiling of women is one of the most visible aspects of fanatic Islamic fundamentalist movements, but there are many other symptoms that are less visible but more dangerous.

The veil is a fashion now among upper-class women. They ornament the veil with jewellery, put on glittering silky dresses, big shiny earrings, heavy makeup, artificial eyelashes, and high heels on which they sway. Most of the Islamic fundamentalist groups allow women to show their faces only; they are not opposed to ornaments or high heels or makeup. A few of these groups, however, insist on the face also being covered; they force their women to wear the *niqab*, which is a thick veil covering the whole of the woman except two small slits in front of the eyes. One of those women came to my office with a mental problem because of such oppression and contradictions. I wrote her story but not a single newspaper or magazine in Egypt would publish it.[3]

Some poor women put on the veil for economic reasons, or to protect themselves from men in the streets. Some Muslim women put on the veil as an anti-Western protest, or to assert their authentic, Islamic identity and indigenous culture. They do not know that the authentic identity of a Muslim woman is not to be veiled, and that the veil is not an Islamic dress. They think that they can protest against foreign invasion and Western economic exploitation just by putting a piece of cloth on the face. Some upper- and middle-class women import their veils from the West; some of them do not know their indigenous language or culture. They do not participate in any struggle to liberate their country from Western economic and political exploitation. Still, they think they are challenging the West by hiding their hair or face behind a veil.

Western colonial circles praise such superficial battles against them so long as economic exploitation goes on. They portray Muslim women in their Western media as either veiled creatures or naked belly dancers. Some progressive left-wing people in the West tend to support the veil under the name of multiculturalism, or as a symbol of the authentic identity of Muslim women. But the veil is just a piece of clothing. How can an authentic identity be reduced to a piece of clothing? How can multiculturalism depend on confining women or hiding their faces?

Traditional leftist groups

Some left-wing groups or individuals are fundamentalist or adhere to the fundamentalist teachings of Marx. To them Marxism is another religion with fixed ideas, though Marxist philosophy is based on *change* as the eternal law of everything.

The most progressive men and women belonging to such groups criticize outdated customs and traditions that limit the mobility of women, in so far as education and work are concerned, but tend to consider that women's main role is that of wife and mother, and that work outside the home is to permit a woman to assist the husband economically. They make a distinction between economic or political exploitation and sexual, social and psychological issues.

They do not follow the changes happening in reality to women. They do not follow women's liberation movements and new feminist ideas. They accuse women's liberation groups in our countries of being Westernized, or of being agents of some external or internal power, or of dividing the ranks by antagonizing men or separating the cause of women from that of the nation.

They do not recognize that it is they themselves who make this division between women's liberation and national liberation, because they ignore the basic needs of half the nation (women). Women and women's issues can be easily sacrificed not only on the altar of reaction and fundamentalism, but also on that of national liberation. These progressive groups ignore the historical fact that the class system was founded on the slavery of women and children in the family, and that the basic profits of the patriarchal class systems which prevail in our world, are rooted in the accumulation of surplus value derived from the unpaid labour power of women and children.

Arab women are still a marginal minority not exceeding 10 per cent of left-wing political parties. Their percentage decreases as we go up to higher posts and decision-making levels.

Traditional left-wing parties do not hesitate to sacrifice women's rights to placate the more powerful conservative groups. For example, in 1985, when all political forces in Egypt, government and opposition, left and right, responded to the conservative Islamic groups' campaign against the family code of 1979, the result was the family code of 1985 in which women lost some other rights.[4]

What is an authentic identity?

We Arab and Muslim women know that our authentic identity is based on unveiling our minds and not on veiling our faces. We are human beings and not just bodies to be covered (under religious slogans) or to be naked (for consumerism and Western commercial goods). We know that veiling of women is the other side of the coin of nakedness or displaying the body. Both consider women as sex objects.

One of our slogans in the Arab Women's Solidarity Association is 'unveil the mind'. We speak and write in Arabic. We join all struggles of liberation for ourselves and our countries. We study our history, and try to redefine Islam in intellectual terms. We question the dominating Islamic tradition defined by men. There is nothing in Islam that prevents women from participating fully in all political or religious activities.[5]

The authentic identity of the Arab woman is not a straitjacket or dress, or veil. It is an active, living, changing process which demands a rereading of our history, and a reshaping of ourselves and our societies in the light of present challenges and future goals. Arab women employ Islam, history, culture and heritage for the sake of greater freedom and justice for themselves.[6]

The enlightened men and women in the Arab countries are fighting against all fundamentalist groups, whether Islamic or Jewish or Christian. We know that our battle is economic and political, against both external and internal exploiters. But those exploiters try to transform political and economic wars into religious ones. This has been very visible in Lebanon.

The Palestinian Intifada should be understood as a political and economic battle against Israeli military occupation of the West Bank and Gaza Strip, not a religious war between Muslims and Jews. But Western circles have tried to show it as such, though Palestinian Christians have fought side by side with their Muslim sisters and brothers. Historically the most radical Palestinian factions were Christian.

The fundamentalist movements are a mask for other battles, and a distortion of all religions. It is therefore necessary to create an enlightened interpretation of different religions, since it is the right of all people to believe, if this is their wish, and since faith will continue to play an important role in the lives of most of the people in the world.

Islam and other religions in their early revolutionary eras loosened the chains of slavery and declared that no man or woman should kneel except before God. Faith in God as a symbol of justice and freedom can add fuel to revolutionary fervour against all types of exploitation and injustices. Islam in our region can be a spiritual force in the struggle against foreign penetration. But this must not blind us to the fact that 'God' in the eyes of the oppressed is different from 'God' in the eyes of the oppressors. Under the name of 'God' as a symbol of absolute power our oppressors try to justify dictatorship.

[1990]

Notes

1. During April 1990 the Egyptian Minister of Education omitted a piece of poetry (by the Arab poet Nazar Qabani) from preparatory school books.

2. In their newspaper published in Egypt, *Al-Nour* (4 October 1989 and the following issues), the fundamentalists published articles insulting and degrading our Arab Women's Solidarity Association. We hired two lawyers to sue them in court. The male judge stood with the fundamentalists and we lost the case on 5 March 1990. We appealed before a higher court and we still [1997] await the result.

3. It was published in our magazine *Noon*, No. 3, November 1989, and in *Index on Censorship Newsletter* (London) 15 February 1989. [Reprinted as Chapter 10 of this volume.]

4. *Women in the Arab World: The Coming Challenge* (papers of the First International Conference of AWSA, held in Cairo, 1986), Zed Books, London, 1988, p. 14.

5. Nawal El Saadawi, *The Hidden Face of Eve*, Zed Books, London 1980, p. iii and p. 196.

6. *Women in the Arab World*, Zed Books, London, 1988, p. 21.

The Impact of Fanatic Religious Thought: A story of a young Egyptian Muslim woman

An Egyptian man had been very strict with his daughter only permitting her to work outside the home on condition that she be completely isolated from men. She found that 'ideal' job. Many months later, in the spring of 1988, this same man brought his daughter to my office to see me in my capacity as a psychiatrist. The following is based on the young woman's true story. Egyptian television wanted to produce a film based on this story – on condition that the protagonist not be a veiled woman, as she was in real life.

A few days ago a young woman came to me. She told me her story and asked me to write a prescription. I didn't prescribe any medication. I don't believe that pills can cure this young woman. The problem seems to be psychological and social. This is why I would like the readers to consider this case.

Last year the young woman began staring into space at night without sleeping. When she goes off to sleep she sees a flood inundating the land and the Prophet Noah embarking on his ship and leaving her behind. She finds herself in life after death, walking on a narrow path with the inferno lying below her. Her feet are bleeding and her body, off balance, is about to fall. She opens her eyes and finds herself asleep in bed under the blankets drowning in her own sweat. She reads the opening sura of the Qur'an and thanks God that she hasn't died yet and has a chance to repent. She goes to the bathroom and washes five times. She dresses herself in a long, loose robe and wraps her head with a thick cloth. After she prays she sits with God's book in her lap, reading and asking God for forgiveness for her grave sin. There is nothing in her life except that sin.

Since she was born she has gone to bed hearing the voice of her father reciting the Qur'an. Since infancy her face has not been seen by a stranger. During her student years she never talked to anyone. After graduation she went to work in a place where there was no one other than herself – a storeroom in the basement of a small museum never visited by anyone. There she would sit at her desk with a register in front of her recording the number of mummies that came in to be stored or registering the ones already there. She would dust the mummies with a small yellow cloth. She would count them and record them in the register. She would close the register and put it in a drawer. Then she would open up God's book and read until the time the employees leave work. Carrying her handbag she would walk for an hour and a half to her home. She would cover the distance with a steady, controlled pace, no movement of her body discernable under her thick robe.

Her head, wrapped in the black cloth, she kept inclined towards the ground. In the heat and cold she walked the distance twice a day, back and forth. She did not ride the bus so that no one would brush against her from behind. She did not take a taxi alone with an unknown driver. At home she washed off the dust from the road, performing her ablutions and praying before she ate. After she ate she would go to sleep with God's book under her pillow. She would wake at the sound of her father's voice calling her to fix his food. After he eats he prays and asks God to protect his daughter from the Devil. If it were not for the forty-seven pounds every month he would not have let her leave the house. He is an old man without an income and she has no husband to support her. Nobody approached her for marriage except the son of his sister, who is penniless and unemployed. If God had sent her a husband in sound financial condition she would not have left the house.

In her room she would pace up and down in prayer. She did not ask God to send her a husband. Since childhood she has dismissed the idea of marriage. Her mother died haemorrhaging when her husband hit her after she had gone to bed. Death was inevitable, but she wanted to die in a different way, not by being beaten. There was no man in her life. She knew nothing about the other sex. If she heard music or singing coming from the neighbours' houses she would plug her ears with her fingers and shut the windows and doors tight.

One day last April she was sitting as usual at her desk. She had finished counting the mummies and statues when she discovered a statue that was not there the day before. She looked back over the entries in the register, closed it and put it back in the drawer. She opened God's book and started to read without a sound, her head bowed. While she was reading, her eyes peered through the two narrow holes of the black cloth and moved around the mummies and statues.

They became fixed on the face of that statue. The features were carved in a strange way. The strangest of all were the eyes. They were looking at her with a movement in the pupils that she had never seen before in any other statue. She asked God's forgiveness. She asked God to protect her from the Devil. She bowed her head to continue reading but her eyes moved involuntarily towards the statue, which was smaller than the other statues. The dust covered it as if it had been neglected for years in the storeroom. She removed the dust from the statue, putting it near the window. She returned to reading God's book but her eyes peered through the two small holes, attracted by the face of the statue and its eyes with their strange movement. The eyes were slanted slightly upwards like ancient Egyptians' eyes. She held the statue in her hand covered with a black glove and started looking for a symbol or letters that might reveal the name of the person or the time he lived. There was nothing. She put the statue back and returned to her seat behind the desk. Her eyes settled on the lines in God's book. But the question turned around in her head: Has anybody else before her seen this movement in the eyes of the statue?

No other person worked in the museum except the old woman who was the manager. She would come down to her from time to time inspecting the entries in the inventory and passing her eyes over the statues one after the other; she might stop at one that would draw her attention. That day her eyes passed over the small statue without being attracted by anything. The young woman was puzzled. Why hadn't the director seen the movement in the eyes of the statue that she saw? The same question nagged her every day.

Now, as soon as she enters the office and sits down, her eyes settle on the face of the statue. The movement in his eyes is still there. Now it becomes a movement especially for her. He looks nowhere with these eyes except at her. Since she saw the statue for the first time she has never stopped looking at it. If she turns her head away or leaves the office his eyes are always in front of her, continually looking at her with the same expression, as if he were alive now, not seven thousand years ago. In his gaze there is no arrogance of the Pharaoh gods nor humility of the slaves. What is in it? She does not know. Every day she is overcome by her desire to know. This grows day after day into a sinful desire. Whenever she sits at her desk she looks around her, afraid that the director might suddenly appear and catch her while she is looking into the statue's eyes. The thing she fears most is that an order will be issued to transfer him to another storeroom. When she goes to bed she is unable to sleep. What happens if she returns to her office in the morning and does not see him? Since finding him she has started to walk to her office with a faster pace, and when she opens the door and enters, her eyes peer through the two holes looking for his face among the faces of the other statues. When she sees the movement in his eyes her closed lips part with a faint sigh beneath the black cloth.

One day she entered her office and she did not find him. She searched all over the storeroom but he wasn't there. She looked in every corner, below the legs of the large statues, on the floor where hundreds of small statues were lying. He wasn't there. She returned to her desk to sit down. She couldn't write anything in the register and she couldn't read a single line in God's book. Her head was bent and her heart was heavy: Where did he go? His place next to the window is vacant. The whole universe is empty. There is nothing in her whole life. Nothing at all. Her hand under the black glove is cold and the blood in her veins stops moving. All around her she sees nothing but death in the shape of stone statues. Sitting at her desk she herself is also dying.

She lifts her eyes with an abrupt movement, in the same way that air rushes out of the chest before the last breath, and sees him hiding behind the windowpane. The director, if she had appeared at this moment, would not have understood what has happened. The young woman's outside appearance is the same. She is sitting in her chair behind her desk with the register in front of her. Her head is bent and nothing in her moves except the black pupils visible through the two holes and the hot blood rushing in the veins under her skin.

Before leaving that day she hid him in her handbag to take him home with her. In the morning she brought him back to his place. The director did not notice his absence and reappearance. At home her father did not notice that the statue was inside her wardrobe. At night after her father sleeps she takes him out of the wardrobe and places him in front of her and does not stop looking at his face. She sleeps with her eyes fixed on his eyes. In her dream she sees him standing while a flood inundates the earth. She sees him standing in front of her in flesh and blood. And the flood inundating the land and the Prophet Noah climbing into his ark and leaving without him. Could it be that he is the son of the Prophet Noah who did not get into the ark and was drowned? Could it be that he is a sinner who followed the Devil and not a believer who followed God? And, more important, is it possible for him to come back alive after dying seven thousand years ago?

In the morning when she opens her eyes, the question spins in her head. She walks down the street to her office with her head bent, afraid to raise her eyes. Afraid she will see him in front of her in flesh and blood the same way she saw him in her dream. Through the two small holes in the black cloth her eyes start to move, to rise slowly, glancing cautiously in the faces of the passers-by. Perhaps among these human beings there is a face that resembles his? Or eyes with the same look?

Two months pass and she does not stop this thinking. Her eyes do not stop stealing a look at the faces of people on the street as she moves back and forth between home and office. Sixty days pass and among the faces she does not see a single one that looks like his or among the eyes any that have his look.

She sleeps restlessly and while she sleeps the dream recurs. She sees the earth inundated in a sea of water and herself standing at the entrance to the city, and suddenly she sees him in front of her. Now he does not notice her presence. He walks calmly forward, then turns around and looks at her. In his eyes is the same look, which never changes. The water covers him from all sides. He keeps looking at her until he disappears under the water. His eyes are the last to disappear.

In the morning she opens her eyes with the roaring of the water still in her ears. The voices screaming for help are muffled by the sound of the crashing waters. In the moment between sleep and wakefulness the dream seems to be the destruction of her town seven thousand years ago which she has seen with her own eyes. He was drowned seven thousand years ago among those God took in the flood. She continues lying on her bed. It is late for getting to the office. She rises, her body heavy, and in the mirror she sees her eyes red and full of tears. With a touch of her finger she recognizes real tears. She knows she was weeping over his drowning. What made her weep most was that he was not a follower of God.

She recognizes clearly that he was a follower of the Devil. No matter, tears continue to gush from her eyes as she stands in front of the mirror. It is as if he has died at that very moment, not seven thousand years ago.

On her way to the office that morning as she stopped at an intersection, she lifted her eyes to look at the traffic light when suddenly she saw him among the people crossing the street. She recognized him immediately. The face was his face – the ancient Egyptian features. The eyes were his eyes. In them there was the movement and the look. Involuntarily her body lunged towards him. She was about to grab him by the hand but she stopped at the last moment. Her closed lips parted under the black cloth crying, 'You?'

The street was crowded with people rushing along their way. They stopped, amazed at the scene. They saw her rushing towards him, and him fleeing from her. It is not normal for a young woman, walking in the street, to rush in this way towards a man she does not know. And she is not just any young woman. She is a creature of whose being nothing is visible except through two small holes in a black cloth. She is rushing towards him and he is escaping from her with fast steps. The scene appears to the onlookers both strange and amusing.

Their laughter rang in her ears and she shrank under her thick clothing. She continued to shrink all day long sitting at her desk with the register in front of her. Her head was bent. Only her eyes moved towards the window where he stood in his place. His face was the same, and his eyes had the same movement and a look more human than the eyes of the people in the street even though he died seven thousand years ago with those who drowned in the flood. She wept for his death. Every human being dies but the stone statue lives seven thousand years. Is the stone more permanent than humans?

The question turns around in her head without an answer. Now she has a friend made of stone. She feels his presence more than the presence of any human being with a body. The word *body* escapes from between her closed lips without a sound. The word in itself produces a shiver in her own body. She doesn't know exactly where the shiver is. Through the two holes, from under the thick cloth, her eyes steal a look at her body. In her chest there is a heart that beats. In her head there are veins through which blood flows hot as air. Her mind understands that her friend is nothing but a statue of stone. But she sees in his eyes the look of one about to speak.

Is it possible he will speak? And in what language? In Arabic or ancient Egyptian? Is it fantasy or reality? And if it is fantasy where does it come from? Does her imagination mix with the blood in her veins and head? The question turns in her head with the movement of blood like a whirlpool in the sea. And the water drowns her like a flood and he is standing in front of her and in his eyes there is a human look. Deep inside herself she is sure he is a human being – more human than all the people in the universe. He cannot be an evil person. She can swear in full consciousness that he is follower of God and not of the Devil.

She was fully conscious. If anyone saw her they would have no doubt about this. Her father sees her the same way he sees her every day: full of modesty, totally covered, going to her office and returning home on time. The director of the museum sees her sitting conscientiously with the register in front of her and when she finishes the inventory there is nothing in front of her except the Book of God. On the road she walks in her measured step with her head lowered.

One day while she was walking she turned her eyes and through the two holes saw him step out of the door of a house and cross the street with calm steps, mindless of the screaming horns. She saw him. The same person. She could not mistake him after all these days.

Her feet were nailed to the ground. Her hand inside the black glove was raised over her heart. He was standing in the middle of the street. Around him the cars were rushing like the flood. She thought he would fall and be drowned among the wheels but he did not fall. He continued walking in his calm pace towards Nile Street. Her body rushed after him.

She recognizes that he is a phantom and not a reality. But she sees him with her eyes. So long as she sees him with her eyes she doesn't care whether he is a phantom. Her feet walk behind him. In her ears she hears the sound of his shoes on the pavement. He is only a few steps ahead of her. If she speaks to him it is possible he will hear her. She does not know what to call him. He doesn't have a name. Her sealed lips under the thick cloth part with a sound: 'You.' She sees him turn around and look at her, face to face. She recognizes that it is him. The eyes are his eyes and the expression is his expression. She hears him say, 'Who are you?' His surprise silences her. She stands nailed to the street. He spoke in Arabic not ancient Egyptian. She thought he knew her as she knows him. How is it that she knows him all this time and he asks, 'Who are you?'? She stands looking at him, without moving. Then she directs her eyes towards the ground. Her head remains lowered for a long time as she shrinks in shame inside herself. After all this he asks her who she is. Her mind does not believe it. She lifts her eyes once more to be sure what is happening but he has turned around and gone his own way, disappearing among the people.

The second day on the way to her office her head is lowered as usual but her eyes are moving like two bees behind the two holes looking at the faces of the people. Her mind says to her that he is no longer living, that he lived seven thousand years ago, but her eyes never stop searching. Her mind tells her he exists. She has seen him. So long as he exists she can see him again. She is overtaken by the wish to see him in any shape. Let him be made of flesh and blood or of spirit without body. What is important is that she sees him. What is the difference whether he is a spirit or a body so long as she is able to see him?

She waited in the same place where she had met him yesterday. When he appeared in the street, fully conscious she lunged towards him. It was him, with his face and eyes and human expression. Nothing had changed except that a black moustache had grown over his upper lip. Her closed lips part underneath the thick cloth emitting a word without a sound: 'Male!' Never before in her whole life could she utter that word. She thought, he was simply a human being without sex but this moustache means that he is.... Her feet remained nailed to the ground, her hand inside the black glove was raised up to cover the two small holes in the thick cloth.

When she lifted her hand from her eyes the street was still crowded, but he was no longer standing in front of her. She was still standing modestly, completely conscious. Hanging from her shoulder, secure in the cavity between her arm and chest, was her leather handbag. It pressed through the thick cloth next to her left breast. She felt the touch as if it were electricity. Her mind recognized that it was only a leather handbag with nothing inside it except her purse and the small statue of stone. But the touch continued to run from her left breast like electricity.

She went home that day without her handbag. Without opening it she threw it in a large dump. She even left her purse inside. She imagined that if she opened it she would see him. She had become afraid of seeing him. She did not know why she was afraid. But she started to shake with fear. The fear accompanied her all the way home. She lay down on her bed. She realized that the handbag was no longer with her. She thought that the fear would leave her but until morning the fear never left her. On the second day the fear continued to accompany her in the street, in the office, in the house, everywhere. It accompanied her like the trembling of a feverish person. One night her father heard her moaning in a low voice. Her body shook with the trembling like a person racked with malaria. Her father took her to a doctor. She took medicine for thirty days but the fever remained. At night her father heard her speaking to somebody as she said her prayers. He thought she was speaking to God asking him forgiveness. But her voice became louder and her words became clearer. She was not talking to God. She was cursing the Devil in words that could never come from the lips of a pure young woman. He believed that she had committed a sin that she was keeping to herself, not daring to reveal it to anyone. He took her to a holy man people repent to of their sins. But after her repentance her fever continued. And once more the pills the doctor prescribed failed. When the director of the museum visited her she said the young woman was not suffering from malaria but from a psychological condition. That is how she came to me.

[Paper presented to the Second International Conference of the Arab Women's Solidarity Association, 'Contemporary Arab Thought and Women', 3–5 November 1988. Translated from the Arabic by Ali Badran and Margot Badran. Later published in *Noon*, No. 3, November 1989, and in *Index on Censorship Newsletter* (London), 15 February 1989.]

CHAPTER II

Fundamentalism: Old friend, new enemy[1]

We squatted cross-legged on the rooftop of a huge white house in the Cairo district of Al-Hilmiya Al-Gedida. All around us we could glimpse rows of faces – their features barely revealed in the flickering torchlight, young and bearded, or veiled – looking upwards in rapt attention at the Supreme Guide, Hassan al-Banna, as he spoke in his quiet rhetorical, sometimes rambling style. Other people seemed lost in thought, their heads downcast, their eyes brooding with the distant vacuous look common in people who spend their lives in prayer and in muttering verses about God.

It was a clear night in the summer of 1945, some time during the middle of the fasting month of Ramadan. Hassan al-Banna, a short man dressed in a suit, wearing a squat red fez on his head with prayer beads dangling in one hand, stood in front of the crowd. That was the period when the Muslim Brotherhood began to have a visible influence on the lives of Egyptians.

The Muslim Brotherhood had been founded by Hassan al-Banna, a schoolteacher, in 1928. He started his *da'awa*, or preachings, in the city of Ismailiyya, bastion of the Suez Canal Company and advanced command of the British occupational forces. It was started in the very arms of the 'enemy' so to speak; a detail perhaps worthy of attention. After the Second World War, the Muslim Brotherhood grew rapidly, encouraged at a distance by the British and King Farouk to become a force that could oppose, or deviate, the movement for national independence led by the party of the Wafd, and to channel the movement's energies into other paths. At the university and schools the Muslim Brotherhood countered the slogans raised for national independence and democracy with other slogans against drinking alcohol, for 'moral' rectitude and the need to obey the ruler (King Farouk) and worship Allah. 'God is great' was the organization's battle cry, and to impress this on our minds they beat students up with iron chains or stabbed them with long curved knives if they happened to belong to the Wafd, to another nationalist group, or to the left. Together with the semifascist Misr Al-Fatta (Young Egypt) and the reactionary political group Gabhat Misr (Egyptian Front) led by Ali Maher Pasha, who was known for his close links with the palace, the Muslim Brotherhood formed a coalition against the Wafd and other national democratic or left-wing movements.

Bidding for power

After the Arab–Israeli war of 1948, which enabled the Muslim Brotherhood to train and arm a military wing, it made a first bid for power. In the process, members assassinated Nokrashi Pasha, the prime minister, after he outlawed their movement, which had started to engage in various terrorist attacks. The regime retaliated by assassinating Hassan al-Banna.

When the Free Officers movement challenged the rule of King Farouk in July 1952 and gradually took over the reins of power from the old ruling class, the Muslim Brotherhood flirted with the movement, hoping to exercise a leading role and eventually complete control over the revolution. In 1954 Nasser wrested full power from Naguib, the short-lived president of the Revolutionary Council. Naguib, in an attempt to consolidate his position and his views, had conjured the support not only of forces within the army, but also of the old political parties and the Muslim Brotherhood.

Now that he held the reins of power firmly in hand, Nasser felt free to engage in negotiations with the British for an eventual withdrawal of their forces as part of a new agreement emphasizing the independence of Egypt and the severing of its remaining links with colonialism. The Muslim Brotherhood, after some time, started parallel secret talks with the British, perhaps as a pressure game on the new regime, but also in an attempt to replace Nasser as interlocutors in this process and to present themselves as an alternative force. When Nasser cracked down on their movement, they tried to assassinate him in Alexandria in the summer of 1955 while he was addressing a quarter of a million people in the huge square of Al-Mansheya.[2]

Who pulls the strings?

All this does not mean that the Islamic political movement has no popular basis and no potential as a liberating force. It could mean, however, that since it was founded, most if not all leaders of this movement have tended to use the fervour of its adherents for ends that have little to do – or, more often, have nothing to do – with the hopes of the majority of people in Egypt. They long for real independence, social justice, and democracy, which, when expressed in concrete measures, would lead to a better life.

It would appear that religion – especially in societies where economic, social and democratic development has been retarded by colonialism, neocolonialism, and the corrupt autocratic regimes linked to them – has been, and still can be, a suitable instrument for deluding the masses. The British colonialists and the corrupt ruling classes which collaborated with them saw that political religious movements were a powerful force with a popular following, which could be channelled to serve their purposes.

However, the leaders of this powerful and explosive movement were always tempted, whenever the occasion arose, to take over power themselves and rule directly. It was at such moments that they clashed openly with the ruling regime.

Is history only repeating itself again?

When Sadat came to power in Egypt after Nasser's death, he quickly emerged as a ruler who had different views and represented different interests to those of Nasser and his immediate collaborators. For Sadat, the future of Egypt lay in a complete dependence on the USA, which had replaced the British and the French as the capitalist world power in the Middle East after the tripartite invasion of Egypt (by Britain, France and Israel) in October 1956.

This old/new vision of things necessitated peace with Israel and a complete reversal of Nasser's economic and political strategies that had attempted to chart a middle course between capitalism and socialism, between the USA and the Soviet Union, between Western democracy and an autocracy built on a one-party system and Arab unity. For Sadat, the solution of Egypt's problems lay not in a planned economy but in a market economy which would give free rein to competing forces: even if the result, or perhaps because the result, irrespective of official discourse, would be an ascendancy of the richest and most powerful over those who had neither money nor power, or little of either; even if it meant the big fish eating the little fish; even if it meant an increasing gap between the rich and the poor, and between men and women. Even if it meant replacing British colonialism with the economic and military ascendancy of the United States coupled with growing dependence of Egypt on the West, more freedom for speculators and brokers at the expense of industrial and agricultural production, and a foreign debt growing by leaps and bounds. Even if it meant replacing Nasser's anti-democratic politics by other anti-democratic measures hidden behind the thin veil of a multiparty system controlled by a few, who danced to the tune of a ruling party with a rigged majority. Even if it meant replacing partly controlled corruption by a corruption let loose. Even if it meant throwing overboard any hopes of Arab unity and therefore of a more just peace with Israel for the Palestinians, the Syrians, the Jordanians, the Lebanese, the Egyptians, and the Arabs in general.

Sadat had to overcome those who opposed his views. After naming himself Al-Ra'is Al-Mu'min, the President Believer, he reverted to the old game of reviving the Islamic political movement to use it in the struggle against the opposition composed of Nasserites, nationalists, progressives, liberals and left-wing movements. Once again, the followers of the Islamic political movement started to become visible, the young men bearded and the women veiled. Their slogans, 'God is great' or 'Islam is the solution', reappeared on the walls or were shouted into microphones. This time, however, there were significant changes: a greater complexity and sophistication, and more violence. The movement seemed to have split. On the one hand there were numerous radical groups, like Al-Gihad and Al-Gama'a Al-Islamiya, susceptible to terrorist teachings, methods and attacks. On the other there was a softer, 'moderate' mainstream, the Muslim Brotherhood. This group, after learning from past experience, was now prepared to play the electoral game, to infiltrate into professional, cultural, informational and other institutions, into the administration at all levels (central and local), and into parliament and the judiciary. It also set up a network of social services. Most important of all, many members of the Muslim Brotherhood who had worked in the Gulf countries and gone into voluntary exile had learned how to make money and had understood the importance of an economic base composed of a network of banks with Arab, Islamic and international connections. After all, way back in history, and even in more recent times, some Arabs had been wily traders. The Islamic fundamentalists, who were not worried about art or culture, or the future of our life on the planet, could fit in very well with an economy built on brokerage, trade and speculation. They were at home in a world order and a national or regional system where money was the commodity to be played with plus a sideline in drugs or in arms. Why not? 'God forgives all sins except that of giving your allegiance to another god.'[3]

This way, the roles were nicely divided. The Muslim Brotherhood no longer had any need for a military wing. The 'radical terrorist Islamic groups' could throw the bombs for them. This way they were not responsible. Their role was more important and strategic. They provided the ideology and presented themselves to the government, and to everyone else, as a moderating force. They alone could deal with the fanatics and save us from them by coming to power. They would restore our lost security, our vanishing stability, and save us from chaos. So while the radicals threw the bombs and disrupted the economy, the Muslim Brotherhood could steal to power by gradually expanding its base in the governmental and quasi-governmental institutions, including Al-Azhar University, the state religious institution.

But the Muslim Brotherhood's plan was cut short momentarily. As the Islamic political movement became stronger, its opposition to Sadat, who had conjured them up, grew vociferous. The growing opposition in the country was threatening his reign. So on 5 September 1981, seized by panic, he arrested all the oppositional parties and groups in one swoop. Some 1,352 people were rounded up in thirty-six hours.

One month later, on 6 October, the Islamic 'demon' that had been let out of the bottle assassinated its master as he stood reviewing his troops. This setback was only temporary. Two months after Mubarak took over, he released all the people whom Sadat had imprisoned. But as time went on, it was clear that his policies would not differ much from those of Sadat. The 'liberalization' process continued more rapidly under the watchful eye of the World Bank, with the help of the pressures exerted by 'aid' donors. Prices continued to soar; this inflation was a monster which devoured the meagre earnings of a population that was forced to import what people needed most rather than produce it through their own work as all human beings prefer to do.

The government continued to encourage the Islamic political movement in a multitude of ways, and to knuckle down to the pressures exerted by Saudi Arabia and the other Gulf countries, especially after the Gulf War had eliminated all resistance from Iraq or anyone else. Perhaps the oil countries could be enticed to invest – a hope that has not materialized except to a limited extent. (The governments of the big oil countries are now in debt; only private capital has the money to invest, and it has been quite hesitant, concentrating on food and clothing for the rich, luxury buildings and hotels, and speculation in urban development and currency trade – all the things that make things worse, marginalize the poor and women, push them to the edge.)

Religion has been and still functions as a safety valve, so the government pampered the Islamic political movement even while at the same time it tried to hold it back. But the government kept losing ground. The new strategies of the fundamentalists were proving themselves.

Inflation served them well and so did the policies of the capitalist West, backing Israel all along the line, knocking down the Arab countries one by one, and tightening the economic clamp.

The West: a central player in the game

The policies followed by the Egyptian government under Sadat and then Mubarak have been largely supported by the USA and the other Western powers. The Islamic political movements were used to fight in the Afghanistan War, supplied with money and arms through Saudi Arabia and Pakistan, with technical aid from the CIA and other sources of help. Recourse was had to the most fanatic and terrorist groups such as Al-Gihad and Al-Gama'a Al-Islamiya. Sheikh Omar Abdel Rahman, the spiritual leader of the latter group, who was arrested in the USA in connection with the bombing of the World Trade Center in New York, is known to have been involved actively in the Afghanistan War.

Today in Egypt the Islamic political movement feels strong enough to make a decisive bid for power. Its success or failure depends on many things, not least of which is the position of the army, whose favour the present government has done a lot to woo.

Fundamentalism, women, and the intellectuals

On 15 June 1991, the Egyptian government closed down the Arab Women's Solidarity Association which we had founded in April 1982 along with a group of other Arab women and men. This closing-down was the culmination of systematic attacks on the association and its founders emanating from the different Islamic political groups, from Saudi Arabia, and from different governmental institutions and administrations.

Women's rights and women's movements have always been considered anathema to these Islamic political movements and to the state religious institution. Only a small minority of progressive Islamic intellectuals and thinkers had some sympathy for the efforts made by women to struggle for their rights.

One of them, Farag Foda, was assassinated by a terrorist group on 8 June 1992, and today many other intellectuals and independent thinkers are threatened by a similar fate. Several professionals, journalists, and writers have been killed in Algeria. The names of those under threat have figured on various death lists circulated in Arab countries including Egypt, Yemen, the Sudan, Algeria, Jordan and Saudi Arabia. One of the paradoxes of this situation is that a number of them are being protected against fundamentalists by security guards employed by the very governments they oppose. But the fundamentalists have infiltrated many government administrations, including those responsible for security, which is hardly a comfortable thought for those under guard, who have the double task of opposing both the fundamentalists and the governments from whom they are deeply alienated.

[1994]

Notes

1. Written with Sherif Hetata.

2. Since the Muslim Brotherhood was not officially a party, the decree dissolving parties issued by the revolutionary regime did not apply to it.

3. To believe in more than one god is termed *al-Shirk Billah* in Arabic.

PART FOUR

Orientalizing Women

CHAPTER 12

Why Keep Asking Me About My Identity?

Every time I come to a conference dealing with African identity or culture held in Europe or North America, I ask myself why these conferences are held, why the organizers and most of the participants live in England or Germany or Switzerland or the United States, are citizens of these lands, scholars, researchers, intellectuals, writers in different institutions. This conference is being held in the United States with American money, American logistical and informational facilities provided by American institutions. And here I am after a long journey from Africa, sitting in my seat on time, ready to talk about my 'identity', an identity which I am asked about over and over again. It makes me turn your question round and round. Why does no one ask you what is your 'identity'? Is it that the American 'identity', American culture, does not require any questioning, does not need to be examined, or studied or discussed in conferences like this?

So far I have not heard of a conference held in Africa or Asia or even in America dealing with *Pan-Americanism* as related, for example, to North and South America ever since the Munro Doctrine made of South America your backyard. Neither have I heard that Pan-Americanism, just like Pan-Africanism, requires some updating so that we can understand a little more of what is going on in this world of ours – so that 'identity politics' does not remain the exclusive tool of the powerful against the peoples who are being postcolonialized.

Words whose meanings are obscure sometimes open up vistas in the mind. They may, however, be a shroud, a mask that hides: such are 'God' and 'Satan', or 'free trade', or 'democracy' in my country or in the countries of the West. The game of words continues all the time. Some years ago my 'Arab identity' was a fact of politics and culture and of life. Today it has become a taboo, a curse for those who insist on saying they are Arabs. Now a new identity has been coined for me by the global powers. Our region is 'the Middle East', refurbished to include Israel, Turkey, and perhaps a subdued Iran. If I am asked I should say my identity is Middle Eastern, not Arab at all. That way I can be postmodern, updated, moving with the times. The Arab nation, Arab unity, Arab nationalism are over. These are the relics of the past, like other backward national identities that belonged at one time to the 'third', or the fourth or perhaps even the fifth world, not euphemistically designated as the 'South' where the marginalized 'Confucian', or 'Islamic', or 'Hindu' hordes teem, and starve and die, threatening to clash with the 'Christian' civilization of professors Huntington and Bernard Lewis. My backward national identity has been replaced by more advanced, more civilized identities. A 'Middle Eastern', or 'American', or 'Israeli', or maybe a global identity with no place for secondary national identities like mine.

Recently I was asked, 'What country are you from?' I said Egypt, and the man said, 'Do you consider Egypt to be in Africa?' So I found Egypt being uprooted from Africa too, after it had ceased to be a part of the Arab world. Now I no longer know the continent in which Egypt can be found, nor do I know if I am Arab, or African, or whether I should be here at all. And in early 1996 I watched the leaders of the world as they sat in Egypt, in Sharm Al-Sheikh, beside the Red Sea, discussing so-called terrorism and updating things. They called themselves the 'makers of peace' and established a new map for Africa and the Middle East. Their friends and business partners and followers of their creed were identified as the 'angels of this peace', and others who did not agree to their view of things were called 'terrorists', backward barbarians with no soul. These 'makers of peace' forgot that Hamas had been nurtured and used by Israel against the Palestine Liberation Organization. They forgot Deir Yasseen and the children of the Intifada with broken bones and plastic bullet wounds to their heads.

People asked me where I stood, did I identify with the angels, makers of the peace, or with the devils, the makers of war, the aggressors, the terrorists. I am not a terrorist, nor will I ever be. But I believe that without justice there is no peace. Ever since I was born, the events in my region have proved that to me. 'Identity' is a discourse, and it is essential to know who is using it, who decides, who labels me, what all this interest in 'cultural identity' means, where does it lead.

That is what I want to keep in mind as I address the issue of identity and language. When I was a child I was told to 'hide' my brown complexion under a coating of white powder. I was born in the early thirties and at that time Egypt was under the rule of the British and the royal descendants of the Albanian Turk Mohammed Ali who over-threw the Mameluke dynasty. At that time a 'white' skin meant that one came from the upper classes, for both the British and the Turks had fair complexions. Beauty was therefore to have white skin. To be brown or dark-skinned was ugly, related to the lower, poorer classes of society. I wasted many years of my life before I would feel comfortable with a brown skin, before I gained sufficient self-confidence and understanding to see that my brown skin could be different and yet beautiful, before I could wash off the coating of white powder and live in the world with my real face, my real identity.

Later I asked myself a question: 'Is my identity related to the colour of my skin and what was I doing covering it with a coating of white powder? Does not the coating reflect a *migration* of the mind, an alienation from my mind?' Migrating words and worlds is a theme I relate to the general problems we are facing in the countries of our African continent. These problems to my mind are not, as some people tend or like to think, related to questions of identity or to what we now designate as a 'global culture' crossing national, ethnic and geographic boundaries and overcoming the frontiers, the delimitation resulting from land, language, state, colour, race and religion.

For four years from 1992 I lived in the United States in what may be considered a form of exile. Before they were over I realized that I had to go back *home* to my country, my land, my people, my language. My home, my country, could not be the United States. In the USA I am a stranger, an 'alien'. There I discovered that Americans are attached to their country, to their nation and their national identity to a greater degree than most peoples of the world. They take great pride in being American, in being patriotic. Yet they are surprised when other people take pride in being African. Perhaps they think that the only country worth being proud of is the United States. And this is the case even amongst learned people in the academy. This probably has a lot to do with how the world is divided today despite the fact that we have moved out of the so-called modern era of thinking into the so-called postmodern era, which implies an important step forward.

But in this postmodern era the struggle has intensified over sources of wealth and power and therefore over people's minds, over culture. What decides the issue of these struggles, however, is not justice or human rights but multinational economic power and monopoly, intensified a hundred times by the backing of military power at the core of which resides the club of states possessing nuclear and postnuclear weapons. Much effort goes into the drive, led by the United States, to break down boundaries, destroy frontiers, dissolve nation-states and national entities. But it is these multinational powers who decide which frontiers, which boundaries, which entities should disappear and which should be maintained and injected with new strength. The black peoples of Africa, the poor of Africa, are required to 'overcome the limitations of' their blackness, their languages, their international or national frontiers in the name of 'one world', of humanity, of a 'human universalism'. They are required to soar towards the ever-widening horizons of postmodernism, where everything is fragmented, diffused, splintered to the advantage of a handful of rich people.

The economic and the cultural

Never before in the history of the world has there been such a concentration and centralization of capital in so few nations, and in the hands of so few people. The countries that form the Group of Seven, with their 800 million inhabitants, control more technical, economic, informational and military power than the rest of the world's people, the approximately 430 billion who live in Asia, Africa, Eastern Europe and Latin America. Five hundred multinational corporations account for 80 per cent of world trade and 75 per cent of investment, and their number is dropping each year as a result of mergers and the elimination of the relatively smaller ones. Half these multinational corporations are based in the USA, Germany, Japan and Switzerland. The OECD group of countries contributes 80 per cent of world production.

Since around 1970, technological advances have reduced the amount of raw materials used per product by more than one third. This *de-materialization* of production has resulted in a tendency for the real prices of fifty principal raw materials to fall. Price deterioration has been ever more pronounced in recent years. Dematerialization of production combined with automation means that labour loses value. People are losing their value or are no longer needed. The South including Africa, which depends on raw materials and labour, suffers most.

Plunder of the South, including Africa, is now taking place under new names, such as 'aid' or 'free trade' or even 'development'. About $220 billion were transferred from the Third World to commercial banks in the West during the period 1986–92. What the World Bank calls structural adjustment is potential *economic genocide*. Its essence is to raise prices in the so-called developing countries to world levels – yet average earnings in the South are seventy times lower than in the North. 'Free trade' means an expanding world market for the multinational corporations. It means breaking down customs, subsidies, tariffs, quotas, ending cheap adaptations of patents – breaking everything that protects the weaker. It means protection when necessary for the stronger. Witness the wrangles between the USA and Europe or Japan over 'free trade'. Double standards have always been used to defend privilege.

To expand their world market, the multinational corporations use economic power, buy governments and rulers, play politics, and have recourse to armed force where necessary through the UN, or away from it, according to circumstances. It becomes easier, however, if people can be convinced to do what the masters of the global economy want them to do.

This is where culture comes in. And culture includes identity, migrant words, and migrating worlds. Culture can serve in different ways to help the global market reach out all over the world, expand to the most distant regions. Culture can also serve to reduce or destroy, or prevent, or divide, or outflank, the resistance of people. At the disposal of culture today are powerful means which function across the whole world: the media.

To expand the global market, to increase the number of consumers, to make sure that they buy what is produced for sale or offered as services, to develop needs and desires, and to multiply them, to create a fever for consuming; culture must play its role in developing certain values, certain patterns of behaviour, certain visions of what is happiness or success in the world, certain attitudes towards sex, beauty, and love, including a cult of pornography and desire and violence. Culture must fashion the global consumer.

Africa: a giant suffering fragmentation

In this global economy Africa, so rich in potential power and resources, remains the poorest of the poor. It has a debt of $317 billion – on which $10 billion are paid as interest every year – 50 per cent of the cases of malaria in the world, 17 million cases of tuberculosis, and 45 per cent of all the people below the UN poverty line.

The global culture which aims at expanding, homogenizing and unifying the world into one market seems to be contradicted by another movement towards cultural division, fragmentation and strife, towards the multiplication of ethnic, cultural, linguistic and religious identities. It militates against Pan-Africanism or, more precisely, against *African unity*. It serves the purpose of the multinationals. It is a postmodern application of the old adage 'divide and rule'.

The movement towards a global culture is therefore not contradicted by this postmodern tendency towards cultural fragmentation and identity struggles. They are two faces of the same coin. To unify power, economic, or cultural, at the top it is necessary to fragment power at the bottom. To maintain the global economy of the few, of the multinationals, unification must exist at the top, amongst the few, the very few. It must not take place at the bottom, in Africa, and especially not amongst the many, amongst the African peoples. There should be no African unity. People should remain divided, fragmented, confused. And new slogans, new catchwords, new worthy causes must be found to hide this truth. 'Identity', 'multiculturalism', 'respect for other cultures', 'cultural studies', the list will go on proliferating, so that as soon as we unveil one world another is found to replace it, so that our African peoples remain perpetually confused, so that our African intellectuals and thinkers and writers are drawn into the noose. Instead of struggling for economic identity, for political identity and for cultural identity, instead of making links between them, they forget that there is no culture without an economy to support it, without political institutions to defend it, without a land in which it can strike its roots. That 'cultures' and 'identities' are doomed without a material base, condemned to wither away. That the struggle for 'identity' is a total struggle, like the struggle for my personal identity depends on my integrity, my originality, my mind, my thoughts, but also on my material existence, my economic independence, my capacity to earn and produce.

Otherwise culture, identity, multiculturalism become an exhibition, a spectacle for the pleasure of others to see, to consume. Like the festivals of African culture I have seen in London, or Copenhagen or New York. Like the visibility of African-Americans in music, dance and sports and their almost total exclusion from the decisive levels of banking, production, business and other areas linked to intellectual or administrative or economic power.

Migrating words, migrating worlds

Globalization has meant different things at different levels for different categories of people. Millions of farmers, immigrants, poorly qualified urban workers, youth, and especially women in Africa suffer globalization's negative consequences. They are marginalized and excluded from the new world economy as a result of structural changes imposed by World Bank policies and multinational intervention. Africa, with its rivers and fertile lands, imports 10,000 million dollars' worth of foodstuffs every year.

The phenomenon of globalization has brought with it massive international migration on a scale never seen before in history. Whereas in the nineteenth century Europeans left their homes in great numbers to colonize the United States, today the poor populations of the South are travelling in an opposite direction. Accepted at one time as cheap sources of labour or in order to lure the best brains of the South into the scientific, technological, academic, information and intellectual institutions of the North, they are now being sent home again. Multinationals can exploit their physical and mental capacities more effectively in their home countries. Borders are closing, immigrants and refugees are being rejected, and xenophobic ideologies are once more on the rise.

Xenophobic, chauvinistic and fundamentalist movements are also multiplying in the South. Fuelled by the quasi-genocidal economic difficulties, despair and loss of faith in past experiments and in the leaderships imposed by the new colonial powers, these movements are being used in the power game to contain progressive forces, exert pressures and provide alternative regimes when others have done their time. They are also part of the identity game of fragmentation and the policies that divide.

So where is the place of the migrant word, the migrant intellectual, the migrant writer from Africa in this global world of ours? What roles can he or she play, and what roles should he or she avoid?

My experience with the migrant world in exile

As I noted above, between 1992 and 1996 I was a migrant from my country, Egypt, to the United States.

I opened my eyes one morning just before dawn to the sound of knocks on the door of my flat in Giza. At the door was a police officer in plainclothes accompanied by two other men. He had come to install armed guards around my home and to place bodyguards who would accompany me wherever I went. He told me the state had decided to take these measures to protect my life. They had information that indicated that my life was in danger, that the religious fundamentalists had put my name on a death list and that they might try to kill me.

My life was now at the mercy of a state apparatus that I opposed and that throughout the long years had done its best to silence and oppress me in different ways. This oppression had included banning my books, firing me from my post in the Ministry of Health, and a period of imprisonment. The last measure taken against me had been the arbitrary and illegal closing down of the Egyptian branch of the Arab Women's Solidarity Association in June 1991 and the banning of its magazine *Noon*.

My life was thus caught in the crossfire between the state security forces and the terrorist movements that concealed their aims behind a religious facade. I did not know where the bullets would come from, who would aim their guns at me, and to what end – to fulfil the desire of the state, or to serve the aims of the fundamentalist movement?

Would the fatal bullet be shot in my back by a bodyguard, or from the front by a youth wearing a religious mask?

As I sat in my home surrounded by enemies on every side, not knowing what to do, fortune intervened. An American student named Elizabeth had come to Cairo to pursue some studies and by sheer accident she decided to take a chance and visit me after failing to get through to me by phone. At one time she had been a student at Duke University, and when she saw the armed guards around my home she suddenly said to me, 'Why don't you leave?' I said, 'Where to? I cannot leave like that just to any place. I must know where I'm going, and what I'll do.'

Next day she phoned up a friend of hers at Duke, Professor Miriam Cooke, who taught Arabic literature, including several of my novels. And that's how I became a migrant and an exile, living in the USA for four years as a visiting professor at Duke. They were good years and I was happy to be there. But as the years went by I felt I must return *even if my life was in danger*. Back in my country even if there is a threat I am where I belong, I am more at ease. I am not an 'alien', as they call me in the United States. In the USA I'm treated as an alien even though I pay my taxes, the same taxes as a US citizen pays. I do not have the same rights. I cannot even get a certificate to say that I pay taxes in the USA so that I can be exempted from paying taxes elsewhere. So when I was in the USA I was paying double taxes, and if I had a book translated, which happens quite a lot, I was paying taxes in three places at the same time.

Within Duke University I was treated like other colleagues who were aliens: in a different way. I was not like a US professor, even though I might be more efficient and more gifted in many ways. It was not only a matter of pay. There was no equal pay for equal work. It was the way academia valued me as a person. It was as though US professors alone had knowledge, alone would deal with theory, alone had higher thoughts. There were a few exceptions of course, but Africans or Arabs like me were of inferior intelligence and standing. And if we had thoughts, or theories, or contributions to make they were necessarily limited, localized, one-sided. The higher, holistic, global thinking was the realm of the American. He or she alone could see across the world, englobe it in a total vision, explore the horizons as they opened up, soar with daring up, up and far away. He or she was not limited by geography, or history, or language, or culture. He or she could speak of Africa with authority, deal with so-called Third World culture better than I could. To them this seemed natural, despite the outward veneer of polite tolerance. After all the USA was the leader of the world, with a global reach. And English was the global language. All other languages were limited, local, they could not leap across frontiers to reach as far as English went. American culture alone was universal. All other cultures were narrow in scope, backward, biased, prejudiced, unable to deal with the world as it is today, unable even to deal with their own problems and find a way out. People in my part of the world were corrupt, accustomed to bend their backs, knew little about the human essence, and less about human rights. This is how identity was seen by the bulk of academics.

Their postmodern vision and thinking fragmented us into a colourful mosaic. Interesting they would say, delightful. To study the other gave them a thrill. But the other was not of great weight, not of real value in the future of the world. The other could not become a part of self. Identity was there, but it was there for intellectual fun.

Yet US academic life has left open a space, a limited space, for us African migrants. We can find a corner in which to rest, perhaps to find some peace from ruthless tracking down by corrupt states, from the gangs in the political game, or the bands of fundamentalists pointing guns. And we must admit that, after all, the US academy is more tolerant, more flexible, than the academy in Europe, or the universities of African countries from which we come. Here there is more room to learn, to argue, and to think.

I would never have found a place in England, or in Germany, or in France. Even Switzerland, the 'neutral' paradise, was closed to me. In the US academy there are men and women who welcome us, open their arms, help us to find our way, exchange their thoughts with us. They learn from us and we from them. We exchange on equal terms. We become friends. And together we forge a new image of what America is, of what it can be, a new image of Africa and of what it can become – a new image of a future world in which our identities are genuine though distinct, yet unified by a common endeavour for what is human and best in both of us.

I lived in North Carolina for four years. I was at the margin of the intellectual life in Duke, and of the wider spaces of thought outside the narrow confines drawn by forest trees around the campus grounds. I was hemmed in. My voice was not able to reach into the media because I was the bearer of a different thought, of an Arab–African identity misunderstood and distorted by those who monopolize the word, including the word of migrants like myself.

For despite all the talk about diversity, difference, respect for other cultures, despite the postmodern discourse about multiculturalism and identities, there is no space in the media, or even in the academy, for a real, in-depth discussion of who I am, and who you are. Of who each one of us really is. In the United States the same process of exclusion operates that we have in Africa. The mechanisms are different, more sophisticated, more economic, less evident. Africans appear here and there as samples.

My experiences with American TV and radio have shown me time and time again that my real identity is something that should be concealed. My sentences are amputated, my words are rearranged, my thoughts are distorted, even my features are made to be angry when I should smile, made to smile where I am rebelling. *Fresh Air* radio programme wanted to interview me after the publication of one of my books by California Press. But when I expressed some of my opinions on the phone, the person responsible for the arrangements cancelled the interview. For when I, as an Arab woman, say what I think about what is happening in my region I am made to disappear or portrayed as an Arab terrorist thirsty for blood. If I say something with which my US interviewers agree, I am called a peacemaker, or a postmodern thinker. Never am I allowed to be myself and yet an Arab woman. At each moment I am robbed of my true identity to fit in with the views of those otherwise in control.

After four years of exile I decided to go back to my country where I belong. To the land where I was born and where I shall die. To the people who speak my language and understand what I say. To the men and women with whom I have shared the struggle and with whom I will share the hope and the pain of the future.

My identity

I have tried to tell you about my identity. I hope I have been able to make you understand what African woman I am. But we are so engrossed in defining our identities, when they are changing all the time. Instead of stressing what is different perhaps we should spend more time discovering what is common to you and me. Or perhaps we cannot do one without the other. Our humanity is common but it takes many forms.

For me there is no identity without home, no identity without a land on which I can stand, without a language, without the means to keep it alive and help it to flourish and grow, without an organization and a pen with which to struggle for freedom and justice and love and peace, for women to know that they are human beings, for blacks to feel that all the colours in the world are what make it glow.

I am an Arab woman fighting for a peace that will last. Not a surrender to the US and Israeli nuclear arsenal, nor the peace that fundamentalism wishes to impose by bullets and terror in the United States and also in Egypt. Not the peace of fanatic religious movements, whether Muslim, or Christian, or Jewish.

I am against the identities built on religion because the history of religion was written in the endless rivers of blood flowing in the name of God, in the name of a land chosen by Him for His people, in the name of any god-chosen race or nation on earth. I am against a nationalism, a patriotism, that does not see the rest of the world. I am against privilege of the rich against the poor, against privilege of man against woman.

I am an Arab woman. But in my body run the rivers of Africa, that flow through Africa from Jinja and Tana. I am African and Arab and Egyptian because my genes were drawn from all these, because my history goes back in Egypt for seven thousand years, to Isis and Ma'at and Noon. I am a woman who is Arab, who writes in Arabic, struggles in the Arab region and belongs to the world.

Is my identity Mediterranean? Some people say Egypt is not an African country but is in fact linked not only geographically but also culturally to the Mediterranean basin. They organize conferences and meetings, establish institutions and carry out other activities which group the Mediterranean countries including Egypt in a cultural com plex. They bestow upon us a new 'identity', separating culture and economics, culture and the right of people to self-determination, culture and the rights of the Palestinians to their land. They forget that the Lebanese have been chased out of south Lebanon and that the Syrians have been forced to accept the Israeli occupation of Golan.

Am I a woman whose past and future are linked to Black Africa? Or am I a white Egyptian whose land is bathed by the Mediterranean Sea like Italy and Greece and France and Spain? Does this make North Africa a part of Europe rather than of the continent from which it draws its name? Does the Sahara Desert decide my culture for me?

This difference of opinion related to identity involves an argument about the statue of the sphinx that lies at the foot of the pyramids not far from my house in Giza. Was Abul-Houl black or white? Was his nose fleshy and flat like that of black Africans or was it sharp and prominent but lost its shape when Napoleon fired his guns during the French invasion and clipped it off? And Cleopatra: were her ancestors black or white? Who discovered the continent of America? Was it a black man from Mali who sent his ships across the ocean more than two centuries before Christopher Columbus set out from Spain? Was the beginning of Greek civilization a movement that spread across the Mediterranean from Egypt as Martin Bernal maintains in his book *Black*

Athena?[1] Or was Greek civilization newborn in Greece and therefore European in origin, untainted by the Egyptian civilization that had preceded it and developed over thousands of years before we heard of Greece?

Do I inherit my identity from my female ancestors Ma'at (the goddess of justice and truth), Isis (the goddess of knowledge and freedom), Sekhmek (the goddess of medicine and health) and Hypathia (the philosopher born and burnt in Alexandria with the library of the city)?

The struggle over history, over identities and their origin, is part of the struggle over power which has never ceased throughout the centuries. It is those who possess military and nuclear and economic power, those who invade us and take away our material and cultural sustenance, those who rob us of our own riches and our labour and our history, who tell us what our identity is. Throughout the ages it has been like this.

How can I, Nawal El Saadawi, have an identity if my history is effaced? If my female ancestors are forgotten, buried in oblivion? If Ma'at, Isis, and Sekhmet are not spoken of? If Khadija the wife of Prophet Muhammad (who was the first to call him Prophet, to tell him not to fear or doubt but go on with courage) is not spoken of, although if it were not for her courage Islam might have been born not through him but perhaps through someone else.

Is it I who decides what my identity is or those who have the power, and the money, and the arms and the media, and the global market and the multinational corporations in their hands?

How can I defend my real identity against the international and national forces that wish to take it away from me, or distort it, or change it into something else, into the identity of a slave who does and says what he or she is told, who speaks the language of the masters of this world?

A few days ago, in Cairo, I read the weekly issue of the most important weekly women's magazine in Egypt (24 March 1996). This women's magazine was first published after the Egyptian government authorities took the decision to ban our women's magazine *Noon*.

The magazine in question, *Nisf Al-Dunia*, whose Arabic name means 'Half the World', was celebrating 8 March, International Women's Day. The first page was an editorial written by a man whose name is Ibrahim Nafi. He is head of the biggest newspaper complex in Egypt, Al-Ahram. In his editorial defining feminine identity, or rather women's identity, Ibrahim Nafi took as his reference Jean Jacques Rousseau, whom he quoted as having written that a woman is like a cat – if you show affection to her she keeps rubbing up against you. This is the identity that the man in charge of this women's magazine finds suitable to describe the traits that distinguish a woman. If she is treated well she turns her back on those who were good to her: she is traitorous and not to be trusted. If she is treated badly she becomes servile and tries to endear herself.

On the front page there was the photograph of a woman ostensibly depicting the ideal woman, with a demure face like a kitten's, covered in makeup: a postmodern veil hiding her real features just like the *hijab* hides the face of women, their history, their authenticity, their true identity, in the name of religion.

A role for migrant intellectuals

Many of those who have migrated from Africa have built their lives, and see their future, elsewhere. Some of them would like to go back but cannot for political or other reasons. What role can the migrant world and the migrant word they carry with them fulfil?

1. When speaking of cultural, multicultural or intercultural writings and studies in the academy, in various institutions, or in conferences, we Africans should struggle against the tendency to deal with issues of identity, of ethnicity, of language and of national or local or subaltern cultures as such, separately. To separate, to deal with culture and identities apart from the economic and the political, serves the purposes of the neocolonialist approach. We cannot understand the role which culture plays, or how it is and what it does, if we fail to link it to the power struggle, to the dynamics of gender and class, to rulers and people, to economic interests.

Perhaps cultural, multicultural and intercultural studies need to identify themselves more clearly. What path or paths would enable cultural studies to prove a greater concern with and solidarity for people and their cultures in the African continent? How can we transfer knowledge and technology to those working in the area of culture without appropriating them to the power system? Does this not involve avoiding being appropriated ourselves or at least maintaining a sufficient distance so that we see through eyes that remain focused on Africa as it is and can be in the twenty-first century?

The forces of globalization are homogenizing indigenous African cultures everywhere. In villages that continue to be deprived of the basic necessities of life it is possible to see Star TV, MTV, Zee TV, cable TV and blue movies. The cultural invasion by consumerism is spreading, creating a severe conflict between what is available and what is desired.

The invasion by images is critical. For the first time in the history of cultures like ours we are watching the homogenization of Western or Northern culture into a consolidated, alluring image of the other, of a liberal, capitalist, materially and sexually enticing market, of a world that in comparison with our life we can see only with envy and even reverence.

What can writers and multicultural scholars or academicians from Africa do to appraise critically the image created, which we know is quite *false?*

2. When cultural and identity studies speak of the 'other', the two poles involved are usually North and South. Yet I as an Egyptian and we as Africans can look in our continent to many directions, to the north or the south, to the east or the west, to the sixty or so countries or entities that exist in Africa. Religious, ethnic and racial strife are increasing the gaps and reinforcing barriers between people in many parts of the world. The 'other' is a matter related not only to North and South but also to South and South, to differences and similarities between African countries where culture and cultural identity are concerned. What we might call intracultural studies and writings can therefore be useful in bridging the dichotomies of a bipolar world, in coming closer to a global world not from above but from below. In such a global world, people would understand one another and come closer – despite 'identities' and 'diversities' – through joint ventures, writing, and research, rather than maintaining a hegemonic, pyramidal world where culture and identities are decided in the boardrooms of multinational media, companies, and institutions run or influenced by them.

The Orient, or the South, or Africa have served long enough as sources of self-definition to the West or the North. This process has been going on for over four centuries. The mechanism used has remained the same: taking the societies, the ways of life, in Africa and elsewhere in the South out of their socioeconomic and historical context so that they appear unreal, strange, foreign; distancing them as much as you can. And this process still happens on a wide scale today. Time and time again I have attended African art festivals, or cultural events, or exhibitions, that were displays of disparate samples brought to entertain and to delight without any reference to the societies, the miseries, they represent and the factors behind them, including relations with the North.

3. Books that are translated are a glaring example of this tendency to choose the exotic or the strange or to misrepresent. French publishing houses are past masters at this art, more often than not aided and

abetted by North African Arabs or sub-Saharan Africans living in France. US publishing houses are rapidly picking up the same trick. The modern writings, novels produced in Africa and the South, especially if they deal with the reality of relations between Africa and the North, or with gender and class, are not considered to be suitable consumption in the North.

4. New media technology has opened up wide vistas to small groups, and even to individuals. In the countries of Africa even the production of long feature films is relatively inexpensive, probably around $300,000. My son directed a short feature film called *Bride of the Nile* for a production cost of $12,000, and it won six international prizes. The possibilities opened up in the cultural field by film and above all by video are enormous. Africans in academia, in media and other institutions can think along these lines; the material costs are limited and can be found. Migrant Africans can cooperate with local groups, and this form of North–South networking can do a lot in many fields. Problems exist, but how much have we Africans in northern countries, including the United States, been oriented to think this way? How much have we thought of building up the expertise and knowledge of people still living in the countries from which we came?

There is so much that migrant Africans can do. They are living in advanced countries. They have access to knowledge and technological means that their brothers and sisters at home are deprived of. By networking with them they can help in many ways, build up a global solidarity from below. Step by step, over the years, they can help to resist marginalization of the millions back home. Step by step they can participate in creating a global force from below, an alliance of peoples united in a universal human endeavour which is able to respect cultures and identities and yet unite in struggle for true democracy, justice, peace and a better future for all people.

5. Some of the African emigrants in the North are working in academia, in culture, in science, in the media. Many of them are intellectuals and writers, and quite a number have become prominent or even eminent contributors to the fields in which they work.

It is natural that those of them who are involved in literature, the arts, the humanities, in writing and culture should become involved in multicultural and intercultural thought, in the problems of identity, of migrants' words, migrants' worlds, and migrants' thoughts. They represent more than one culture or possess a dual one. They reflect this dual culture and are better equipped to navigate between the two cultures to understand the changes that are producing a new international body of mankind and womankind. The mutual fertilization of two cultures is an asset, or can be an asset if well used, used for their people, for their migrant communities, and for their fellow citizens in what has now become their home. The dual culture can give insights into the twin poles of North and South, Africa and the United States. Migrant intellectuals have at their disposal all the accumulated knowledge provided by modern information technology, and its means, as well as the discipline, the training, the frame of mind, the habits, which motivate research, understanding and initiative. If courageous, these intellectuals can help to bridge the gap between Africa and the North, to bring people closer, to emphasize what is good, and to criticize what is negative on both sides.

However, they cannot replace those who continue to struggle and work at home in Africa. Representation is never easy. And there is no real representation if you are not part of people's everyday life, of their failures and their successes, their misery and their joy, their despair and their passion, their margins of freedom and their prison bars. Some Africans have thought that they can represent their people better than their counterparts in Africa because of the sophistication, the means, the knowledge at their disposal. This is an illusion. This is what the global powers tend to encourage. They want to separate the intellectuals and the peoples who resist at home. They want to play another power game, to stand them up one against the other. We Africans should not let them play that game.

In the early part of 1996, I was invited to Paris to celebrate International Women's Day on 8 March. The invitation came from Iranian women exiled in France and in other countries of the world. Those women have never ceased struggling to change the Iranian regime, which under the Shah oppressed women and the poor in the name of modernization and now oppresses them in the name of the mullahs and Islam. They have formed an alliance, a front of women and men, which is growing in strength. Their resistance movement is well organized and enlightened in its approach. They have a parliament in exile composed of 560 members, of which 52 per cent are women.

In 1993 this parliament elected a woman as president of the new Iranian regime that they are struggling to create. These people have succeeded in developing a new personality for both men and women, a new identity, where gender discrimination is disappearing through the conscious effort of women, but also men. They want to build a different country, a different economy where the gap between the rich and poor is gradually bridged, where Islam, or 'aid', or 'development' under the guidance and the pressures of the World Bank can no longer be used for the benefit of the few at the expense of those who work.

This is a new identity. It is created by people who struggle in exile, who see exile not only as the path to self-improvement, but also as a chance to help in changing things in their own country. For them, exile is no longer just exile. It is a way to change the world, by changing the societies from which we came. The migrant word is no longer just a changing word, it is an *act*, it is a part of the struggle against injustice and oppression.

This struggle for change, for revolution, can unite us across differences in colour, in race, in language, in culture, in sex, in identity.

To end, let me quote from an interview given by the former Black Panther activist and journalist Mumia Abu Jamal, while on death row waiting to die (*Al-Ahram Weekly*, Cairo, 21–27 March 1996):

The color of power in the courtroom can often be white. And the color of dispower in the courtroom can often be black. But the most consistent variable that determines power in the courtroom is the color of green, the color of money, the power of wealth.

He says:

We spent our energy in professional illusion: fighting with words, debating identity, culture, and diversity without understanding that the essential truth, the essential element that is real, is revolution, and that revolution must enthuse, feed and give life to every facet of our being or else will fail.

And he says:

The spirit of freedom, of human liberation, cannot be held within one vessel. It is like holding air in a glass: The rest of the area around that glass is not a vacuum, it doesn't stop there. It's the same for the spirit of revolution. I am just one vessel. There are many other vessels. Let's keep pouring and pouring it on until it becomes the air we breathe.

[Keynote address to the African Literature Association Twenty-second Annual Conference, 'Migrating Words and Worlds: Pan-Africanism Updated', held in New York, 27–30 March 1996]

Note

1. Martin Bernal, *Black Athena: The Afroasian Roots of Classical Civilization*, Rutgers University Press, 1987.

CHAPTER 13

Women, Religion and Literature: Bridging the cultural gap

The two sides of the cultural gap

The notion of 'bridging the cultural gap' implies that we are dealing with two or more cultures between which there is a gap. In our case, Islamic culture and another culture: namely, Western or Christian culture. In recent years I have been invited to several conferences in Europe and the USA which dealt with the conflicts, or differences, or 'cultural gap' between Islamic and Western or Christian culture. In all these conferences, the speakers and the papers confined themselves to Islam or Islamic culture. The Western scholars who were invited to these conferences were professors or authors specializing in Islamic studies or Islamic culture, and not Christianity or Western culture.

If we want to know the gap between two religions or two cultures, I think we should examine both equally and compare one with the other. In addition, we have to place each religion or culture in its historical, political and economic context. To my knowledge, this is never, or very rarely, done in studies or conferences dealing with religion or culture in the Arab region (or in the South in general) and Western or Christian culture. Sometimes I feel that Islam or Islamic culture has become like a guinea pig in the Western lab, to be examined, dissected, analysed, gazed at. This gaze is never directed in the other direction, to the Christian or Judeo-Christian culture or religion.

Is the gap mainly religious or cultural?

To me, the main problem is not what is called the 'cultural gap', nor is it religious differences or conflicts. The Qur'an teaches us that a good Muslim has to believe in the three holy books, and the prophets of Judaism and Christianity. I spent many years studying the Old and New Testaments and the Qur'an. Many of my writings and novels are related to the three. religions. The similarities, the common foundations between them, are striking. I cannot believe that the 'cultural gap' and the conflicts between the West and our peoples, are the result of religious differences. We must look for reasons elsewhere, even if sometimes these conflicts wear the garb of religion, or hide behind its cloak. To me, the main problem is economic and political. We cannot look at the cultural gap without looking at the economic gap or at the inequality between countries, the inequality between classes in each country, and the inequalities between the sexes in the family and in the state. All these inequalities are linked together. They feed each other in the pyramid of hierarchy and are inseparable. At the top of this pyramid are the leaders of the New World Order.

We are living in one world (not three worlds). It is dominated by one international, patriarchal, capitalist, military system. Countries in our region, in what is called the South, do not progress towards real democracy or real development, culturally or economically.

The problem in our region is not culture or religion or Islam. All regions are flexible and tend to change with the political and economic system. The Christianity of the Middle Ages is not the Christianity of today. The feudal Church is very different from the capitalist Church. Wahhabite Islam in Saudi Arabia is totally different from Islam in Tunisia or Iraq or Syria or Egypt. The situation of women in Saudi Arabia is very different from that of Muslim women in other political systems where Islam is the religion.

Religion can be interpreted to help in liberating women and the poor, and it can be interpreted in a way that increases their oppression. Its meaning depends on how it is interpreted by the power groups in the state or the society. However, almost all conferences in the West dealing with this issue have asked almost the same question regarding the cultural gap.

I remember a conference held in Switzerland in 1992. The organizers sent me a preliminary position paper in which they referred to the 'gap' between Islam and the West. There was nothing about the economic or political or military gap. The questions were restricted to cultural differences or differences in relation to human rights, women's rights, and democracy. They considered the conception of human rights in the West as a model. I still remember a phrase which stated: 'Based on the ideology for equal rights between men and women, the situation for women in Islam seems to be objectionable, because it is oppressive, sexist, and patriarchal.'

This gives the impression that the Christian West is living under a nonpatriarchal, nonsexist, nonracist system! Western democracy was depicted in this conference as the model. The paper maintained that the central difference between Islamic and Western culture lies in the Western conception of sovereignty, that the highest authority in Islam is God, Allah. The individual and the state must follow the will of Allah, whereas Western democracy relies on the principal of state sovereignty, which protects the human rights of the individual and has a humanitarian social character. From this conception arises the need to articulate and protect human rights whereas in Islam, the idea of human rights is unnecessary.

Why is there a gap?

In the countries of the South the direction of our cultural and economic development is not something we have much freedom to choose. It is dictated to us by our local governments dominated by colonial or neocolonial powers in the West. The problems facing us, and which increase the gap between the so-called North and South, are therefore not rooted in religion or specifically in Islam. They are rooted in the North and in the local authorities or dictators collaborating with what is called the New Economic Order. This order is both economic and cultural.

Today, we live in a world dominated by a unipolar power, by one superpower, the USA. The USA dominates the United Nations, the World Bank, IMF, and the General Agreement on Tariffs and Trade (GATT) and is able to dictate the terms of SAPs (structural adjustment programs). The results of development carried out in our countries (in line with the policies of these international institutions) are increasing poverty – both economic and cultural – a resurgence of fanatic political religious groups, and increasing oppression of women.

This new global policy has emerged since the end of the Cold War. It has led to more hunger, more violence, and new wars. All this is often called 'cultural' or 'religious' conflict. Women, youth and children, and the poorest sectors of society, are the main victims.

The New World Order was inaugurated in our region by the launching of the Gulf War. The nature of this war was veiled in the mass media (the international information order) by means of a false universalist culture built on phrases such as 'democracy' and 'human rights', or religious ideas such as fighting the devil or corruption. This was repeated with the war in Somalia and other wars. The reasons for wars have always been concealed behind humane or religious pretexts. If we read the Old Testament we discover that the war to invade the land of Canaan and kill thousands was considered a holy war waged according to the will of Jehovah in order to give his chosen people the 'promised land'. Religious motives are still used in our era to rob other people of their economic and cultural resources.

The other half

Perhaps the problem of the world has always been the 'objectification', the nullification, of he 'other'. For the West or the North, the South is the other which exists only as an object to be exploited and oppressed. Christianity or Western culture sees Islam and Arab culture as the other. And in all religions, all that does not belong to God is seen as emanating from the devil. The problem of our world is to ignore, to dismiss, to destroy, the other. To do this, the other must be 'satanized'.

Men see women as the other (the other half). This may explain why women and the devil (Satan, Iblis) are often related to each other, why women are often dismissed from religion, why God speaks in his holy books only to men, why prophets, priests and all religious authorities are almost all men. In the three holy books of the monotheistic religions, we find that women have an inferior position if compared to that of men. The status of women varies in degree from one religion to the other. Their inferior position is most glaring in Judaism, as a reading of the Old Testament shows clearly.

In the Jewish state of Israel women's groups have been fighting for three decades against gender discrimination in civil and state laws, as well as the family and personal status laws. The Jewish fundamentalist groups in Israel oppose women's rights, and force women back to the home away from political or public life. When I read their literature I see how they use the same anti-women language used by other fanatic religious groups in the Christian North or the Islamic South.

In the Western media and in Western popular thinking, the term 'fundamentalist' is almost restricted to Islamic groups, and yet the New World Order is characterized by the upsurge of so-called fundamentalist religious movements. Fundamentalism is a universal phenomenon, which increases with increasing poverty and racism.

Christian fundamentalists in the USA have grown in power and number since the Reagan–Bush era. They are fighting fiercely against women's rights, black rights, working-class rights, and the rights of other oppressed groups in the American society. They are violent and use guns.

When one tourist is killed in our region by an Islamic fundamentalist the whole Western media becomes superactive, as if thousands of tourists were killed, or as if all Muslims are bloodthirsty killers. When a Christian fundamentalist shoots a doctor and kills him in an abortion clinic in Florida it is shown as a single incident, and all other Christians are represented as good and peace-loving. This double standard is political, economic, and military. It is related to who has the power and who has the media or international conferences. I have not heard of a conference organized in recent years on Christian or Jewish fundamentalism.

Why is it that Islam attracts so much criticism and attention whereas the Old Testament, Judaism, and Israel are either enveloped in silence or presented as a model of democracy? I quote from a study on women in Israel:

> Women, not men, are harassed on the street and in the workplace, and men, not women, murder their lovers and spouses (35 in 1991, and 18 in 1992). Women's body parts, not men's, adorn bus stations and magazine advertisements, and pornography is the *sine qua non* of advertising, not only in adult magazines, but also in teenage publications. Women comprise no more than nine per cent of the knesset and eleven per cent of local governing bodies.
>
> Another major impediment to gender equality in Israel is the lack of separation of religion and state. The fact that Israel is defined as a Jewish state means that Palestinian Arabs, who comprise 18% of the Israeli citizenry, cannot be full-fledged members of society. It also means that the religious establishment – including the religious political parties and the Rabbinate – affects the lives of all Jewish citizens of Israel, religious and secular alike. Since 1948, no political party has been able to form a government without the participation of at least one religious political party. The price of these coalition governments has been the imposition of a certain degree of adherence to Jewish law on all Jews living in Israel. The element that has had the greatest influence on the lives of women, both Jewish and Muslim, is the jurisdiction of religious courts – Rabbinic for Jews and Sharia for Muslims – in personal status matters. This means that in domestic litigation women are at a disadvantage: their status is inferior at the very outset, they cannot be judged by other women, and they have to plead their cases in the framework of laws prejudicial to females.[1]

The postmodern veil

The International Information Order is working together with the International Economic Order to veil the minds of men and women in the South as well as in the North.

The New World Order is fostering globalization, or global multinational capitalism, to expand its markets in the South. The globalization of the economy requires globalization of information and culture. That is, the breaking down of national economies and cultures to permit the free flow of capital, commodities, films, TV serials, contraceptive drugs, beauty products, similar patterns of consumption, etcetera. Global capitalism requires global flexibility to ensure the free market (freedom of the powerful to dominate the weak). Similar patterns of consumption are constituted by similar outlooks on life, and similar values and cultures.

Women are exposed to what may be called the false femininity or beauty culture, and its material products such as makeup, powders, perfumes, earrings, etcetera, which are sold globally and advertised by the media (films, TV, radio, magazines, newspapers, songs, music, dance, etcetera). The aim is to create a conception of femininity and beauty that becomes part of the culture and has its set of values, feelings, and desires that are absorbed by the conscious and the subconscious mind. The cultural unconscious is not separate from the conscious.

The relation between culture, religion, gender and class is very important. This is true not only of the economic and political processes within which the cultural and religious take form, but also in psychic processes which are engaged in its production and reception.

Images of femininity or female beauty have increasingly become the reflection of a globalized mentality. The American or Western white upper-class image of femininity or beauty represents a conception of femininity for all women throughout the world. In my village I noticed after the introduction of television and its advertisements about beauty products, perfumes, high heels, makeup, etcetera, that even the poorest girls who sweat in the fields and who cannot even afford to buy soap to wash with, or eggs to eat, are buying perfume and makeup powder in order to hide the smell of sweat or cover up their brown skin. They are also buying high-heeled shoes, which are not at all suitable for them or for the type of rough streets on which they walk. I also noticed that some of the village girls who had never worn a veil on their faces started to cover their faces. They heard on TV or radio or read in a booklet that this is what a good Muslim woman should do.

When I travel in the Arab countries, I notice that the TV screen often shows two contradictory images one after the other. A religious man talking about the need to veil women appears on the TV screen, and immediately following is a half-naked woman or belly dancer advertising some makeup or perfume. Girls and women in our countries are torn between these images. According to the moral and religious system, they are supposed to be veiled, but they are also supposed to be exposed and naked (fashionable, feminine, beautiful) in order to conform to the media advertisements and the global culture.

In fact, veiling and nakedness are two sides of the same coin. Both mean that women are bodies without a mind and should be covered or uncovered in order to suit national or international capitalist interests. Men in our countries are not victims of this contradiction.

Why does the West want to bridge the gap?

A few days ago, while I was writing this, an American scholar, an expert in the Middle East, was invited to give a lecture on Islam in the University of Washington in Seattle. (I have never heard of an Arab or Islamic scholar being invited to give a lecture on Christianity.) The American scholar mentioned that in recent years Islam has been associated in the public mind of the USA with violence. In his opinion, this 'distorted image of Islam as an anti-West and militant movement' began when Ayatollah Khomeini initiated a revolution in Iran and started to orchestrate acts of terrorism throughout the Middle East.

Many people, including myself, will disagree with this view. In history the conflict between the Islamic countries and the West did not start with the Iranian revolution. It dates back much further than that, and is related to the history of colonialism in the region, to the domination of the capitalist West over our resources, mainly the oil. But as often happens, this economic and political conflict remains hidden under the guise of a religious or cultural conflict between the North and the South.

In his lecture the American expert said that not all Muslims are fundamentalists and that not all Muslim fundamentalists are terrorists. He made the distinction between different shades of fundamentalism, dividing them into two distinct groups: nonviolent fundamentalists and violent/terrorist fundamentalists. At the end of his lecture, he said that the United States should create more friendly communication with nonviolent Muslims who are willing to work within the law or within the existing governments to instigate changes.[2]

In US newspapers and in the European press for some time, news items and articles have tended to express a changing Western policy towards Islam, and towards Islamic countries. It is a policy that aims at improving relations with nonviolent Muslims. This is what is called, in other terms, bridging the cultural gap, or overcoming cross-cultural misunderstandings.

The gap between North and South, or between the West and our countries in the Arab region cannot be reduced to a cultural gap, or cross-cultural misunderstanding. To bridge the gap, we have to overcome political and economic exploitation, we have to replace the present world order with a different world order based on justice, peace, and real democracy, on freedom and equality between men and women, and on reducing the gap between the rich and the poor. But so far this has never been the policy of the West. The gap is defined as 'cultural', and bridging it has come to mean improving and strengthening the relationship between the ruling powers in the West and the Islamic political movements which are gradually moving towards power. It has come to mean seeking new allies to replace the old ones – the local rulers, the governments supported so far by the West, who have lost all popular support, are discredited and are facing crises caused by their corruption and their inability to ensure the stability of Western interests in the region.

It is from this that the growing desire to bridge the gap with the Islamic movement in our region arises.

The role of women and literature

Since the beginning of the slave system, women have been struggling against oppression. They can become a great force in our attempts to create a more equitable and just international order. This is natural since they are the first victims of the existing order.

During the second half of the twentieth century, the writings of women in the Arab world, and elsewhere, have played a growing role in unveiling the links between gender, class and race oppression, and have moved human struggle to a higher level of understanding. Women's literature, fiction and nonfiction, has opened up new horizons of thought, new readings of history, and new interpretations of the holy books. This is a recent phenomenon in our century. However, in all periods of history since the discovery of alphabets, women have tried to play this role. Recent anthropological research seems to indicate that the first alphabets were evolved by women in Ancient Egypt and Mesopotamia.

In the Arab peninsula, women composed poetry and participated actively in the cultural, political and economic life of their tribal society before and after the advent of Islam. It was Khadija who allayed the fears of the Prophet Muhammad when he came to her trembling after the revelation of the first Qur'anic verse, which begins with the word 'Read'. It was she who helped to interpret the meaning of this verse, and to encourage him to start his mission. We can remember many other women, such as Rabi'a Al-'Adawiya, the leader of Sufi thought. She evolved her own interpretation of Islam which is different from other Islamic schools.

During the last two decades, despite the backlash against women's rights fuelled by both secular and religious forces, new generations of women writers have taken up the challenge, and are advancing on the path to a more comprehensive understanding of the problems that face their societies, and of ways to express this understanding in their writings.

Women writers in our region encounter many obstacles, not the least of which is the refusal of men – including literary critics – to see what is new in the field of women's literature.

Those who sit astride the status quo have always opposed change and have always ended, sooner or later, in defeat.

[Paper given to the PEN conference held in Denmark, Louisiana, USA, 27–29 May 1994]

Notes

1. Marilyn P. Safr, 'The Interface of Feminism and Women's Studies in Israel', (in Liza Fiol-Matta and Mariam Chamberlain, *Women of Color and the Multicultural Curriculum: transforming the college classroom*, Feminist Press, New York, 1994).

2. Talcott W. Seeley, lecture at the University of Washington, Seattle (*The Daily*, university newspaper, 17 May 1994).

CHAPTER 14

Women and Development: A critical view of the Wellesley Conference

Why do we feel the duty to write our experience at Wellesley? First, we want to make sure that we shall never have to face the same situation that we faced in Wellesley. We realize that the people who organize international conferences did not learn anything from their experience in Mexico.

Second, we want to explain the feelings of Third World women who have to confront one of the latest developments of neocolonialism: materialism.

Third, we believe that encounters between people from different cultures and geopolitical areas can be very fruitful and highly inspiring. We therefore think that improvement of the methodology of international conferences is possible, to make them truly international – if people make the effort to understand each other, and take upon themselves the arduous task of critical self-analysis.

Fourth, we want the organizers and convenors of such meetings to be more sensitive to the cultural differences of women from different parts of the world; that can be achieved if equal participation at all levels of decision making is realized.

Fifth, we want to destroy the myth that the mere fact of being women will unite us all and that women are not political beings – that political discussions at women's meetings mean 'diverting from women's issues'.

Sixth, we want to emphasize the fact that the 'explosions', 'conflicts' and 'disruptions' which have occurred in conferences such as the one in Wellesley are healthy; because of them, we believe that the conference was a success.

The predominance of Western women at all levels of decision making

The people involved A glance at the official programme of the Wellesley conference reveals that in spite of the fact that the conference was titled

'Women and Development' the contingent of women from developing countries at the levels of organizing, panel convening and paper giving was ridiculously small. The people who got involved in the organizing of the conference can be divided into four groups according to national origin and place of work. Third World contribution was minor if you take into account that most of the organizers, paper givers, and panel convenors were either Westerners based in or outside their own state, or women from developing countries based in the USA often for many years. More than three quarters of the conference papers were given by Western women or women from developing countries living in the West.

It is worth mentioning that one of the regions of the world where change in women's condition was a priority for government in recent decades, that is, the socialist countries, was hardly represented.

The time structure The numerical underrepresentation of women from developing countries in the panels could have been partially compensated by a better time structure. There was hardly any time for discussion. If the panellists were left to themselves, they usually took up all the time and the discussion period was often shortened to a ridiculous extent. If there had been equal time for papers and discussions, the women from developing countries, who often had to listen to Westerners talking to them about their own cultures, could have had more opportunity to contribute by correcting information and thus raising the level of discussion from trivial corrections to more substantial, meaningful exchanges. The insistent requests by Third World women for more discussion time, and their impatience at the lengthy reading of papers – full of incorrect information and interpretations of their cultures – were interpreted by the organizers as disruptive behaviour. A series of meetings was held by the Third World contingent in order to persuade organizers to change the conference structure. It appeared after repeated clashes with the organizers that they expected us to sit quietly and listen respectfully to the papers, no matter what their content was, and certainly not to hurry the speech makers. Evidently for them our contribution was irrelevant. Otherwise they would have structured the time differently. This disregard for active involvement of the women from developing countries was clearly illustrated when the issue of publication of the outcome of the conference was brought up, in an *ad hoc* meeting convened by concerned participants from outside the USA.

Publication of the conference proceedings When Third World women real-

Table 14.1 Organizers of the Wellesley Conference

	Organizers	Panel conveners	Paper givers
Western women based in Western countries	9 (90%)	18 (82%)	44 (56%)
Western women based outside Western countries	0	1 (5%)	4 (5%)
Women from developing countries based in Western countries	1 (10%)	3 (14%)	12 (15%)
Women from developing countries based in developing countries	0	0	19 (24%)
Total	10	22	79

ized that the organizers were not willing to make any changes in the programme so as to meet their demands, they decided as a last resort to give up any attempt to play a part in decision making as far as the actual conference was concerned, and decided to concentrate on the issue of the proceedings. Hours of nightly meetings were spent in trying to have some say in the proceedings by restructuring the editorial committee, which was heavily if not totally American. To their dismay, the Third World women realized that the organizers, who were often members of the editing board as well, were not willing to give in on that issue either. The strange, laborious arguments that went back and forth between organizers, the committee members of the editing board, and Third World participants was so degrading that one participant from Turkey became so upset that she decided that the only thing left for her to do was to withdraw her paper, so as not to be part of the outcome of the conference, whatever it might be.

The clash between women from developing countries and organizers, which was bound to happen anyway, given the composition of the organizing committee and the panel convenors on the one hand, and the time structure on the other, was clearly illustrated at two levels. The first was the issues chosen as priority issues by the organizers, which were not considered so by the developing countries' participants. The other level was that of personal interactions, where the words used varied from cold restraint to straightforward insults.

The panel topics as a subject of discord

It is very revealing that the World Conference on Women held in Mexico City in 1975 was split into two separate groups which happened to divide along the lines of women from developed countries and women from developing countries. The first group, led by women from Europe and North America, thought it was a pity and a failure of the women's international movement to forward political claims. According to their 'feminist' ideology, to talk about politics is a diversion from women's issues, and a deliberate attempt by Third World women, who allegedly lack 'feminist' awareness, to minimize the women's question by linking it to bigger political issues. *Example*: talking about the effects of so-called 'development' and 'modernization' on the degradating economic conditions of women in developing countries in both the modern and the traditional sectors, without linking these effects, among other factors, to the role of the multinational corporations. The Western women put the emphasis on the conditions of oppression of women in developing countries; the causes of this oppression became secondary. When Third World women tried to attract attention to the role of the multinational corporations, they were accused of being nonfeminist, of imitating the 'male' in his political games, and of 'splitting the spirit of sisterhood in the women's movement'. A logical outcome of the depoliticization of the women's issue is the minimization of the politics of economics, trade, and money. The Mexico pattern was reproduced in the Wellesley Conference, although it assumed a substantially different aspect.

One of the painful surprises of Third World participants at the Wellesley Conference was the absence of papers on US women, be they black, white or brown. One of the topics on which the Third World women expected information was how the development process geared by the multinational corporations' priorities affected US women of different classes and races, and the mechanisms that make US women powerless in the system. This absence made us Third World women realize that we were invited to attend a conference where mostly US 'scholars' were interpreting for us our conditions, our culture, our religion and our experiences. The fact that the time for discussion was eaten up by the verbose panellists (who tried to make up for their lengthy expositions by speeding up their diction, making it a heroic attempt for us to understand their English at all) combined with the absence of papers on US women to restore for us the hardly healed colonial experience – where detached outsiders define your world for you. To feel like a fish in a glass bowl is a very uncomfortable feeling, especially if you are women coming from far away, expecting a rare opportunity to shed oppression and passivity and engage in a meaningful egalitarian dialogue.

The absence of analysis of US women's situations, as these relate to development, outlines another shortcoming of the conference: the lack of any questioning of the narrow classical concept of development, often equated with material and technological growth divorced from human growth. This issue, which should have been the main focus of a conference which labelled itself 'Women and Development', became a marginal issue dealt with in subsidiary discussions.

Money and economics are vital issues to be studied and discussed by women in any attempt to create a new international economic and social order, of which women's issues are an important component. The lack in the Wellesley Conference panels of in-depth analysis of economics and money as they relate to international trade and multinational corporations, on the one hand, and the lack of analysis of such critically important factors as health on the other, illustrates the US women academicians' way of designing topics for international encounters. Moreover, no panel was devoted to the important question of credit and women's access to money and banking, which is the key to power.

The provision of information on the latest decisions made by multinational corporations on their activities in and outside the USA, and how they affect the lives of women in and outside the USA, could have been a valuable contribution by US women to the international conference, because that kind of data is hard if not impossible to get in Third World countries. We are the last ones to know what has been done to us. The national leaders in this respect are as cautious as the multinational corporation manager about letting information leak out.

Patronizing and materialistic attitudes in personal interaction

The power issue, which was the main cause of the clash between Third World participants and organizers, became very clear at the level of personal interaction. A few events illustrate the misunderstanding that arose on a personal level between organizers and Third World participants. Oblivious of the power issue, the organizers became adamant defenders of the conference 'law and order' they had designed, and failed to take into account Third World women's protests, which they labelled as 'disruption'.

The organizers and panel convenors, who were all Westerners with one exception, did not understand why Third World women felt humiliated and manipulated because they did not participate in the organizing and the design of the panels. The organizers thought that this issue was completely irrelevant. They acted just like the man who organizes meetings involving women's issues without getting the women involved in planning and policy decision-making.

The organizers did not understand at all why the Third World women were uncomfortable, from the first panels, at their power-lessness to contribute in any meaningful way to the rigidly structured conference. The well-meaning US organizers and panel convenors had and probably still have no idea how maternalistic and condescending they sounded, in both words and attitudes, when they read papers or talked at the participants, telling them how to behave, how not to interrupt when paper deliverers were reading false data about develop-ing countries. For the US organizers, power was not the issue because *they* had it, and thought it normal for us not to participate. Here are some examples of this.

When a Third World participant working with an international organization, who because of her work has to have knowledge of the work done by the US women's movement, voiced the concern of many Third World women participants about the absence in the conference of the American experience of development, she was told by the key organizer that she would be provided with information on the research done by US women on the US women's issue. The organizer interpreted her claim as a lack of *knowledge* of the research currently done on US women. The organizer, once again, managed to restore the traditional colonial relation. Instead of receiving the real message voiced by the Third World women, the organizer revealed herself unable to hear what she was told. *The American academician perceived herself in this case, like men do, as a highly informed and well-read individual expert dealing with an inferior being whose knowledge cannot but be defective.*

Another very revealing incident which illustrated the organizers' capacity to turn the Third World women's protest into 'personal defects' was the dialogue that took place between a key organizer and a Third World participant at the end of the conference, after two days of heated discussions in desperate attempts to understand each other.

Key organizer: Many of us think that you played a very destructive role insulting panellists, preventing people from reading their papers.
Participant: It never occurred to me that my role is a disruptive one. I saw my role as a positive contribution to the conference, in correct-ing when I heard misinformation about the data on my region delivered to us by a so-called 'regional expert'. As the panel structure leaves very little time for discussions, I have to do it for the sake of

other participants who would otherwise be misinformed. Anyhow, I did not interrupt the panellists systematically regardless of the nationality of the paper given. Some were a delight to listen to, and were very instructive to us from the Third World who are involved in doing research. There are many American women in this conference whose contribution is highly valued and respected.

Key organizer: You disrupted all the panels in which you were not a member. You liked only the one in which you delivered your paper.

Participant: This is absolutely inaccurate. Do you realize you are insulting me right now?

Key organizer: [silence]

Participant: If you say that I only interrupted panels in which I was not participating, you are implying that I am trying to break the other specialists to further my own career and establish my own name. What a mediocre professional, who can only establish herself by using the American academic conventional tool, stepping on colleagues and discrediting high-quality American specialists on the Middle East. By doing so, you are refusing to hear my protest. Instead of doubting that there is something wrong with the organizing of the conference, you are reducing my argument to shortcomings of my personality.

This is a very common syndrome of the colonial 'dialogue', in which the oppressor blames protest and dissent on the character defects and the hangups and shortcomings of the colonized. According to this syndrome, the people who ought to adjust are the Third World women and not the US woman organizers, who are perfect by definition. This syndrome needs to be scrutinized seriously by US women genuinely interested in breaking down the male colonial pattern for two reasons:

First, according to this explanation of the clash that took place at Wellesley, the blame lies with the Third World women who failed to 'adjust' to the perfectly well-organized conference. The US women organizers had no adjustment to make and were unjustly attacked by ungrateful, wicked Third World elements.

Second, according to this explanation of the clash, the issue that is preventing international dialogue between women is a matter of individuals and personality defects, not a matter of clashes at the level of global structures and values, choices and priorities. In this explanation, all you need to do is to get rid of the unruly Third World elements and replace them by 'smiling', accommodating, understanding 'sisters' from developing countries – hence the vital importance of the interpretations of what happened at Wellesley.

Conclusion: the successful internationalization of the women's movement

The Wellesley Conference on 'Women and Development' was a historical, and will probably become a trend-setting, event in women's attempt to transcend national, ideological and political boundaries; that is, in women's attempt to escape the male-imposed divisions and create a powerful international movement. This conference was successful precisely because it was a painful clash between on the one hand well-meaning American women academicians who believed themselves to be ahead of American men, and freed from colonial and imperialist limitations, and on the other hand overly optimistic Third World women who had believed that the impossible dialogue between people from developed and developing countries could be restored by women, between women, and for women.

The results of the Wellesley Conference could be interpreted in two ways.

The first interpretation is the one shared by some of the key organizers, according to which US good will was thwarted by unruly, disruptive, ill-willed women from the Third World. These American academicians threatened that they might cut the dialogue with Third World women who did not understand their courageous attempt and live up to their expectations. These interpretations revealed that these US academicians felt that the fault lay solely with Third World women who in their view are irrational, emotional and therefore rebellious and disruptive. The overwhelming majority of Third World women invited from outside the USA were deeply hurt and insulted – as professionals, as human beings and, worst, as women.

A second interpretation of the results of the Wellesley Conference is that it was premised on the asset of united power which, however, when closely analysed, turned out to be naive and unrealistic. The notion of united power is based on the erroneous belief that the mere fact of being women is a binding enough characteristic to create instantaneous international sisterhood beyond and above political differences and an unequal distribution of power. The basic assumption here is that women are not political beings. This assumption could generate an apparent 'sisterhood', but sooner or later this could only explode, with even more damaging and demoralizing results than if we face the contradictions among women across the world realistically, scientifically, now.

The conference may have been one step ahead of Mexico, where Third World discontent was felt and voiced but not analysed. Wellesley could have offered an occasion to begin this analysis, but did not, unfortunately, get to it. We feel that what was wrong with the conference was that it was meant to be an international gathering when in fact it was a US-planned and US-organized conference. Third World participants were, therefore, misled in anticipating fruitful encounters between researchers of different nationalities. They were reduced to passive, accommodating audiences rather than participants. This was well expressed in one of the organizers' own words when urged to change the conference structure: 'We spent a whole year organizing this panel; people worked hard at the papers; the least you can do is to go and listen to them. If you are not happy with it, don't come. Nobody forced you to come.'

Recommendations

The fact that until now these international gatherings have failed to be really international in the full sense of the word, does not mean that the potential is not there. On the contrary, the fascinating thing about women now is that, throughout the world, they are the only group that feels an urgent need to create international solidarity, and this need could materialize if a few changes are brought about in the structure and nature of women's international encounters. One could already think about two alternatives (and they are far from being exhaustive): encounters organized internationally and encounters organized locally.

1. *Encounters organized internationally* For a conference to be genuinely international, women from developing and developed countries have to be involved on an equal basis in the organizing of the conference from its very beginning, starting from fundraising, topic choice, designation of panel convenors, panel convening, etcetera. This will lead us to inquire who should be invited to such conferences, and here we will define some characteristics of women participants from developing countries that seem to us very relevant in this respect.

The US academic system has serious hangups about publication. That is up to Americans to deal with. But this idiosyncrasy of the US academic system should not become a stumbling block in the choice of researchers from developing countries. Much insightful research and many studies have been done by people in developing countries, often in their native languages, without them being published. The reason is that publishing is still one of the most safeguarded monopolies of developed countries. Ironically, those who publish are not necessarily those who are the most creative and innovative in their thinking; often they are those who have access to West-based publishing networks.

Therefore the criteria for participation so far as Third World women are concerned ought to be creativity, and not publication. If a woman has done research and produced papers, no matter in what language, she should be entitled to attend these meetings. These meetings will also bring forward facilities for translation at or prior to the conference, which will help to transcend the language obstacle, and which should be funded as a priority item. Breaking down the language barrier will maximize the contributions of all the participants, and mainly of those who do not speak Western languages, thus helping to create real internationalization of knowledge about women's issues.

The other very important element that made this so-called international conference so rigid was the exaggerated importance accorded to publication of the proceedings. The investment of so much money and effort into bringing together knowledgeable people ought to have broader aims than the narrow academic reading of papers to one another. Interpersonal communication between the participants ought to be considered an important component. Free time and flexible scheduling ought to be a characteristic of these meetings.

2. *National conferences* National conferences organized locally, where participants from outside the host country would have the status either of fully-fledged participants or of observers, could serve two purposes. They would give a chance to US scholars to feel helpless, awkward, in a foreign setting they do not control, which would give them new insights into interdependency relations. These conferences would also give more visibility to local young up-coming talents.

3. *Audiovisual materials used at the conferences* Films, slides, pictures, and so on shown at the conference should be selected by a responsible committee that is knowledgeable about the material available in different societies. It is interesting to point out that despite the existence of a quantity of great films on the changing status of the Arab women, the Wellesley Conference chose a vulgar, low-quality film portraying Arab women only as belly dancers, or as veiled, motionless, thoughtless sex objects in harems.

4. *Personal relations* Personal relationships between women from Western countries and women from Third World countries should be based on equality and mutual respect in spite of differences in race, colour, social class, and culture.

Racist phrases such as 'The reason why Ms X did not get criticism from Third World women is because Ms X *knows how to talk to Africans and Asians*' should not be used at all in conferences.

5. *Donor–recipient relationships* Organizers of international conferences should take care not to encourage superior attitudes in representatives of the funding agencies by putting participants from Third World countries 'on the carpet' to solicit money for their research. A comment like, 'Here are all the representatives of the funding organizations: you researchers from the developing countries should come up to meet with them and show them *your worth*. You should also ask them for their funding criteria for research in developing countries', hurts the feelings of people from developing countries and puts them in a 'rich master and beggar' relationship with the funders.

[Written jointly with Fatima Mernissi and Mallica Vajrathon following the Wellesley Conference held in Boston, Massachusetts, 2–6 June 1976]

PART FIVE

Decolonizing the Imagination

CHAPTER 15

Dissidence and Creativity

I started writing this paper on the first of January 1995. I wrote it in English though my language is Arabic and my country is Egypt. I was born and lived in Egypt and have lived there almost all my life, but for the last two years I have been teaching at Duke University as a visiting professor. I hope to be back in Egypt in 1996. All my books, whether fiction or nonfiction, are written in Arabic and are published and read in Egypt and other countries of the Arab world. When I am faced with censorship in Egypt I publish my work in Lebanon or another Arab country. This context is important for me when I try to understand what we mean by dissidence or the dissident word.

Today I will be speaking about the intrinsic dissidence of the creative word, and the languages of imperialism and oppression which authors have forged into instruments of liberation. But it is difficult for me to do that without speaking in Arabic, difficult for me to be creative both in mind and body when using a foreign tongue. What I am doing now is translating my Arabic into English. When I do that, a part of the meaning is lost or changed. But although my English is different from the English in use here and may have its defects, it expresses my thoughts better than if I had given my lecture to an English translator.

What is dissidence?

I have tried to find the Arab word for dissidence. In Arabic we say protest (al-ihtijaj) or opposition (al-mu'arada) or disputation (al-mukhasama) or rebellion or revolt (yatamarradu or yathuru). But each of these words has a different meaning according to the context in which the dissidence or struggle takes place. For me the word 'struggle' in Arabic (al-nidal) sheds most light on the meaning of dissidence. The dissident in Arabic (al-munadil) means the fighter who cooperates with others to struggle against oppression and exploitation whether personal or political.

I believe there is no dissidence without struggle. We cannot understand dissidence except in a situation of struggle and in its location in place and time. Without this, dissidence becomes a word devoid of responsibility, devoid of meaning.

Demystifying words

Can I be dissident without being creative? Can I have the passion and knowledge required to change the powerful oppressive system of family and government without being creative? What do we mean by creativity? Can we be creative if we obey others or follow the tradition of our ancestors? Can we be creative if we submit to the rules forced upon us under different names: father, god, husband, family, nation, security, stability, protection, peace, democracy, family planning, development, human rights, modernism or postmodernism?

These fifteen words are used globally and locally by both the oppressors and the oppressed. I chose them because we read or hear them all the time, whether we live in Egypt, the United States, Brazil or India. These fifteen words constitute a large part of the language of imperialism and oppression. But they are often used by the oppressed with a different meaning, as part of the fight against imperialism and oppression.

For example, the word 'protection' seems a very positive word. British colonialism in Egypt was inaugurated by a military occupation in 1882.[1] It hindered our economic and cultural development for more than seventy years. Instead of having the freedom to develop our agriculture to satisfy our needs, we were obliged to produce cotton for the needs of British industry. The result was increasing poverty in Egypt and increasing wealth in Britain. This was done in the name of protection, not of colonialism or exploitation. The British used military power and terrorism to achieve these ends. The rulers of Egypt, the Khedives,[2] submitted to British power. The royal family and the ruling class collaborated with the colonizers to protect their joint interests. Egyptians who challenged the government or the British were labelled dissidents, communists or nationalists, and were killed, imprisoned, dismissed from their work or forced to live in exile or starvation.

Today the neocolonizers do not use the word 'protection' any more. The colonized people in Egypt, Africa, India and elsewhere have seen through it. The word 'protection' was demystified through people's living experience; 'protection' to us in Egypt now means colonialism. Another word therefore had to be used by the neocolonizers. It had to be just as positive and innocent, but more progressive. So the word 'development' came into use in the early seventies. Many people in

Egypt and other so-called developing countries were deceived by this word, but the results of development proved to be even more pernicious than the results of protection. Much more money travelled from the so-called developing countries (or Third World) to the First World than in the opposite direction. The gap between the rich and poor increased both locally and globally. Even the United Nations could not hide these facts. They appeared in statistics and in UN reports written by field workers in Africa, Asia and Latin America.

In 1979 I was one of the UN field workers in Ethiopia. I worked with the UN for two years before I left. I discovered that development projects promoted by the UN and Western corporations and agencies hindered development in Egypt and Africa. They were a disguised form of economic genocide, more pernicious than military genocide because they killed more people but were not as visible as blood shed in war.

When the word 'development' was demystified the neocolonizers shifted their terms. The new term was 'structural adjustment', now being promoted by the World Bank. Few people understand this word. But when 'structural adjustment' is implemented in Africa and other parts of the so-called South, the effect is no different from that of protection or development. The result is even greater poverty in the poor South, and greater riches for the rich North. Just one example: from 1984 to 1990 structural adjustment policies (SAPs) led to the transfer of $178 billion from the South to the commercial banks in the North.

Another neocolonial word is 'aid'. It is another myth that is becoming demystified. Many countries in the South have started to raise the slogan 'Fair Trade Not Aid'. Just one example from Egypt: between 1975 (when US aid to Egypt began) and 1986, Egypt imported commodities and services from the United States to a total of $30 billion. During the same period Egypt exported to the United States commodities worth only $5 billion.

Egyptians who stand up and challenge the global neocolonialist powers and their collaborators in local governments are labelled dissident, communist, nationalist or feminist. They are punished according to the effectiveness of their dissidence; this ranges from losing their job and censorship of their writings to imprisonment and even death.

In Egypt, under Sadat, we had to demystify some of the words and slogans he used. One of his slogans was the 'open door' policy. It proved to be no more than opening doors to a neocolonial assault on the economy of Egypt and its culture. American products (Coca-Cola, cigarettes, nylon clothes, McDonald's, makeup, TV series, films, etcetera) invaded Egypt, destroying local production. Sadat inaugurated his rule with what he described as a 'Corrective Revolution'. The Corrective Revolution in fact was no more than a correction in the flow of money to ensure that it ended up in the pockets of the ruling groups that came to power after Nasser's death in 1970.

Mutual responsibility

Our struggles are becoming more and more difficult. They need more and more creativity. There are always new words emerging that we have to demystify, words such as: peace, democracy, human rights, privatization, globalization, multiculturalism, diversity, civil society, nongovernmental organizations (NGOs), cultural difference, liberation theology, religious fundamentalism, postmodernism, and others. We need to discover new ways of exposing the paradoxes or double meanings in the many new and old words that are endlessly repeated. This needs greater knowledge and more understanding of modern and postmodern techniques of oppression and exploitation.

We cannot acquire this knowledge through books, through formal education or the mass media. All of them are controlled by the global and local powers of domination and exploitation, and they help to veil our brains with one myth after another. We have to acquire this knowledge by ourselves, from our own experience in the daily struggle against those powers globally, locally and in the family. This is creativity. It is inspired and stimulated by our living our own lives and not by copying theories of struggle from books.

Every struggle has its own unique theory inseparable from action. Creativity means uniqueness: innovation. Discovering new ways of thinking and acting, of creating a system based on more and more justice, freedom, love and compassion. If you are creative, you must be dissident. You discover what others have not yet discovered. You may be alone at the beginning, but somehow you feel responsible towards yourself and others: towards those who are not yet aware of this discovery, who share your struggle with the system. Towards those who have lost hope and have submitted.

Can there be any struggle or dissidence without responsibility towards oneself and others? Is there any human who does not struggle against oppression? We are all born dissidents to a greater or a lesser degree. But since I came to teach in the USA I have ceased to consider myself a dissident. I have been a dissident since childhood. My name was put on the Egyptian government's blacklist in 1962. I had to face censorship. I lost my job in 1972, and our health association and magazine were banned soon after. In 1981, I was put in jail and in 1991 our women's association (the Arab Women's Solidarity Association, AWSA) and magazine, *Noon*, were banned. In 1992, my life was threatened and security guards were placed around my house.

Now I am a visiting professor at Duke University in the United States. I teach creativity and dissidence to students. But can you really teach these things? All you can do is to open up closed doors. Undo what education did. Encourage students to discover their own dissidence in their own lives.

Dissidence and distance

I watch what is happening in Egypt from a distance. In November 1994, floods in Upper Egypt left thousands of people homeless. I received a letter from a young woman student who lives in Cairo. Her family lives in a village in Luxor (one of the places hit by the floods). She said: 'I went to visit my family and my village when I heard about the floods. Thank god my father and mother survived but they were left with no home, no shelter. The authorities were busy with a big tourist show, busy preparing to mount the opera *Aida* in front of the Temple of Hatshepsut. Priority was given to satisfying the needs of American tourists and not the homeless thousands. Each tourist sat on a blanket to warm his seat while he was watching the show. My family received no blankets to sleep in the cold nights. They lost their cane sugar farm because the local authorities took it over together with other roads and bridges for tourists, so that they could reach Hatshepsut's Temple easily. Four hundred acres of cane sugar were taken by force from homeless people. Other farms were taken from people to secure a space around the open *Aida* stadium (a security belt to protect the tourists from the so-called fundamentalists). The average yield of each acre is 50 tons, the price of each ton is £90 – constituting a loss of about £2 million to the people. Two other bridges were built on the Asjun canal for tourists to cross on their way to the show, and more farms were taken from people. This will result in an acute drop in the local production of cane sugar. An American company called Orascom built the bridges and the stadium in collaboration with Onsy Saweeris who opened a McDonald's eating place as well. The waters of the flood were quickly pumped out of the graves and temples of the dead pharaohs. The local authorities were boasting to the tourists that the waters did not spend one night in Siti the First Temple in Korana, or, rather, that Siti the First did not sleep one night in the waters. But thousands of homeless people were left to the floods with no shelter.

In front of the Karnak temple there was another big tourist show. One thousand five hundred girls and boys danced for six weeks. Each one of them received £10. The police were everywhere to protect the tourists and the dancers. The fundamentalists are against music shows and dances. The tourists call them terrorists. But the tourists are terrorists too. They frightened everybody, even the local authorities, who were so afraid of the fundamentalists that they destroyed hundreds of cane sugar farms.

'They said that the fundamentalists used these cane sugar farms as hiding places. My father and mother are among these people. I do not know how I can help them. I have to go to Cairo and let a friend of mine who is a journalist for *Roz El-Youssef* magazine write about it. Our government does not help anybody unless the journalists write about them, or the TV or CNN broadcasts something about their story. During the population conference in Cairo last September, CNN showed something about female circumcision. After that everybody in the government and in the media was speaking about female circumcision. Even Al-Mufti, the highest Islamic authority in Egypt, wrote in *Roz El-Youssef* opposing this operation. The Sheik of Al-Azhar also wrote in the same magazine, but he supported the operation and said that it is an Islamic duty. I will send you a copy of this issue. It was published on 17 October 1994. I hope that the government listens to Al-Mufti and prohibits the circumcision of girls, but the government is afraid of the fundamentalists, who force people to circumcise their girls and to veil them.

'After the show of *Aida* people caught an old tourist with a girl dancer hiding in Karnak temple. The girl was veiled. The tourist was very drunk and he told the people that he is more excited by the veil than by belly dancing.

'The fundamentalists are becoming more and more harsh on girls and women. They prevent them from going out even to school. They tell the girls that they are protecting them from being raped by tourists.

'In the Cairo International Population Conference I met a young woman in the AWSA workshop. I was glad to know from her that you have started an AWSA branch in North America. Her name is Amina Ayad. She read the paper you prepared on AWSA. It made me aware of the fact that increasing poverty in Egypt is due to the development forced on us by the West rather than the high fertility of Egyptian women.

'I used to come to the AWSA weekly seminars and to read *Noon* magazine. I met you many times. You may remember my face but you do not know my name. I was not a member of AWSA but I was very sad when the government banned it in Egypt in 1991. I read in *al-Ahali* that you have taken the government to court. But the court is part of the government. I have no hope in this government. Nobody is helping my father and mother. I have to leave them and go back to my school in Cairo. I took your address in America from Amina Ayad. She told me that she met you in the University of Washington. You may know someone in CNN who can broadcast something about my family in Luxor. If this happens the government will hurry up and build them a home or a shelter or at least give them blankets. It is very cold at night in Luxor, more cold than Cairo. I am crying while writing to you.'

In Durham, I am ten thousand miles from Egypt and from women and men whose struggles I have shared: against British colonialism, Egyptian governments, neocolonialism, fanatical religious and political groups, the oppressive family code and other forms of oppression in our private and public lives. In Durham I look at my country from a distance. Sometimes I lose hope. But we cannot be dissidents without hope. We cannot be dissidents from a distance or if we are not in the struggle. When we struggle we do not lose hope. We feel responsible towards ourselves and others.

Intellectual terrorism

The relation between self and other becomes simple and clear when we struggle, but it becomes very complex, very vague, very difficult to understand when we read books or listen to lectures, especially by so-called postmodern philosophers. It becomes a puzzle or conundrum. We find ourselves lost in an avalanche of words which appear very dissident, and which multiply and reproduce themselves endlessly, breeding more and more complex words. We drown in these words, we are suffocated by them. It is a zero-sum game of words in which you lose your power to understand.

In the spring of 1994, a friend of mine, a South American scholar at a US university, attended a conference at Duke University to which Derrida had been invited to lecture. He was very attentive during Derrida's lecture but understood very little. He felt frustrated and did not have the courage to ask questions. When others asked a question the answer complicated matters. That night, he had a nightmare: Derrida's fingers were around his neck trying to suffocate him. The nightmare was of course unreal, but this does not mean that it was insignificant. It had symbolic truth for the person who suffered it. Another friend of mine, an American scholar, attended the same lecture. He considered it a dissident postmodern lecture. The South American scholar discussed it with him and became even more frustrated. He felt the lecture was an act of intellectual terrorism.

In November 1994 I found myself sitting in a huge solemn hall, listening to men and women scholars, the women with big earrings, very red lips and thick makeup, the men wearing neckties, their finger-nails manicured, smelling of aftershave and deodorants, their teeth and shoes shining in the electric light. Some of them are well known in the United States and Europe. They are not known to the majority of people who live in Africa, Asia or Latin America, or even to the people in their own countries who do not read books. But they call themselves global scholars or international philosophers.

Their language was so dry, so complicated, that the huge hall full of young students seeking knowledge was almost empty after the first session. These scholars drowned in abstract theories and words taken out of context. They sometimes used Marxist ideas about capitalism and imperialism. They criticized the separation of economies from culture. But this was only a philosophical judgement which was quickly forgotten in order to adopt other ideas from Foucault or Derrida and again distinguish between the cultural and the political or the social and the economic.

They spoke about the responsibility of the intellectual towards op-pressed people in the Third World, whom they called the 'subaltern', the 'docile bodies' or the 'subject'. We, the people in the so-called Third World were reduced to bodies (docile or not), we were de-capitated just as happened to women in the name of god in the three monotheistic religions. But then they forgot these ideas and solemnly announced the death of the intellectual, looking furtively around as though suspicious of whether they, the intellectuals, still existed and still had a function.

As usual, they quoted Michel Foucault and Gilles Deleuze's phrases: 'Those who act and struggle are no longer represented either by a group or union that appropriates their right to stand as their con-science.' Once more they used this paradoxical statement which could mean one of two contradictory things: (1) the end of the role of intellectuals who replace the language of struggling people with their own language, a positive interpretation since it is aimed at liberating the voice of the oppressed and thus empowering them; or (2) dis-empowering oppressed people by divorcing their struggle from the struggle of other groups or collectivities.

Here the word 'struggle' is itself ambiguous. It can be a genuinely dissident word if struggle means action and not just words to be replaced by other words which do not change the systems of oppression and exploitation at any level. Struggle is both action–thinking and speaking out. There is no separation between the practice and the theory of struggle. But these simple ideas were totally absent in the conference. Here also 'responsibility' towards the self and the other is transformed into a conundrum, since the struggling/dissident creative person, who has acquired new knowledge or demystified certain myths, can, it is said, no longer represent the struggle of his or her group. In the same way I might say that 'groups or unions' are formed out of a nonfragmented struggle and this, too, might be just empty words. On the other hand, it might equally refer to a progressive idea, that of liberating those who struggle from the power of the leading dissident: the so-called hero.

Dissidence and heroism

The creative dissident is not a hero or heroine. He or she should be the first to be killed in the battle. The concept of heroism or leadership differs from that of dissidence. In battles the leader is often the last to be killed, while unknown soldiers are shot at the front. The dissident is not a hero or leader. The hero is worshipped as a demi-god, but the dissident is punished and cursed like Satan (*Iblis* in Arabic). The devil is responsible for what is called evil. Since the evolution of monotheism, Satan has become the symbol of dissidence, or disruption of the existing order.

The devil is responsible for disasters, defeat and misery. But the devil has no power relative to god. Though god has all the power, he is not responsible for any disaster, defeat or misery. The split between power and responsibility has lain at the core of oppression and exploitation from the advent of slavery to this day. Dissidence is the antithesis of power divorced from responsibility for the misery of people. Responsibility does not mean aid or charity; it means trying to eradicate the causes of poverty and oppression. The concept of charity or aid is as pernicious to others as the concept of replacing the other's language or mind.

For creative dissidence does not believe in the dichotomy 'god–devil' or 'self–other'. Both are to be challenged and criticized equally. This means directing a critical gaze at the self as well as at the other.

If we wanted to translate these ideas into postmodern language, we might say that the deheroization of self and other is at the core of real dissidence: of radical ethics, an aesthetics of creativity or a critical ontology of self and other. Real dissidence avoids lapsing into the reverse essentialism of a cult of self or the other. It also avoids one-way reflexive self-monitoring by including the other in this process. It is thus that the analytical links between ourselves and our social context are maintained.

Dissidence and fundamentalism

Radicalism is a part of creative dissidence. But postmodernists do not question the established canon of neocolonial economic–political– cultural imperialism. They do not question the hegemony of male philosophers in the so-called First World, of male gods and male prophets. They limit themselves to cultural imperialism: to the problems of power/knowledge and of self-knowledge and identity. This established philosophical canon began with the patriarchal slave or class system and is still prevalent today.

Fundamentalism, like radicalism, is a positive and original way of thinking necessary to any creative dissident work. But both of them have come to be labelled negatively, like communism, socialism and feminism.

Individual identity or individual responsibility is inseparable from social identity or social responsibility and the word 'identity' is a positive word, like democracy and freedom. But these words are all used by neocolonialists to obstruct the freedom or identity of the others, to favour the development of so-called modern or postmodern democratic free societies.

So we find that concepts like radical ethics, religious freedom, liberation theology and cultural autonomy have not led to greater freedom or to fundamental cultural and economic changes that improve our lives. They have led to what is now called religious fundamentalism and fanatical spiritual movements using religion or culture to abolish the other (the devil). These fanatical religions and political movements are spreading all over the world. Christian, Jewish, Islamic, Buddhist or Hindu, they have become very prominent in many religions.

Postmodernism itself is a form of cultural fundamentalism. It is the other face of religious fundamentalism. Both are products of neo-colonialism. Perhaps we would do better to name them pseudo-modernism and pseudo-fundamentalism since they both function and combine to maintain the global capitalist system.

The concepts that we have mentioned are new forms of imperialism, terrorism and tourism: they make use of indigenous culture or religion as a tool to serve their own economic and intellectual interests. Philosophical imperialism and its discourse are inseparable from cultural and economic imperialism.

Just one example from Egypt: in 1994, the US government threatened to cut off so-called US aid to Egypt if a law was not promulgated to protect US films and cultural products. The Egyptian Ministry of Culture was obliged to draft a new law under the title 'Protection of Intellectual Rights'. This law will apply only to US 'cultural' products. The Egyptian government was not able to resist US government pressure on this issue. Yet few in Egypt still believe in the mystique of US aid. The problem is not only one of demystifying or acquiring new knowledge. It is a question of economic, political, military and cultural power.

Knowledge is power. But the power of knowledge alone is not enough in a world where military power can intervene at any moment to protect the economic interests of neocolonialists, as it did in the Gulf War or Somalia under slogans like 'human rights', 'democracy', 'humanitarian aid'.

The US government is using the postmodern GATT agreement (signed in Uruguay in 1993) to impose cultural imperialism on people everywhere: in Africa, Asia, Latin America, the Arab countries, Russia, Eastern and Western Europe. American cultural products (films, TV series, books and music) have become a profitable export industry in the so-called free market – almost as profitable as the trade in arms; almost as profitable as the trade in beauty products for women; big earrings, makeup and even oriental veils for women who want to be exotic or choose what they call their authentic Muslim identity.

But the free market is being demystified rapidly, being exposed as the freedom of the powerful to exploit the less powerful. In the year 1994, everybody in Egypt was talking about the bad meat scandal.[3] The European Community threatened to obstruct the sale of Egyptian exports because the Egyptian government was not being flexible enough to disregard the most elementary health rules for imported meat. These prescribe that fat content should not exceed 20 per cent and that the expiry date should be respected. Large amounts of bad meat, in which the fat content reached 35 per cent or more, were imported into Egypt, threatening the health of thousands of people. Often the expiry date was almost due. This kind of meat is fed to pigs and other animals in European countries since it is no longer suitable for human consumption.

This kind of pressure is exerted in the name of freedom of the market. Non-flexible governments in the Third World are considered bad or 'dissident' governments. The global neocolonial powers are able to punish them in ways corresponding to their level of 'dissidence' or 'inflexibility'. Punishment includes the threat of economic or military sanctions and of defamation: publicizing their human rights violations in the global media.

The United Nations and human rights organizations are often instruments of this neocolonial game. In the same way the so-called nongovernmental organizations (NGOs) or movements in 'civil society' have become new instruments to outflank local governments that are still sufficiently powerful and organized to put up some resistance.

'Privatization', 'nongovernmental organizations' or 'civil society' are all considered positive words for men and women who are fighting against local dictators and oppressive governments. But, in the hands of neocolonialists, they are transformed into swords directed against local people. Swords and words are used to divide the people in the name of diversity, while the neocolonialists globalize in NATO or in transnational corporations.

This is a game in which 'god' has all the power of both word and sword and is always the winner while the 'devil' – ourselves – is the loser. The devil is dissident and the angels are docile, obedient, tolerant, moderate and flexible groups and individuals.

In 1991, our 'NGO' (the Arab Women's Solidarity Association in Egypt) was banned by the government. The AWSA was considered locally and globally a dissident group. Why? Because we did not distinguish between patriarchy and neocolonialism and we protested against the Gulf War. But how can women, who are half the population, be liberated in countries that are neither economically nor culturally liberated?

Our concepts in AWSA emerged from our experience as women struggling against all kinds of oppression exercised in the name of god, the father, the husband, the state, the United Nations or international law.

Dissident philosophers

The word 'philosophy' in Arabic is *al-falsafa*. There are important Arab philosophers but most of their work is in Arabic and the most important parts of their work have not been translated or studied in the West. Many Western scholars think that philosophy, like feminism, is a Western invention. People who read history think that philosophy started with the Greeks. This idea is related to nineteenth-century colonialism. Egyptian history is reduced to what is called Egyptology, to stones and ruins looked at by tourists.

Colonialism uses military terrorism and cultural tourism at the same time. Cameras in the hands of tourists are like guns in the hands of colonialists, like pens in the hands of postmodernists. The upshot is words in books or images on the TV screen about 'clean' neocolonial wars, whether physical, economic or cultural.

Egyptology is an example of cultural genocide or terrorism, in which a whole nation and its civilization and philosophy are violently reduced to a few stones or ruins. Egyptian philosophers have disappeared from history. One of them was a woman philosopher called Hypatia. She was killed twice: the first time in AD 415 by foreign invaders who killed her physically and burned her books together with the whole library of Alexandria in Egypt;[4] the second time was in the nineteenth century when she was assassinated culturally and historically by the Egyptologists.

Not all philosophers are, like Hypatia, killed because of what they write or think. That depends on the effectiveness of their dissidence or challenge to the political system that rules over them. If a philosopher produces many works that change nothing in the power system because they do not reach people and are not understood, he or she may remain safe and secure, even prosperous. The dissident word must be effective in real life, otherwise it loses its meaning and is no longer dissident. Thinking that is isolated from real life is not part of the struggle. The dissident word is an expression of a struggling woman or man whose body and mind and spirit are inseparable. Can you have a dissident mind and a docile body or a cold heart with no passion? A dissident writer is both a philosopher and an activist.

A philosopher who is not an activist in a struggle ends up as an empty shell: as a shelf of books in academia. S/he struggles in closed rooms, using words to fence with other users of words. S/he has a love–hate relationship with poor oppressed women and men who are struggling to live. S/he worships them, calls them the 'subaltern', glorifies their authentic identity or culture, but at the same time looks down on them, considers them as docile or struggling bodies unable to produce philosophy or as local activists but not global thinkers. S/he abolishes subaltern philosophies and replaces them on the global intellectual scene; s/he becomes the philosopher of the subaltern who knows more about them than they know about themselves.

Tourism and postmodernism

There are important similarities between tourists and postmodernists. Both appear to be physically present in nature, but in fact they are empty shells: ghosts haunting what are called cultural differences. Both consume cultural differences, diversity, multiculturalism, authenticity, creativity, and even dissidence. For them indigenous people do not exist. They have become a piece of stone, a collection of images, words and symbols, an abstraction of nature–culture.

Both postmodernists and tourists consume the other or use the other as a tool for consumption. To them everything (including the subaltern) becomes a commodity to be used materially, culturally or intellectually. Multiculturalism, diversity, cultural difference, religious difference, ethnic difference, authenticity, specificity are the new commodities. The postmodernists even go back to glorifying blood relations, feudal patriarchal family ties and tribal societies. Like pagans they worship the gods or statues which they have created out of stone or words or images.

I have seen tourists in Egypt kiss the stone of the pyramid in Giza like pagans or pilgrims kissing the black stone in Mecca. In my village in the delta of the Nile, an American woman scholar kissed a veiled girl and praised her veil as a sign of her authentic identity. Another American woman scholar produced a film about subaltern or Egyptian women who are going back to the veil, back to their authentic culture. She praised the veil in her film and said: 'Nowadays Egyptian women have their own revolution and are not imitating Western women.' The title of her film was *A Veiled Revolution!* She is considered an expert on Middle Eastern culture, and has the money and equipment needed to produce such films. We Egyptian women are considered ignorant of our culture. We have to be guided by American experts. They mediate our experience for us and then sell back to us their image of ourselves.

The veil is forced on Egyptian women by religio-political groups. It is no different culturally from the postmodern veil made of cosmetics and hair dyes that is forced on Western women by the media and beauty commercials. In an international women's conference, a French woman scholar said the veil was linked to Islam. I mentioned that veiling preceded Islam, and existed in both Christianity and Judaism, that it in fact arose with the slave system. She said: 'I am Christian but I am not veiled.' While she was speaking I noticed that she had a thick coating of makeup on her face. She was not aware that she herself was also wearing a veil. This postmodern veil is seen by the global neo-colonial media as beautiful, feminine, a sign of progress, though it is as pernicious to the humanity and authentic identity of the woman who wears it as the so-called religious veil.

The dissident god

At a conference an Arab scholar tried to glorify his culture, his religion, his 'Islam', by proving that women in Islamic societies could be heads of government, as in Pakistan and Turkey, and as Shajar al-Durr was in Egypt in the past. He meant that the veiling of women does not prevent them from being heads of state or going out to work. The veil, he said, was just to protect Muslim women from Western values, which permit sexual freedom for females and homosexuality for men, both of which lead to AIDS. For him Islam is the 'good' religion or the 'absolute truth'; it represents virtue for women and men, which prevents adultery and disease.

Islamic positional superiority is established by avoiding criticism of the self relative to the other. The other here is the 'unbeliever', *al-Kafir* (the devil). This attitude is viewed positively by postmodernists as reflecting cultural difference, and they separate freedom of belief from critical thinking about freedom or cultural difference. They worship freedom and difference even if they lead to cultural and economic exploitation.

The same can apply to Christian and Jewish scholars and to so-called liberation theology movements, in which Christian scholars say that Christianity is based on love and compassion but Islam is based on justice, and justice is an abstract word that leads to violence or war. They forget that love and compassion are abstract words too and may serve in even bigger wars. Inter-cultural or inter-religious dialogue takes place on the conference platforms at a distance from real life and its struggles. Cultural or religious comparisons are used as a proof of superiority and thus as a new instrument of domination.

Postmodern liberation theologians are widely honoured in the global and local media. They are products of neocolonialism but they serve as the intellectual face of the fanatical religio-political movements called religious fundamentalists. Fundamentalist religious movements do not oppose or expose neocolonial economic exploitation. They are religious movements fighting against Western values, protecting women or the nation of Islam against Western materialism. They put more energy into veiling women and fighting against 'abortion' than into fighting against the sale of bad meat or the shipment of nuclear waste into our country. They encourage Western banks by putting their Muslim money into them. The US government calls them moderate (nonterrorist) Islamic fundamentalists and has started negotiating with them so that they can replace insufficiently flexible governments which no longer deliver what the global powers need.

Western Christian or Jewish scholars on the other hand consider 'Christianity' or 'Judaism' the 'good' religions because they did not block the way to modernism or postmodernism or prevent the libera- tion of Western women. To them Muslim women are victims of the veil, virginity, sexual inhibition, polygamy or Islamic fundamentalist terrorism. They forget that Christian fundamentalists in the United States terrorize doctors in abortion clinics and even kill them as part of the so-called pro-life movement. This is not theological liberation but theological competition, in which each group tries to defame the other.

In 1993, in one of these conferences, a young Muslim scholar from the Sudan was wearing a veil. She said that she was proud to be a Muslim veiled woman, proud that she was not Westernized or elitist; the veil was part of her authentic identity and culture, and she was a part of a women's revolution struggling against Western cultural imperialism. (I noticed that her veil was made of silk and probably imported from Harrods in London.) For her, identity and culture had once again become an issue separate from the economic and the political. She ignored or was ignorant of the fact that women are oppressed in the three monotheistic religions (as in other religions), that class, gender and racial discrimination are universal phenomena which originated in the slave system and have been kept alive by colonial and neocolonial powers.

Postmodernists and religious fundamentalists present themselves as new groups rejecting cultural imperialism. Today culture and religion have become the issues around which our struggles seem to centre. For postmodernists 'culture' is the new god. This new god takes on the aspect and form of a new dissidence, to be set against the old gods of the socialists, which were 'the economy', 'anti-capitalism' and 'anti-imperialism'. But if god becomes a dissident himself, we have to declare the innocence of the devil. The word 'god' has to be demystified like any other word. Since the advent of 'the Word' in holy books, it has been used to invade other people's land (justified because this was a 'promised land'), economy and culture.

Since the beginning of human history men and women everywhere have struggled against foreign invaders and economic and cultural oppressors. They make no distinction between their minds and bodies. And they seek after song and dance just as they seek after bread and vegetables. Dissidence is a natural phenomenon in human life. We are all born dissident and creative. But we lose our creativity and dissidence partially or wholly through education and the fear that we shall be punished here or in the hereafter. We live in fear and we die in fear. Dissident people liberate themselves from fear, and they pay a price for this process of liberation. The price may be high or low but there is always a price to be paid.

Non-dissident people pay a price too: the process of subordination.

So if we have to pay a price anyway, why not pay the price and be liberated?

Pseudo-dissidence

The word 'dissidence' itself needs to be demystified: like the word 'philosophy', like the words 'East' and 'West', 'North' and 'South', 'Occident' and 'Orient'.

I met an orientalist philosopher who lives in San Francisco and writes his books in English. He is a scholar in a Californian university and is considered a dissident writer on the so-called Orient, that is, a scholar for people who do not live in the West or Occident. (I have tried to find an occidentalist philosopher or scholar, but it seems that occidentalism does not yet exist.)

In the postmodern era we meet a lot of orientalists both white and coloured. Most of them are postmodern. Some of them live in the United States and others live in Europe. None live in Egypt or Morocco or Palestine or Algeria or in other Third World countries. They may go to Egypt or other countries for a short touristic visit or to make a film about Egypt or to write a book on ancient or contemporary Egypt. Then they go back home to the West, to Europe or the United States. Some of these orientalists were born in Egypt or Morocco or Palestine or Algeria, but they have lived most of their lives in the United States or Europe. They have not participated in any real struggle in their country of birth, or even in their country of residence.

The orientalist whom I met was invited to give a lecture in the summer of 1991 in Egypt. He was deeply imbued with orientalist arrogance and exclusivism. He wanted to be our philosopher and replace us, we who live and struggle in Egypt. He wanted to remain both in the Orient and the Occident. He insisted on the privilege of 'hybridity' as his birthright. He quoted occidental postmodernists from Foucault to Derrida. He criticized US cultural imperialism severely. He was smoking US cigarettes. Some members of our association (which was banned a few days before his lecture) tried to meet him but he was too busy. He met the Minister of Culture and other ministers. He was a star on Egyptian TV as a dissident orientalist or anti-orientalist.

The neocolonialist star system works very successfully, rather like the transnational corporations. The difference between the current postmodern orientalist and the old colonial orientalist is often his/her country of birth or skin colour. The similarities between white and coloured postmodernists in the West are great. Both quote Foucault and Derrida. Both use ultra-elite complex discourse, and maintain traditional exclusionism: Orient or Occident. Both compete in the market of publishing, scholarship, the media and CNN. Both have become a commodity; both are addicted to the production and consumption of dissident words kept at a safe distance from real struggle. Most of them are also addicted to the production and consumption of culture and cultural products. The products they consume are mostly American, especially Hollywood films and other US mass culture. Even when they leave their homes for a trip to the Third World they see only American films or TV series. Local films and cultural productions have been overwhelmed by American products and will cease to exist as a result of the new GATT agreements. These pundits often smoke American cigarettes, in spite of the increasing anti-smoking campaign in the West. In Egypt smoking advertisements are increasing. The US government gives grants to tobacco firms to promote smoking overseas. The sale of American cigarettes in Egypt has become as pernicious as the sale of bad meat from Europe, as pernicious as 'sex crime' films from Hollywood.

If you visit Cairo or any other city in the Third World today your eye cannot miss the advertisements everywhere, the huge posters with half-naked women carrying a cigarette or a bottle of Coca-Cola in one hand and a gun in the other as they dance under the dazzling neon lights.

Conclusion

It is not so difficult for us to see through and unveil the techniques and discourses of oppression and exploitation both locally and globally. Then it is important for us to identify the new victims and the new victimizers in the neocolonial era – for we do not live in a postcolonial era as the postmodernists claim. We must struggle together both locally and globally. The local struggle must be combined with global or international struggle and solidarity. We must fight on all fronts. We must not separate the political from the sexual, economic, religious or cultural. We must carry on a continuous resistance, a continuous dissidence, which will forge the way to a better future for *all* the peoples of the world.

[First published in *Women: A Cultural Review*, Vol. 6, No. 1, 1995. A longer version of this paper was published in Chris Muller (ed.), *The Dissident Word: The Oxford Amnesty Lectures 1995*, HarperCollins, 1996.]

Notes

1. Egypt was declared a 'Protectorate' in 1914, when Britain went to war with Turkey; it had been under English 'administration' since the 1882 invasion, the pretext for which had been anti-European demonstrations [Ed.].
2. The title Khedive was that of Viceroy under Ottoman suzerainty [Ed.].
3. *Roz El-Youssef*, 21 November 1994, p. 18.
4. Hypatia was 'torn to pieces' in AD 451 'by a mob of Christians at the instigation of their bishop (later Saint) Cyril' (*The Oxford Classical Dictionary*, ed. N.G. Hammond and H.H. Scullard). She was an influential teacher of the pagan Neoplatonist philosophy, who revised her father Theon's *Commentary on the Almagest*. In Chapter 47 of *The Decline and Fall of the Roman Empire*, Gibbon specifies Cyril's motive as jealousy of her influence: 'On a fatal day, in the holy season of Lent, Hypatia was torn from her chariot, stripped naked, dragged to the church, and inhumanly butchered by the hands of Peter the reader and a troop of savage and merciless fanatics; her flesh was scraped from her bones with sharp oyster-shells, and her quivering limbs were delivered to the flames' (Everyman edition V, 14–15).

CHAPTER 16

Culture in the Dialogue of Civilizations

Introduction: clash or dialogue?

Words, language, culture, information, education and communication can all be tools in the hands of the ruling minority or elite, at both the international and the national levels, to control the minds of the vast majority of the women and men they rule. The opposite is also possible: words, language, culture, religion and history can become tools in the hands of the popular masses with which they can resist the tyranny of the minority ruling the world, ruling within each state or tribe or family.

Ever since the beginnings of the system of slavery, or the so-called patriarchal class system, the ruling minority has been dominant at three levels: the world, the nation and the family. It came to own language, culture and religion just as it owned the economy and the wealth, the military weapons and the police, as well as the legislative, executive and judiciary powers, the press, the media, Internet networks, television and satellite channels.

Talk of the clash of civilizations or the dialogue of cultures becomes some kind of nonsense, an extract from the theatre of the absurd, in our modern or postmodern world where culture has beaten a retreat before the nuclear bomb, where the word 'civilization' has become meaningless in the presence of genocide by chemical warfare and laser beams. A recent example for us Arabs is the Gulf War of 1991 which killed half a million Arabs for the sake of controlling oil. This war is still, in 1997, claiming thousands of Iraqi lives because of the economic embargo; it is still killing and scattering the Palestinian people to the present day. All this is committed in the name of so-called international law, in the name of democracy, in the name of peace, development or cooperation. Other massacres are perpetrated, causing great poverty, famine and conflicts over the material necessities of life; these are essentially economic conflicts, not cultural conflicts of civilizations.

I have attended several conferences in the USA and Europe since 1992. Most of them were about so-called globalization and its relation to culture in African, Asian and Arab countries, what the conference organizers referred to as the 'Third World'. They also refer to our present age as the 'postcolonialist age', totally disregarding the fact that our Third World is living a neocolonialist age, more savage than the previous colonialist age because it is destroying us intellectually and economically without bombs or bullets, just by drowning us in false information, lies, modernist and postmodernist theories that only serve the interests of the US and European masters, not ours, and which beget greater cultural and economic poverty.

Undoubtedly there are scientists and thinkers in Europe and in North America who enthusiastically defend the interests of oppressed peoples in the Third World. They are a small minority: their ideas do not reach the majority in their own countries; they also do not reach us. The global information network is ever capable of flooding us with all the ideas and information necessary for distorting awareness, and burying the truth.

A new war is in progress, with a flow of information, like a smoke-screen, blinding the eyes and stifling the air. The clash, or conflict, of today is a struggle against the false information brought to us by the fatal global information network, it is not a dialogue between our civilization and theirs.

We are engulfed in this war while the revolution in the areas of information, technology and communication is manipulated by the international ruling minority, or the minority controlling world trade and the world market. This market has changed its way of producing and consuming information; it has also opened up markets in the countries of the Third World that were once closed to it. It has become difficult for many small states to defend their economic and cultural independence in this international jungle called the 'free market' – a market that is far from free, unless it is the freedom of big states to devour the smaller ones.

The so-called global economy, or the globalization of economy, is nothing but a commercial and economic siege of Third World countries, in the name of international unification or of global unity at the level of the minority ruling the world. Parallel to this supra-unification, there is another movement aimed at fragmenting and weakening the strength of the peoples, their solidarity and their unity, a movement disguised as cultural, religious and racial pluralism, or as respect for the differences and specificities of all groups and sects, including the Hare Krishnas, the devil worshippers, the onion lovers or the carrot adorers.

This religious madness is accompanied by a flood of scientific ideas informing us that we are now witnessing the end of history, and the last of the ideologies, whereas a new ideology is sneaking in on us under the smokescreen: the global neocolonialist ideology, one that does not, in essence, differ from the ideology of traditional colonialism. This new ideology bears different names such as multinational companies, the World Bank, the Security Council, the United Nations, the International Monetary Fund, 'international law' or others.

In recent years, some strange and contradictory phenomena emerged under the guise of reviving folklore, or local cultures, or identity or religions. We saw groups of youngsters armed with bombs, knives or chains and in adoration of an 'emir' or 'supreme sheikh'. We saw other groups carrying the cross upside down and glorifying Satan. We saw parties dubbing themselves 'the partisans of God' or the 'partisans of the devil'. Others yet called for a return to Islamic, Arab or national heritage or identity; some others called for privatization, partnership, cooperation, alliance or dialogue.

What is elite culture and what is popular culture?

How can we get to know the role of the culture of the elite or the role of popular culture in cultural dialogue or in the clash of civilizations without knowing what we mean by popular culture and the difference between it and elitist culture?

What is Egyptian popular culture in Egypt for example? How do we get to know it from its original sources: the women and men, old and young, workers, peasants, soldiers, artisans, etcetera, known as the Egyptian people? This popular culture is composed of the stories, the tales, the proverbs, the axioms, the songs, the legends, the jokes and the anecdotes that people invent, that they produce and consume, that they exchange in their daily life, that become part of their talk and nightly gatherings, orally passed down from one generation to another, preserved in the individual and collective memory (grandmothers and mothers play a major role in this, followed by retired old men who reminisce and repeat all the stories etcetera to their children and grandchildren). That is how popular culture is preserved to become an intellectual heritage that is physically inherited, just like the colour of one's skin, as an intellectual matter called 'memes' (in modern genetic science) carried by certain genes in the brain cells to form a people's collective memory, exactly like their physical features are formed.

In recent years, scientific breakthroughs have led to the revelation of many secrets of the living cell, of genes, of the atom and its components such as the electron and the even smaller quark whose greater power is still a mystery, perhaps soon to be discovered and become quarkic power, even greater than nuclear power. It has now become possible to know much of what used to be unknown in the process of transmitting material and intellectual characteristics from one generation to the next. Ideas or memes materialize within the brain cells through biological, physical, electronic and chemical processes which link the organic to the inorganic, which connect biology, thought, economics and culture. These processes are almost similar to what takes place in the computer: the recently invented computers are very much like a living organism, an organism fed with ideas and programs instead of bread and water.

Popular culture is a mixture of the conscious and the subconscious in the past and in the present. It is a merger of the organic and the inorganic within the body, a merger of matter, spirit and mind. That is why popular culture is more expressive of experienced reality than the culture of the ruling elite or the intellectual elite which usually stems from books and from scientific, religious or cultural texts. The difference is certainly great between a culture born of the printing press and a culture born from the very life of people, from their own individual and collective daily experiences.

Letters and language hide more than they reveal of what goes on in people's minds. Yet popular culture strives to overcome this obstacle with gestures, dances, singing, plays, tales and anecdotes, all of which help language and words to express the emotions and the thoughts of human beings.

One of the strongest human emotions is anger against the patriarchal class oppression that has prevailed in human history since the slave system, and still prevails in a different form. At present, the international community is divided into a minority wielding power internationally and nationally – those who control economies, armaments, armies, police and knowledge – and the overwhelming majority of women and men (particularly in the Third World) who live beneath the poverty line. They cannot afford to buy their daily bread, let alone to buy the words of god or the official or party newspaper.

Popular anger expresses itself from time to time in labour strikes, in student and youth demonstrations, in feminist movements, or in peasant revolutions. Written and unwritten laws often crush those movements of anger, and popular anger seeks other forms of intellectual resistance by way of axioms and proverbs, of political or sexual jokes launched against the elite or the ruling minority. These different forms of popular culture play their role in revealing the contradictions or duality of the dominant elitist culture, revealing also its moral, religious, political or economic values. Such a revelation, the unmasking of falsehood, changes anger or tragedy into laughter and comedy, not devoid of enjoyment or a temporary sense of victory.

Popular culture is often a kind of collective moral resistance, an attempt towards collective cultural liberation from the siege of the ruling elite. Popular culture is often a weapon for the peoples who stand defenceless before armed authority. In our so-called Third or Fourth World, where the majority live deprived of material and moral rights, including clean bread and water, unpolluted air and undistorted information, the peoples have no choice and no means of resistance save their popular culture and their collective memory, with all they contain of tragedy and comedy.

Because popular culture is oral, it escapes censorship and arrest. The authors of popular culture have no name or address, the whole people are the authors, they are both producers and consumers; no state, however tyrannical, can imprison millions, nor can it burn popular culture, because it is not contained in books. Books can be burned, but the collective memory of an entire people cannot.

The word 'people' in our country is glorified or even sanctified in the dictionaries of the ruling class or in the culture of the elite, regardless of whether the elite is liberal (believing in the free market and privatization), Arab nationalist (believing in socialism or Nasserism), Islamic (believing in the Qur'an and religious tradition) or Marxist (believing in class struggle and the public sector). All these types of cultural elite glorify the great Egyptian people. However, their glorification is but empty words. Rarely do they try to get to know the people in their daily reality or to know the different categories of women, youth, workers, peasants, soldiers, artisans and others.

Despite much talk of cultural specificities or popular authenticity or cultural identity, in-depth studies of Egyptian popular culture are rare to find. There may be some studies expressing the view of foreign researchers or of the local elite regarding the so-called folklore, which is different from popular culture in that it expresses the culture of the elite researchers more than it expresses the culture of the people who are the subjects of the research.

In European and North American universities, there is a growing interest in the popular cultures of Third World countries, in order to understand those peoples, and their ways of struggle, resistance and revolution against the ruling powers both locally and internationally. Wherever I travel in Arab or African countries or in Egypt, I come across the North American young man, or young woman, living in a tiny village as one of its own people, dressed like them, speaking their dialect, eating their local food, learning their songs and dances, memorizing their jokes, proverbs and stories, spending the evenings with them in their homes and fields, collecting the details of their popular culture in a notebook, in English. These researchers will leave after a year or two, go back to their respective North American universities where their studies are subjected to analysis, conclusions and predictions to feed the appetite for political information which is part of the military defence of US interests in the Arab region, in Africa, and in Asia.

Information is the modern or postmodern weapon in this age of revolution in the field of information and technology.

The battle to control oil resources and raw materials and the fight to open new consumer markets for US commodities (material and cultural) in the Third World take place through information: who controls it, who analyses it and who is capable of counteracting it with a flow of false counterinformation disguised as truth, science, philosophy and new theories in the areas of politics, economics and culture.

One of the new theories, coming to us from professors at US universities, speaks of global economics or the globalization of economies into a unified force. Along with it comes another theory about the fragmentation of popular cultures into sectarian, racial, ethnic or religious differences.

Popular culture is still unknown in our Egyptian and Arab universities, despite the constant glorification of the people (who are absent from the scene of politics or scientific conferences). The people are sacred so long as they remain absent. If they are present, the sacred becomes profane. One important Arab professor (specializing in the science of the clash of civilizations or 'cultural dialogue') was not too happy when I brought with me to a meeting my old aunt, a peasant in her black, dusty dress, her face wrinkled by the sun, and asked her to tell us some of her village's popular tales and jokes or proverbs. He was not too happy with her shabby looks, or with her unscientific language; he said: 'What does your aunt have to do with the clash of cultures or with cultural dialogue?'

Contrary to elitist culture, popular culture came straight from the mouths of people and from their experiences, it reflects their plans and their dreams; it is the collective, social autobiography of their lives in their homes in their towns and villages and in the shanty towns of big cities. This autobiography is transformed into popular culture in the reservoir of collective memory. By its very nature, popular culture is not subjugated by the critical elite, or what we call 'critics', who are professional literary, political or economic critics within government or other parties. In the culture of the elite, critics try to banish the author from existence so that they can take his place. Hence the modern theory about the death of the author, along the line of the 'death of ideologies' or the 'death of history'. But the author of popular culture never dies, he is ever reborn from successive mothers, from generations. He lives in the memory of the men, women and children of the people, despite a continuous attempt by the powers that be to kill or weaken him.

The culture of the elite always tries to expel or cancel popular culture in the name of scientific, religious or cultural sophistication. When I was a child of seven, I witnessed a clash between the culture of the elite, embodied by our village mayor, and between my paternal grandmother, a poor peasant. The mayor held his prayer beads in one hand and the Qur'an in the other. He accused my grandmother of being ignorant and illiterate, of not knowing god since she had not read his holy book, the Qur'an. She accused him of being unjust, of exploiting the sweat of poor peasants, and claimed she knew god better than he did. Her last shot was to throw at him an age-old popular proverb: 'God is justice, reason led us to him.'

This proverb was the basis for the popular religious philosophy that preceded Sufism in Islam; it also predated the other Islamic philosophical schools that believed in justice, truth and freedom more than in Islamic jurisprudence or determinism.

When, under British occupation, the Egyptian government ordered Egyptian farmers to plant cotton rather than corn and wheat, my grandmother and the men and women of her village were angry. They gathered in the mayor's house and said, 'Are we going to feed our kids cotton, mayor?' Under Sadat, during the 'open door' policy, during which peasant were encouraged to plant cash crops to sell in exchange for US wheat and other foreign goods, Egyptian peasants were planting for the cows to eat, whereas children went hungry. I was not aware of this until one day I visited my village. I heard my aunt say, 'We work to feed the cows while our children die of hunger.' I heard another peasant woman say, 'The plants we have planted, but the food is not for us to eat.'

At an international conference in Addis Ababa, in 1978 when I worked for the UN Economic Commission for Africa, an African woman researcher submitted a paper entitled: 'Africa Produces What It Eats Not And Eats What It Produces Not'. That is exactly the policy of the World Bank and of the global economy: to transform Africa and the rest of the Third World into new colonies that produce the harvests and raw materials needed by the West, while their peoples eat and consume what is sent to them by that very same West, most of which is superfluous and does not satisfy the basic needs of those peoples. The African continent, one of the richest in the world in material and cultural natural resources, has become the poorest of them all.

The neocolonialist global economy, along with the culture of the elite associated with it both internationally and nationally, is robbing the peoples not only of their cultures, of their means of intellectual and military resistance, but also of their daily food and water.

Today a struggle is taking place over water and wheat in our African countries. Africa and the Arab countries have been disarmed of any nuclear weapons, all except the state of Israel. Is that why attention is being drawn away from vital material, military and economic struggles to another imaginary conflict, the clash of civilizations and cultural dialogue?

In Egypt, the popular masses are composed of different groups: women, youth, children, workers, soldiers, peasants, Muslims and Christians (Copts); does popular culture differ from one group to another within the same people? Is there ever a clash or a dialogue between those cultures or groups? What is the difference between clash and dialogue? Are not clash, anger or resistance the normal emotions when one is on the receiving end of aggression? In my village, the women say to one another in the absence of men, 'If your trust to a man you give, you are trusting water in a sieve!' This popular proverb stems from their own experiences with their husbands. The law does not punish the man for adultery or extramarital experiences except in one case: if he commits the act in his wife's bed or home; even then, the punishment is mild despite the ugliness of the crime. Women thus lost confidence in men whose moral sense became as tattered as a sieve.

At the international level too, the African states and the small states of the Third World no longer trust the promises of the big powers, nor the resolutions of the UN and Security Council, nor the agreements of the World Bank and IMF or international cultural or economic conventions such as GATT, for they know that such agreements only deepen the chasm between rich and poor.

The economic and cultural conflict is there between big and small states; it is also there within the state itself between the poor classes and the rich ruling classes; it is also there within the family between the ruling sex (men) and their subjects (women). This is the patriarchal class system to which humanity is subjected at all levels – international, national and family – united from the top by the elite or ruling minority. That is why moral principles usually have a double standard and no single yardstick.

This moral duality stems from a single political philosophy, the separation of responsibility from power. This is obvious in international law which considers the big state (the real criminal) innocent and the small state (the victim) guilty. The Egyptian penal code allows the briber to go free if he gives evidence against the one he bribed; yet the briber is the one who has the means to corrupt. In the family, moral and Islamic laws in Egypt entitle a man to several marital and extramarital relations; he has the right to scatter his children and break up his family as part of his absolute right to divorce. In the case of an immoral sexual relation, the man walks away innocent while the woman goes to jail.

That is why the popular culture of women in our country continues to struggle against double standards. This clash between the sexes is part of women's cultural heritage since the days of slavery; it is not what elitist culture claims it to be, a feminist struggle imported from Western civilization or culture.

Another conflict exists in the village: between poor peasants and agricultural labourers on one side and rich landowners and their henchmen on the other. There are similar conflicts in the cities – between workers and capitalism – and within the government itself between small employees and big bosses. It is a normal class struggle stemming from the duality and the absence of justice; it is not a communist or foreign idea imported from the West or the East.

Clash or conflict has a positive connotation in popular culture. Sometimes it takes the form of resistance or irony against the ruling power. In the culture of the elite, by contrast, it becomes negative, something to eliminate. Is that the reason why some members of the elite are opting for 'dialogue' and 'alliance' rather than 'resistance' and 'struggle'? Has the world order suddenly changed to become just and apply one yardstick so that the struggle may end?

The word 'allies' has a bad reputation in the Egyptian collective memory, in our popular culture. The Egyptian people have not forgotten what the British 'Allies' did in the 1948 and 1956 wars. Nor did the Arab peoples forget what the USA and its 'allies' did in the Gulf War in 1991. This collective memory is part of the popular resistance against the new 'allies' speaking of dialogue, brotherhood and peace.

Egyptian popular culture

Egyptian popular culture is full of tragicomic sayings and jokes that are a kind of intellectual resistance, an expression of the struggle between the oppressors and the oppressed at all levels. Popular imagination may also, sometimes, pierce the veils of sanctity to mock the absence of heavenly justice when it abandons them in their struggle against poverty and exploitation.

In the early sixties in Egypt, during the International Conference of Popular Forces, in a contest among intellectuals to find the right definition for workers and peasants, I happened to visit my village in the province of Qalyoubia. There I heard an anecdote that clearly reveals the contradiction or falsehood inherent in the culture of the ruling elite.

A peasant from the village fled to Libya, across the Western Sahara, hidden in a truck. When he reached Benghazi, people asked, 'Why did you ever come, old chap?' The Egyptian peasant answered, 'Because the police in Egypt are arresting workers and throwing them in jail.' The people retorted, 'But you are a peasant, not a worker!' The clever peasant answered, 'Go tell that to the police in Egypt!'

Some members of the elite sneaked into parliament under the label of workers and peasants, having taken off their three-piece suits and put on djellabas and blues.

Here is another popular anecdote from the sixties and seventies when dictatorship and the police state hid behind a screen of words such as 'democracy', 'welfare', and 'peace'. A small statue of a pharaoh disappeared from an Egyptian museum. The Department of Antiquities failed to locate it. State security and police forces stepped in. In less than twenty-four hours they announced that they had found the statue, identified the king, and discovered everything about his life, his marriage and his divorce. Everyone was amazed. They asked the police, 'How did you discover all that – you must have located his tomb?' 'Not at all,' answered the police, 'the king admitted everything.'

That is how popular culture unveils the link between the imaginary fantasy (a stone statue confessing) and the absurd reality (the use of torture by the henchmen of the police state to extract statements from political prisoners).

In September 1981, when more than 1,500 men and women of the Egyptian opposition were thrown in jail, the following story circulated among the people. A man was seen with his nose swathed in bandages. 'What happened to your nose?' he was asked. 'I had my tooth pulled out,' he replied. 'Why didn't you have it pulled out through your mouth?' people queried. He answered, 'Come on. Is anyone allowed to open his mouth nowadays?'

One of the means used in the seventies to confer legitimacy upon the many decisions adopted against the interests of the people was the referendum. The result was usually around 99 per cent in favour of the decisions concerned. The reaction was the following popular anecdote. At parties, a certain ruler loved to tell the jokes invented by the people against his predecessor. He then heard that jokes against him were spreading too. In his anger, he ordered the police to arrest all those joke- and rumour-mongers. The police searched high and low and came back to the ruler with an old man, in tattered clothes, who had been sitting in a marijuana den repeating the latest jokes. The handcuffed man knelt before the ruler while the latter asked him one question after another.

'Did you invent such and such a joke? asked the ruler.

'Yes, sir, I did,' answered the old man truthfully. It went on and on, and every time the old man admitted that the joke concerned was his. Finally, the ruler burst out in anger and said to the man, 'You wretched man, how can you say all these jokes about me when 99 per cent of the people chose me by referendum?' The old man jumped up and objected: 'No, sir! This last joke is not mine.'

It was well known in the seventies that the ruling power encouraged Muslim and Coptic religious currents and sectarian trends against the Nasserist and socialist forces in Egypt. Just before President Sadat's assassination (by those very same Islamic currents he had encouraged), the ruler realized the danger to his life and to his regime from these religious currents. According to the popular story, he ordered the Coptic pope, Shenouda, and the Sheikh of Al-Azhar to be brought before him and said to them, 'Things have gone too far. The fight between Muslims and Copts has become a danger to us all. What say you I appoint others in your positions?' They answered meekly, 'To hear is to obey.' The ruler started with the Coptic pope and said, 'I have decided to appoint Mamdouh Salem in your place.' Surprised, the pope said, 'But Mr President, he is a Muslim not a Copt.' The ruler retorted angrily, 'Come on, Shenouda, are we back to that thing about Muslims and Copts?'

The collective memory of the Egyptian people is full of tragicomic stories and jokes, which reveal more of the contradiction between power centres than does the culture of the elite which is, in fact, an integral part of the ruling power. Indeed, the part cannot be aware of the whole, nor can the eye behold itself. Yet the unarmed people can look upon them from the outside and see what they cannot.

Corruption and bribery invaded Egyptian society after we became a consumer society in the seventies. One day, a ruler sat at an important meeting with businessmen from Egypt, Europe and the USA. The telephone at his side started to ring. On the receiver, he heard one of his family shout: 'Come quickly! Our house has been robbed by thieves!' He answered, laughing, 'Impossible, son! All the thieves are sitting here with me!'

I do not think there has been any study of this kind of Egyptian popular culture at any time. I have written these pages from my own memory and from the stories and jokes I hear from people. If we want to identify the role of popular culture in cultural dialogue or in the clash of civilizations, we must realize that it cannot be done without an in-depth study of that popular culture as well as of the culture of the elite, its role and how it differs from the culture of the people.

In concluding this rapid study dictated by my personal experience, I repeat what I said at the beginning: so long as justice is absent at the international, national and family levels, conflict or clashes will not disappear. The culture of oppressed women and men is a way of resisting injustice; it is ever-present in history and in the collective memory despite continuous attempts to eradicate or disregard it.

It should, however, be noted that dialogue among the different cultures in the world is necessary for knowledge, for progress and for cooperation rather than exploitation. The cultured elite must open a dialogue with itself and with popular culture in its own country, so that it may, some day, become part of the people, capable of truly representing the people in the dialogue with other, outside cultures. Thus will the elite merge with the people as one force capable of dialogue, negotiation or alliance. Unfortunately, the elite in our country is still divided into separate and scattered groups, vying to cooperate with the ruling powers both inside and outside, all in the name of the people.

[Paper given to the Afro-Asian Peoples' Solidarity Organization international conference 'Clash of Civilizations or Dialogue of Cultures', Cairo, 10–12 March 1997]

CHAPTER 17

Democracy, Creativity and African Literature

The central theme of what follows can be summarized in one word: 'division'. This may seem an oversimplification in dealing with a topic that is extremely complex. And yet it is my conviction that what might appear at first sight an oversimplification is in fact a serious attempt to strike deep into the heart of the issues that face us.

To study the relationships between democracy, creativity and African literature is not an easy task. This is not only because of the vastness and complexity of the subject and the paucity of specialized knowledge, but also because the mutual linkages between these different but inter-connected areas have been either neglected, or wilfully severed, by the various schools of colonial and neocolonial thought.

If we wish to seek the roots of this separation between inter-connected areas it is necessary to return to the early civilizations and in particular to ancient Greece, for its roots are embedded in Greek philosophy, which glorified and idealized slave society, its values and its conceptualization of life. Basing itself on slavery in the social, economic and political fields, Greek philosophy evolved a system of values and ideas that became almost as sacred as the monotheistic religions, draw-ing its inspiration from a pseudo 'higher wisdom' blind to reality, because it was incapable of seeing the inner relationships between things. This official ruling-class philosophy was necessary in order to explain why slave society was the highest good, and it reigned supreme over other schools of thought which made the first attempts to expose and understand the dialectical processes in the world.

Separation between things, and a perspective built on isolation were needed in order to consecrate complete domination over the slave, over the human being whether man or woman. Everything had to undergo division. The human being was divided into body and mind (or spirit) and then raised to a higher, superior level far above the body, far above the flesh. Flesh was the seat of instinctual animal behaviour, flesh was the slave and the woman, both creatures without mind. Flesh later became Africa, whose flesh was sold into slavery. The white colonizer was supreme, was the mind. Black Africa was the strength to be used, the emotions, the instincts, the primitive which functions without mind. By profession, I am originally a medical doctor, and have worked in both rural and urban areas. By inclination from the early days of my youth I have been a writer. As the years went by, my activities as a medical doctor dropped into the background, my creative work as a writer came to the fore. But I have never felt any contradiction between artistic writing and medicine, between science and art, between mind and emotion. Each one of them feeds the other, is a part of the other, is knowledge, is energy, is creation in a different form.

In the culture of the West, very often the seat of art is considered to be in the emotions, whereas the source of science is sought for in the mind. It is as if we are being told that artistic writing or creation is an irrational activity which takes place outside the mind, a form of mental disorder, an emotional disturbance or a neurosis, or madness.

At the very early stages of history before the period of slavery, this dichotomy, this division of the body into flesh and soul (mind) and of knowledge into science and art was not known. With the advent of classes, of slaves, came progress, but this progress was deformed. Inequality, oppression, exploitation could only deform the body and split it from its soul. Specialization, patriarchal class civilization and its scientific discoveries could advance towards vistas of new knowledge but only by abandoning the whole. To the degree that Western colonialism and neocolonialism accentuated class divisions and inequality, to the degree that they evolved more comprehensive and rapacious systems of exploitation, the split within the human being had to be deepened, the separation between fields of knowledge and creativity had to be accentuated, and the patriarchal division between 'superior' man and 'inferior' woman had to be consecrated. That is why history had to forget, or neglect, the earliest origins of civilization in Africa when people were still equal, when knowledge was one, and when women were making the first steps in discovering agriculture.[1]

This separation between body and mind, and between art and science, represents in fact two sides of the same coin. For such schools of thought the mind is the seat of rational thinking, that is, of knowledge and science. The body is the seat of feelings and emotions, that is, of art.

The colonialist, the white mind, is the mind of the world. Black Africa is the body, the primitive, the emotional, the realm of pure artistic expression. We know that rooted in the peoples of Africa (like all other people) is this innate capacity for artistic expression, this natural inclination to reorder things in a beautiful way, and we are proud of talent which reflects an essential creativity. But creativity in our view can only be manifested to the degree that there is a unity in the mind between rational, conscious thought and the emotions, the unconscious, in other words to the degree that the unconscious becomes conscious, and the mind and the body are one.

But separating artistic creation from rational scientific thought is not only a false representation of reality which prevents us from understanding the importance of consciousness and knowledge in the creative process, and therefore of the need to develop them, but it also leads to this very harmful dichotomy between artistic expression and science which is most dangerous for the future of African creativity in the area of literature. For although we have to build on what we have, a dependence on 'spontaneous', 'primitive' traditionalist forms of expression will prevent our literature from expressing a changing reality. This changing reality can only be understood by studying it, by increasing our body of knowledge about it, by marrying art with science. We African writers are therefore called upon simultaneously to be men and women of science, aware of the economic, social, political and cultural characteristics of our society and of the most salient scientific developments in the world. Only then will our novels, short stories, poems and other writings reflect the dynamic reality in our countries, make people aware of it, and therefore help to change and develop it for the better.

We must therefore overcome any arbitrary separation between science and art. And since colonialism and neocolonialism have deprived us of knowledge we are called upon to work all the harder in order to understand our societies, to acquire scientific knowledge and use it in our artistic expression. We are called upon to destroy any false notions of a dichotomy between mind and body, between rational thought and emotions, between science and art.

Socioeconomic dualism in developing African countries

When the capitalist classes of the Western world had exhausted the possibilities of national markets, they sought new possibilities for expansion and exploitation outside the confines of their own countries. Thus was inaugurated the colonial era. In order to make full use of the possibilities available for exploitation, the newly colonized societies had to undergo a process of restructuring This resulted in the development of what is commonly known as a *dual economy*. The word 'dual' arises from the fact that such societies were split into two interrelated and mutually dependent sectors. First, there was a modern sector in the cities built on some industrialization, all geared to the needs of the colonizing countries. Here transport and social services were established, sources of energy were developed, and new educational and cultural systems were introduced in order to mould the urban populations and elites necessary to run the various areas of economic, political, social and cultural activity. Second, there was a traditional sector mainly dependent on agriculture, with mining enclaves (usually isolated from the urban areas) standing midway between the two sectors. The urban populations in the cities, swollen by a continuous movement of migration from the rural areas, were exposed to various degrees of modernization and the top levels were indoctrinated economically, politically and culturally so that they could serve as internal supports and instruments to the colonial system. The rural populations were exposed to only very limited changes; old ways of life and values were largely preserved, and illiteracy was maintained. The feudal landlords, tribal chiefs and, later, rich peasants served as a social support and constituted the leading elites required to implement the policies of the colonial powers in rural areas.

An administrative apparatus was created in the cities and later developed whatever ramifications became necessary to run the traditional agriculture sector of the economy and the mining enclave.

Later, when the old colonial system was replaced by a new colonial system based on the individual rule of giant multinationals, the relations between the 'peripheral', now formally 'independent' but in fact dependent countries, and the 'centre' or metropolis underwent further changes in the same direction. Urban middle-class elites were expanded and strengthened. New efforts were made to bind them economically and culturally to the new colonial system headed by the USA, and some of the values and characteristics of Western consumer societies were exported to the modern sector. Limited reforms were implemented in order to liberalize the economic system and permit more flexible monetary and commercial arrangements. Agrarian relations were also modified in order partially to break down feudal rigidity and permit capitalist development of agriculture.

I have rapidly sketched a picture of this dual economic system because of its impact on culture and therefore the question of creativity in African literature. A dual economy was necessarily accompanied by a dual culture. Amongst urban elites this culture was modern and moulded on Western patterns. In rural areas the culture, despite certain changes, remained largely traditional. The dichotomy in culture, as we shall see, still continues to have far-reaching effects on developments in

African literature. Of course, even in the modern sector the colonial and neocolonial powers made sure only to encourage a modernization that served their needs, and that therefore remained limited in both content and forms. In other words, just as was the case in the economic and political fields, cultural modernization was exploitative in nature, elitist and deformed. It was aimed at achieving a form of acculturation, an alienation from society, and at transforming the urban elites, intellectuals and educated strata into willing or unwilling instruments of colonial and later neocolonial exploitation. This inevitably had important effects on the development of creativity and African literature.

Imitation and originality

One of the important obstacles facing African writers is the direct influence of modern Western culture on the life of our continent. This influence exercises itself in three ways. First, by creating a bias for liberal political structures, it holds up the process of true democratization in African societies, since we need to discover and invent our own forms of democratic functioning and our own democratic institutions, in order to ensure the widest popular participation, and thus to mobilize and free the creative energies of the masses of our people. Every human being is artistic and creative by nature. Creativity is a universal human gift and not a distinction confined to any specific group of people or individuals. Second, the influence of modern Western culture has established systems of learning and education which, in the absence of true development, encourage *imitation* and dependent thinking, lead to rigidity, and stifle creative processes. Third, it has developed *language barriers* since many of the elites have been brought up to use foreign languages; this tends to cut them off from the mass of the people and to bind them culturally to the foreign oppressor.

The problems of learning by rote and of imitating Western culture are two of the factors that exercise a negative influence on creativity and the development of an authentic African literature. The educational system in our schools is built almost completely on memorization, unchanging or very slowly changing texts, passive assimilation, and *intellectual obedience*. This tends to be reinforced by the innate rigidity of traditional culture in a rapidly changing world, an archaic and retrograde value system. The colonizers aimed at creating a limited number of skills and at reinforcing mental attitudes and modes of thinking that would help to maintain foreign domination and its ally, internal oppression. What we need is an educational system that is not only adapted to solving the specific problems of our societies but is also built on developing the capacity for *critical appraisal* and free examination of options. Taboos on thought still hold sway, especially in the three areas of politics (class and national struggle), religion and sex. To remould the educational system is a complex task especially where problems of language diversity, absence of written languages, and foreign-language dominance exist. Nevertheless, this remoulding of the educational system, which can only be carried out by Africans, is indispensable.

In the area of African literature especially, where intellectual elites are linked culturally and linguistically to foreign influences, the problem of imitation still exists. This is in some ways rational and is reinforced by the fact that some literary forms are Western in origin (the novel for example). Nevertheless, an increasing number of writers exist who are trying to break away and blaze their own, African path to creativity. One of the major obstacles in this quest for originality is the problem of those who write in a foreign language, or in a language that is not read by wide sectors of the population. The problem of widespread illiteracy and backwardness also tends to weaken the links between those who write and their audience, and therefore strengthens elitist tendencies, or attempts to obtain recognition abroad.

Yet in some ways those who are masters of a foreign language can be considered to be in an advantageous position. They have access to vast reservoirs of culture, knowledge and science, and this can help considerably to enrich their writings and to develop their style. They can also be of great value to the cultural, intellectual and literary movements in their own countries, by communicating to others what they themselves have learned, by setting up institutions for translation and for the simplification of knowledge. The majority of African intellectuals and writers have done their studies in a foreign language and many of them write in languages other than their mother tongue.

However a new cultural awareness is leading an increasing number of African writers to free themselves from cultural subjugation, whether in content or in form or in the language they use. Since each historical period creates its own needs, and its own responses in the area of literary writing, the struggles against colonialism, against neocolonialism, and for national independence inspired writers in Africa to develop a national identity and to see their roots in a national cultural heritage. The anti-colonial struggle helped them to attain a new stage of consciousness, a new understanding of the past and the present, more capable of examining our societies in a critical light and of Africanizing the novel in its content and in its forms.

A good example is the Senegalese writer Sembene Ousmane, who although influenced by the school of social realism has nevertheless been able to infuse in his works a content and a form that are typically African and Senegalese.[2] The Nigerian writer Amos Tutuola, despite the fact that he is influenced by Western forms of expression, has made an interesting and refreshing use of popular tales and myths which constitute an integral part of oral Nigerian culture.[3] Wole Soyinka also is experimenting with different forms and attempting to marry Western and Nigerian ways of writing.[4] An important aspect of this experimentation is his Africanization of English language forms by a process of adaptation and simplification. He has also developed a creative fusion between the past (that is, history) and the present as it is lived.

African writers are also abandoning the use of Western forms and Western languages to write in their mother tongues. We may cite as examples Ngugi Wa Thiong'o of Kenya, Chinua Achebe of Nigeria, Faraax Cawl of Somalia and Tutuola. In North Africa (Tunisia, Algeria and Morocco) most writers are now beginning to express themselves in Arabic. Ten years ago to be cultured, to be a writer, meant that one published in French. Taher Al-Wattar's novels are in Arabic and therefore making their way in Algeria and in all Arab countries. Rachid Boujidia, who used to write in French, has started to write in Arabic,[5] but others still write in French. Their audience is therefore restricted, but they tend to be better known in Europe and the USA. One of the problems of this divided, dual situation is that some writers who express themselves in their mother tongues have not had the same cultural opportunities, nor do they have the same sophisticated audience, as those who have lived, reacted with, and used a foreign language. In addition they face new problems of artistic creation, they need to strike out over hitherto unexplored paths. An element of simplification, sometimes of superficiality, is inevitable in certain of their works. The 'artistic' level may compare unfavourably with their more versatile compatriots. But the future lies with them. It is not a question of accepting *any* work written in the national or mother tongue without critical appraisal, nor is it a matter of preference for the political over the literary, but we need to adopt an attitude of encouragement to this new national current in literature and art which holds within it untold possibilities for creative thought in Africa. We can already see an early unfolding of these possibilities in the experimentation with new literary forms, new ways of adapting and using language, and new themes that is being developed. The role of literary critics and criticism in this area is important since they can help us to be more aware of the creative processes taking place, to understand them better, and to develop their potential to the utmost. The cooperation and cross-fertilization between those who write in English and French and those who write in national or local languages can help to produce works of an increasingly high standard, combining the advantages of both currents; it can overcome their difficulties, and it can enrich African creativity.

Illiteracy and cultural 'underdevelopment'

The internal division of 'dependent' countries into a modern sector and a traditional sector has led to a cultural dualism. I have described some of its manifestations already. One of the salient characteristics of the traditional sector which encompasses the vast majority of our peoples, especially those living in agricultural and nomadic areas, is the prevalence of illiteracy. Most men and women in the countries of Africa do not know how to read or write. In Egypt, considered a relatively developed African country, the illiteracy rate is 70 per cent. It rises to around 85 per cent among women. The writer is thus faced with the fact that he or she can only address a minority of people, and very often a small minority, since those who read literary works are of necessity very limited in number, not only for cultural reasons but also because of the price of books and the limited economic means at their disposal. A writer must therefore ask himself or herself some pertinent questions. For whom am I writing? And who is going to read my books? Am I writing only for those who can be considered as relatively cultured, as belonging to an elite? Or am I trying to reach those who can read and write but as yet have not had much access to culture? For there are sectors of the population that can be reached by a more simple and direct literature which requires less sophistication and effort to understand, and which must have recourse to the colloquial languages, native tongues, and popular means of expression.

An increasing number of new-generation writers and poets are creating new forms of popular literature that address themselves directly to the less privileged urban and rural masses possessing some elements of education and culture. Very often this tendency to popularize and simplify is the subject of controversy between its proponents and those who wish to keep up with the world movement seeking more novel ways of expressing the creative endeavour, and pioneering to wider horizons that are accessible only to a select public of readers. These are real issues which we all witness in the literary movements of African countries, North, South, East or West. I do not know if we can agree on the position that is gaining strength in my own country: namely, that writing for the less privileged sectors of society is in itself a creative endeavour, since it seeks to discover the unknown, or the obscure, and to arrive at a new literature. Where we are dealing with little-known areas it is understandable that early endeavours in so complex a field as literary creation should not only meet with difficulties but also often lack that wonderful combination of simplicity, realism, poetic vision, and authenticity that is the mark of true art. On the other hand, pioneering experimentation aimed at exploring new and complex horizons – art that may be accessible not for the millions but only for the few – is also required. For it is thus that the human mind progresses and maintains its everlasting quest for truth, its constant endeavour to strike out for the new. We will always need to establish and maintain a laboratory for the future.

If I may draw a parallel, we are dealing here with an issue similar to those that have arisen in other areas such as that of appropriate technology. And here again our answer has been the same. If we wish to become really independent, to forge ahead into the future, we need simple, appropriate technology geared to available manpower resources. But at the same time, in certain areas such as big and heavy industries, we require modern, sophisticated technology, just as we should combine the basic and the applied sciences. Without these combinations in science, in technology and in art, we will never develop in the different areas. We will always be looking through one eye, standing on one foot, faltering, stumbling, groping along on the way. The task of all writers who believe in the future of Africa is to exchange experiences, to cooperate, to learn from one another, to create the necessary links between the two kinds of literature, rather than to eliminate one of the poles of a dialectical and enriching process.

Sexual dualism and African literature

In all African countries, class and patriarchal relations predominate to varying degrees, since even in the countries that have chosen a socialist path the liquidation of class and patriarchal relations is still in its early stages. Under the patriarchal class system, women and children are part of a man's property and he rules over them. Women are subjugated to men and sometimes to the tribe, although varying degrees of matriarchal relations, especially in West Africa, have permitted women to enjoy a better status than many of their counterparts in North America and Europe. For example, the women of Togo, Ghana, Nigeria and the Cameroons engage in various economic activities, especially trade, and have more *de facto* economic and social rights than women in other areas. In the cultural heritage, African women are often depicted in positions of strength, and often play decisive roles in directing the affairs of life. Any attempt to reappraise the history of our continent should take such positive elements into consideration, and build on them in order to create a society in which all inequality or oppression is abolished, including discrimination on the basis of sex. The new relations that can be built up between men and women in the process, the very special contribution that women's thoughts and efforts can make, will certainly bring a new richness to the creative endeavour. Literary production, which is characterized, or should be characterized, by a special sensitivity to the 'human' aspects of life, would be much enriched by a profound and progressive examination of the mutual relations between men and women, their conflicts and their common endeavour to build a better life.

Women in general, and creative women in particular, have been kept in a marginal position, have been isolated from the main stream of life due to the undemocratic nature of our societies, which is maintained by both foreign and national privileged minorities. Women are called upon to bear the double burden of work in the field or the factory, and work at home caring for men and children. The gradual emancipation of women as equal partners in life is an integral part of the democratization process, an integral part of the mobilization of popular forces for independence and reconstruction, an integral part of the struggle for freedom, and therefore an integral part of a new humanity and a new creativity in all areas and in all forms. Freedom is indivisible and cannot use its wings to the full if part of its body is chained. The mind too is indivisible. It cannot fully use its creative potential if there are dark areas maintained by prejudice, ignorance, rigid partitions or fetters of any kind. And the development of the mind, like the development of a country, is a total process in which there is no room for division on the basis of sex.

Emancipation of women does not in any way mean hatred of men. We do not reply to sexism with sexism in return. If it has taken this turn in some countries, we Africans can understand why, but for us the movement for women's liberation is an integral part of the movement for national, political and economic liberation, a common struggle and a common future in which men and women must share the efforts and the fruits of liberation. Creative literature has much to gain from the potential of women, their untrapped human resources, their vision of things. Creative African literature will reflect more and more this struggle against division through sex, and will open the doors wider and wider to the participation of women writers in the literature of their countries.

Racial discrimination

Just as the movement for liberation of women does not mean hatred of men, so the movement for liberation does not mean hatred of the white man. Western colonialism and neocolonialism were built on discrimination on the basis of race, colour, creed, sex and class, that is, on the division of humanity. The basis of the movement for national liberation, however, both in its political and cultural aspects right from the beginning, has always been to fight and overcome all forms of racism, even if in specific situations and at certain times, but always to a limited extent, the movement has fallen victim to racist tendencies. What is commonly known as the Négritude current in literary creation, of which Senghor was one of the founders, is an example. For this school is an attempt to divide literature and art on the basis of colour, just as colonialism divided the human race on the basis of colour, and Africa on the basis of 'Black' or 'sub-Saharan' Africa and 'white' North Africa.

As a result of cultural backwardness and a tendency to reply to racism with a racism in return, such currents of intellectual thought can achieve a certain amount of credibility in our countries. This is a falsification – a deformation – of national consciousness,[6] which all our countries have experienced to some extent and which has been portrayed at certain periods as a progressive tendency since it is directed against the white colonizer. For it is sometimes thought that a black man from Africa, a black political leader or a black writer is necessarily on the side of his people against foreign exploitation. However, as the years have gone by we have learned to discriminate between the colour of men's and women's skins and the colour of their hearts and minds, and to understand the role of class and social interests in determining on which side they stand. Neocolonialism has taught us the lesson thoroughly. For neocolonialism depends on privileged minorities to enable it to exploit and rule indirectly, and on false consciousness to enable it to control people's minds.

False consciousness

One of the major problems that faces democracy and stands in the way of literary creativity in African countries is the process known as 'developing a false consciousness'. Men and women, whether as individuals or as collective communities and classes, are subjected to this process systematically throughout life by being exposed to different forms of indoctrination and brainwashing through the educational system and the mass media. The modern information system built up by the multinationals on the basis of the most advanced technology has become a very dangerous and potent weapon in the battle for people's minds. In order to maintain and accentuate economic exploitation of the 'peripheral' so-called Third World countries, the new colonialists have carried out a process of 'internalization' built on the remoulding of their internal structures economically, socially and politically to serve the interests of the centre. In order to ensure continuity of this 'internalization', it has been necessary to cement it with what we now call a 'cultural imperialism'. A dual cultural structure now prevails. On the one hand there is the modern cultural sector, largely urban, with its upper elitist levels, and on the other hand there is the traditional cultural sector, englobing the vast majority in the African countries.

In order to render the system more effective, the 'internalization' process must be carried deep down into the individual, into his mind and soul, into his psychology, into his awareness – hence the need to create a 'false consciousness' which weaves its own chains round the mind. In one of his songs, the Jamaican singer Jimmy Cliff repeats this refrain:

Take the chains off my body.
Put the chains on my mind.

Cultural imperialism is one of the most dangerous phenomena faced by the peoples of Africa and of the Third World in general. For in the process of developing a 'false consciousness', new chains are added to those that encircle the mind, and change men and women into their own unwitting jailers. It is a new form of subjugation, with resilient steel fetters that we do not see winding themselves around our thoughts and emotions, that we do not feel settling on our bodies. The result is that we do not rebel against them. For how can you rebel against what you cannot see with your eyes, or feel with your senses, or understand with your mind? Cultural imperialism is a deadly poison. It is a mental, spiritual, psychological subjugation. It is the illusion that makes the oppressed and exploited individual think that he is free. It is the process of socialization and acculturation that makes the slave welcome his own slavery and that made woman accept her inequality as natural and beneficial to her life and to society, and led her to seek fulfilment only in motherhood, marriage and the exercise of her feminine sexual and domestic roles.

This cultural onslaught is directed in particular to the elites, since they are the leaders and the decision makers in the different areas of political, economic, social and cultural life. It is directed with redoubled energy against writers and artists. For writers and artists play a primordial role in moulding the minds of others. And they are the conscience, the critical eye, the harbingers of change, the first to rebel against oppression of any kind, for they know that tyranny, lack of freedom, is the worst enemy of creativity. Nevertheless, the cultural onslaught extends beyond the confines of elitist society to the masses in urban and rural areas. These masses are an easy prey to acculturation campaigns through television and especially radio. The transistor, symbol of progress, is at the same time the minute and deadly enemy of the peoples of the world. For technology in the hands of the multinationals is an instrument to oppress the body and the mind.

Where the educational system is concerned, specialization, the division between branches of knowledge, between science and art, deprives the educated sectors of society of their opportunity to achieve true knowledge. It stunts and deforms the human mind by developing certain areas at the expense of others and by preventing the harmonious use of all its potentials and faculties. Whether in the First or the Third World, peoples are victims of an acculturation built on hiding or deforming the truth, and on patriarchy, class, racism and sexual discrimination.

The problem of the elite in literature

I have dealt above with issues related to the literary elites in 'dependent' countries in relation to language, forms and content of literary creation, acculturation and other areas. As we have seen, they do not constitute a homogeneous body but one divided amongst themselves in consequence of a variety of factors.

Part of the elite has assimilated Western culture and is impregnated with the concepts and values of political liberalism to the extent that it has become isolated from the people in its modes of living, its thought, and its language. Members of this group sometimes know more about Paris, London and New York than they know about their own country. Another group has been influenced by Marxism but often in a dogmatic way that depends on imitating patterns of thought, on seeking ready-made formulas not related to the African context. Some African socialist elites in the literary field have been able to avoid falling into this trap however, especially those who have had an opportunity to become more closely linked to the daily lives of their people. A third group is seeking its own 'African' path to development, to democracy and true independence. I myself, being a socialist, believe that the future of our continent lies in socialism, but I also feel that at least in my country some of the socialists know more about what is written in books than they do about the real life and problems of people in rural and urban areas.

The difficulties faced by African elites have been depicted in many of the works written by Africans. To mention only a few, we have the novel *Mission to Kala* by the Cameroonian writer Mongo Beti.[7] He draws a vivid picture of members of the elite educated in French in their own countries or abroad who, either consciously or unconsciously, became servile reflections of Western civilization in all areas of life. When the movement for national liberation grew in strength they mounted its wave and became ardent defenders of everything that was African and black, while still maintaining a completely alien mode of life. Yahya Haqqi, the Egyptian novelist now over seventy years old, dealt with the same theme in one of his earliest books, *Qandil Um Hashim* (The Oil Wick of Om Hashem). The Sudanese Tayeb Saleh is known mainly for his novel *Mawsim al-Hijra ilal Shamal*.[8] This novel deals with the shock between two civilizations through the life of the central character, Mustapha Sa'eed, and the crises to which he is exposed. Other authors have dealt with the difficulties faced by socialist thought and socialist intellectuals of middle-class origin in our countries. I have two writers in mind here, both Egyptian: Naguib Mahfouz, a well-known contemporary novelist, in his trilogy *Bein El-Kasren, El-Soukaria*, and *Zokak El-Medak*) published in the early sixties, and Sherif Hetata's *El-Shabaka* (The Network), published in October 1982, which is drawing wide attention to this new author, who started writing at the age of forty-six.[9]

Personal observations of the lives of writers in Egypt and to a certain extent in other parts of Africa (and the Third World in general) have led me to the conclusion that although a reasonable standard of life combined with modern functional amenities is conducive to literary creation, a writer should be careful not to aim too high, not to ex-aggerate his or her needs, lest he or she be cornered into making concessions, for creativity requires courage – physical courage *and* moral courage. It is a quest for truth, a quest for the new, a struggle for change. Compromise, fear, and too strong an attachment to material needs are liable to cloud a writer's vision.

Democracy and creativity

Although socioeconomic structures in Third and First World countries have much in common, at the same time they have many differences. Problems of democracy are a reflection of this situation, and it is not surprising, therefore, if they present both similarities and differences between the two worlds.

In the face of increasing onslaughts and resistance from the national liberation movement, the neocolonial system – aided by supporting elites within the dependent countries – often has recourse to military dictatorship, which liquidates all vestiges of democratic freedom and imposes brutal tyrannical rule, making the creative endeavours of writers extremely difficult. Nevertheless, where cultural and literary activities are concerned there is often more latitude for action and resistance than in the political fields; enlightened elites should be aware of this fact and take advantage of it to the utmost.

As a result of the maintenance of traditional structures and the prevalence of relatively backward modes of production mainly related to agriculture and small-scale production, it is the case that tolerance, personal mobility and freedom of expression tend to be much more limited than in the West. In the advanced capitalist countries the political and social system permits a greater degree of liberation in areas of individual expression and freedom, because of the strength and resilience of the socioeconomic system as a whole. The ruling classes in the advanced industrial nations have less to fear from the exercise of personal, individual freedom which can serve as a compensatory mechanism for easing tensions, and is necessary for higher productivity and greater creativity in the areas of scientific, technical and productive endeavour. It is the social and political collective freedom of action that tends to be the area of restriction, because of its impact on the system as a whole.

This is not the case in Third World countries, where personal freedoms, and freedom of expression, are bound in a thousand chains, resulting from the lack of mobility that is imposed by tradition, religion, archaic feudal systems, and outdated values. Added to this is the fact that the multinationals and their allies are faced with social and political instability resulting mainly from the extremely low economic standards of living, the result of low productivity and intense exploitation, so that even the smallest degree of democracy and political liberty represents a danger – whence the frequent recourse to military dictatorship and ferocious repression.

Freedom and creativity are indissolubly linked. For the uncovering of new relationships and the invention of new paths are not possible unless the mind is allowed to venture beyond the limits of what is already established; moreover, if these limits are very narrow, it is not difficult to realize the cramping effect of such a situation on creative endeavour. In 'dependent' countries, the lack of freedom tends to affect all areas, whether personal or general. Politics (class struggle), sex and religion are considered taboo subjects to varying degrees in our countries. It is difficult to imagine how literary writings can be creative if the essential areas of life, if the relations of the individual to the totality of existence (religion), to the social system (politics) and to his or her own body (sex) are out of bounds.

Some writers are believers in the liberal freedoms of the West. Others believe that such liberal freedoms are inadequate and inappropriate to the reality of 'dependent' countries and should be discarded, since people are ignorant and easily cheated, or poor and easily bought. When the time for elections comes along, they see parliamentary institutions as instruments for the domination and the enriching of privileged classes or groups in society. To them, freedom of speech is a luxury.[10] Similar views are sometimes voiced by the social proponents of economic and social democracy who often forget the need for political liberty and individual freedom.

However, a harmonious progression on all fronts combining economic and social democracy with political liberty, with the widest popular participation in decision making and in execution, and with personal freedom, is the only way to release the creative abilities of the people as a whole, and of writers in particular. Freedom of thought and speech in our countries are essential if we are to replace false consciousness and traditional consciousness by a real awareness of our problems, and of how to solve them. Creative writers must be both the proponents and the beneficiaries of political and personal freedom.

Restrictions on thought: censorship

True consciousness is a dire threat to the ruling strata in our countries and to the foreign interests that support them. This explains the strong antagonism with which African writers and creative artists are met. For the creative writer is an engineer of new thought, a dynamic force that destroys all that needs to be replaced and changed, whether they be gods, rulers, systems or values. The Nigerian writer Wole Soyinka says that the artist creates new gods and dethrones old ones.[11] Rollo May believes that the creative writer creates the uncreated conscious (the unconscious), or expresses the collective unconscious.[12] Herein lies the efficacy and danger of creative writing. It transforms the potential awareness in the minds of the oppressed masses of peoples into actual awareness. The awareness of oppression is the first step towards rebellion against it. This is the secret of the secret and open war that reactionary forces have declared against creative African writers. This is the secret of the secret censorship exercised by police raids in the dark of night, where books are confiscated from homes or from the press, or by the banning of writers from television, radio, cinema and publishing activities, through written or oral instructions issued by authorities. Sometimes writers are thrown out of work, suffer hunger, are pursued, persecuted, exiled, imprisoned, or even killed.

Prison literature in Africa

Many creative women and men writers in Africa have decided to fight back against oppression in defence of their right to express their ideas and thoughts with freedom. All over Africa such battles go on.

In June 1982 I met the East African writer Ngugi during a seminar organized in Dakar, Senegal. He had just been released from jail in Kenya, and I from jail in Egypt. We talked, and I learned that he had written a prison diary on toilet paper during his detention, just as I had inscribed diary notes on toilet paper in the women's prison of Al-Kanatu. I used to hide my pen and toilet paper notes in a hole in the ground that I had carefully camouflaged. My cell was searched regularly by inspection groups headed by the commandant of the prison. He was wont to say, 'If I find a gun, for me this is less serious than finding pen and paper.' Writing materials were permitted in the sections of the prison that lodged prostitutes, drug traffickers and thieves, but not in the part where the political prisoners were kept. For where tyranny reigns, the tyrants know that the activity of the human mind is extremely dangerous, that pen and paper are a thousand times more threatening to their system than a bullet fired from a gun. When a tyrant dies he can be replaced. When an idea survives it can move a nation.[13] When Ngugi and I talked more, I realized that prisons are all the same, that the tragedy of all creative writers in our countries is the same, and that the new tyranny, the new colonialism in Africa, is more interested in imprisoning our minds and stifling our capacity for original thinking than in chaining our bodies.

> Fear not those who kill the flesh, but fear those who kill the spirit. They cannot kill my spirit even if they kill me as they have killed others. They will not kill the determination of this country to remain free.[14]

Mahmoud Darwish, the Palestinian poet, describes the fate of Palestinian prisoners in an Israeli jail in occupied Palestine in his poem 'The Music of Human Flesh':

> You with bloodshot eyes and bloody hands
> Night is short-lived.

The detention room lasts not forever
Nor yet the links of chains.

Prison literature is one of the distinctive areas of creative writing in all African countries, and reflects the oppression exercised against thought. Prison, in fact, for hundreds of years has remained a part of our daily lives. But now this is more so than ever. It has become one of the heroes of contemporary novels written by authors from different generations.

In Egypt, a number of creative writers and artists have been imprisoned under the successive regimes of King Farouk, Nasser and Sadat, and have reflected their prison experience in writings of genuine artistic value. These writings have taken the form of novels, short stories, poetry, plays and diaries. I quote this passage from Hetata's novel:

> His body could no longer feel the lashes of the whip, the kicking feet, the rain of blows that fell from every direction. The jaws clenched, the lips closed and sealed his mouth, welded the opening so that he could no longer open them to speak. The cells lost their sense of pain, as though his body were disintegrating, melting away, except for a small amorphous circular spot hidden somewhere in the depths, like a star in the night, pulsating, breathing, watching ...[15]

Fear and exile

Writers who have not ended up in jail are very often haunted by fear or by the spectre of prison walls looming over the horizon, even if they have never engaged in political activity and never wielded anything but a pen.

People in our countries are nurtured on fear. They feed on it the moment they are born. Fear of the Father, the Ruler, of God, are all combined. From a very early age, children are taught to fear punishment or Hell, or the father's displeasure, which can end in their being thrown out of the home. Women fear divorce, fear to be left alone without shelter, or a future, or security of any kind. Students fear their professors' whims and are taught to cringe lest they be failed, or given bad marks or refused access to higher studies. Writers are afraid of being dismissed from their jobs, for in developing countries the establishment rules with a heavy hand over all areas of intellectual and artistic creation. Obedience is considered the highest of virtues everywhere, in the family, at school, in religion, morals, administrative systems, and political institutions.

As a result, some writers fall victim to the unpardonable mistake of indulging in hypocrisies which over time can only transform the creative writer into a bureaucratic functionary waiting impatiently for the death of the ruler or a change of system to criticize what now belongs to the past and sing the praises of the new king. They run away from expressing their opposition to those who are in power as long as they are still living. They take refuge in silences or in self-exile, block the wells of their own creativity. For with prolonged silence, or prolonged exile, the emotional and intellectual sources of creation tend to dry up.

For the basic power of creative work is the ability to penetrate the minds and hearts of people. This can only be realized when the writer lives the life of his or her people and shares their sorrows, their conflicts, struggles and aspirations.

Individual and collective action

The integrity of the individual writer, his or her own mettle, inner strength and firm belief in what he or she is doing, his or her readiness to work hard, to observe and to learn, his or her human sensibility to others, can shield him or her against many a pitfall. But the struggle against the forces of neocolonialism and local reaction is a long and difficult one. Mutual support and collective action are therefore essential to preserve the creative forces and artistic talents that exist, to develop them by an exchange of experience and ideas, to add to them by discovering new elements everywhere.

The united forces of retrograde thought and imperialist acculturation can only be faced by means of unity between the forces of national, democratic and progressive thought. Creative writers, artists, and intellectuals should therefore organize their associations, clubs, and unions everywhere on a local, national, regional, pan-African, and international basis, in order to take unified action wherever required, nurture new talents, find new ways and means of expression, support one another in the face of oppression, and carry out a continuous and fruitful exchange.

This need for unity and organized strength poses the question of the relationships between creative writers in African countries and progressive or socialist parties. Creativity is often stifled by an attempt to regiment or limit it within a given framework, and there is always a need for independent thinking which can be an asset to the political parties themselves.

Political parties in Africa suffer from many weaknesses for reasons that it would take too long to discuss here. They are rarely capable of understanding the special problems of creative writers, and lack the horizons and flexibility required to deal with them. Yet the need for organized collective resistance cannot be denied. This is a problem that faces most if not all creative writers in Africa, and there is no one answer for it. We need more effort to evolve mature and fruitful relations between writers on the one hand and political parties on the other. Meanwhile, the question of adherence or nonadherence to political parties still continues to evoke much discussion and to be a purely personal decision. Fundamentally, however, the power of creative writing lies in its ability to implant seeds of revolution in the hearts of oppressed men and women. Revolution is the natural result of creative work, and freedom is the daughter of the revolution. Revolution and freedom, together, constitute the form and content of any creative work.

[Written in Cairo, 1983, and translated from the Arabic by Sherif Hetata]

Notes

1. One of the main goddesses of the ancient Egyptians was Isis, whose name means 'Knowledge'. This symbolizes the fact that the ancient Egyptians were convinced that women had a creative mind. But with time the patriarchal class system became firmly established. Woman became Eve: the body, without mind, the flesh with a weak mind.
2. See Sembene Ousmane, *Le Docker noir*, Présence Africaine, Paris, 1973; also *God's Bits of Wood* (Les Bouts de bois de Dieu), translated by Francis Price, Doubleday, New York, 1970; *The Money Order with White Genesis* (Le Mandat et Vehi Crosanne ou blanche genèse), translated by Clive Wake, Heinemann, London, 1972; and *Xala*, Présence Africaine, Paris, 1973.
3. Amos Tutuola, *The Brave African Huntress*, Grove Press, New York, 1970; and *My Life into the Bush of Ghosts*, Grove Press, New York, 1953.
4. See, for example, Wole Soyinka, *The Interpreters*, Collier Books, New York, 1971; *Myth, Literature and the African World*, Cambridge University Press, 1976; *Season of Anomy*, Rex Collings, London, 1973; and 'The Writer in an African State'. *Transition*, No. 31, June/July 1976.
5. Rachid Boujidia's last novel, *El Tafakok*, was published in Arabic, and was then translated into French under the title *Le Démantèlement*.
6. See Franz Fanon, *The Wretched of the Earth*, translated by Constance Farrington, Grove Press, New York, 1968.
7. Mongo Beti, *Mission to Kala*, translated by Peter Green, Collier Books, New York, 1971.
8. Tayeb Saleh, *Mawsim al-Hijra ilal-Shamal* is translated from the Arabic and published under the Arab and African Authors series by Heinemann, London, 1969, under the title *Season of Migration to the North*.
9. Sherif Hetata, *El-Shabaka*, is published in Cairo by the Arab Centre for Research and Publishing (El Markaz El Arabi Lilbahth Wa el Nashr), 1982, and in Beirut by El Mouassasah El Arabia Lil Dirushat wal el Nashr, 1982.

10. T. M. Aluk, a Nigerian writer, states in his book *One Man, One Match* (Heinemann, London, 1964, p. 150), that freedom of speech is an unnecessary luxury in a poor and backward country, in a country where the masses are illiterate, ignorant, and believe anything that anyone who can read and write tells them.

11. Wole Soyinka, *Myth, Literature and the African World*, Cambridge University Press, Cambridge, 1976, p. 86.

12. Rollo May, *The Courage to Create*, Norton, New York, 1975.

13. After my release from prison in 1981 I wrote a play dealing with this theme. It is called *Twelve Women in a Prison Cell*. The national theatre authorities refused to have it produced, and the national book authorities refused to have it published. The war in Lebanon had made it difficult for me to publish in Beirut, as I had before.

14. Ngugi Wa Thiong'o, *Detained: A Writer's Prison Diary*, Heinemann, 1981 (extract from Waruru Kanja's speech in Kenya's parliament on 13 November 1980).

15. Sherif Hetata, *The Eye with an Iron Lid*, Onyx Press, London, 1982, p. 212 (originally written in Arabic in 1970).

CHAPTER 18

Creative Women in Changing Societies

I would like to begin by expressing the joy I feel in attending this first seminar on 'Creative Women in Changing Societies' organized by the United Nations Institute for Training and Research (UNITAR). This seminar is a unique event, original and innovative in its conception, quite different from the general run of seminars and conferences. Its theme, that of creativity and creative work among women, is closer to my heart, and reaches deeper down into my self than most, if not all of the seminars in which I have participated, for it is in artistic creation and expression, in creative action and thought, that I find my real self, and rediscover it when it is lost. It is in creativity that I am able to shake off the feeling of alienation which creeps over me whenever I am engaged in the routine tasks of everyday work, in the daily grind of some of the posts which I have occupied at different stages of my life, and which somehow seem as though they are destined to be stripped of all that is new or innovative in life.

What is creativity?

To my mind creativity is an innovative process which embraces all the arts and sciences. It includes the love, friendship and cooperation that people develop between one another in the common effort aimed at achieving a better life, and moulding better individuals. It is not confined to the intellectual activity or the mental production of the individual but in its essence encompasses the collective action of groups, classes and nations and the mobilization of the potential of all peoples to improve life, to develop societies materially, culturally and morally, and to ensure that peace reigns among all peoples. Since it is not possible to divide a human being into separate parts, the mind cannot be isolated from the body. Thus physical activity is an integral part of creative action. Dancing, which might appear to be pure physical movement, can at the same time be an elevated form of intellectual activity. The peasant man or woman using a hoe, or carrying a jar of water on the head, is involved in some form of creative action, since optimum use is being made of bodily force to achieve a given objective. The dividing line between craftsmanship, skill and creative action is not as sharply defined as many might think, although it exists within certain limits. I remember how the peasant women in my village, Kafr Tahla, carry heavy jars on their heads without the support of their hands, without dropping the jars or spilling any of their contents, no matter how often they turn their heads or tilt the jars at alarmingly acute angles. They have developed a *creative balance* built on sensory perception and body movements discovered through practice. I have seen fathers and mothers wresting a livelihood for themselves and their children, fighting against death, and winning the battle, by a creative adaptation of work needs, production techniques and the art of survival in difficult circumstances.

Human bodies, whether of men or of women, their minds and their emotions enfold a wide range of dazzling capabilities that reveal themselves through creative action, and also through the manifold activities carried on every day by people who are considered ordinary because these activities, which to us often appear mundane and repetitive, are the result, historically, at least, of a long creative effort. For many dominant schools of thought, the tendency has been to limit the creative and innovative process, and to see it only in some specific, restricted forms of action carried out by an oligarchy of men, a limited class group, elevated by the patriarchal class system to the level of gods, upon whom are bestowed privileges and titles and who are referred to as geniuses, artists, exceptional talents, creators, extraordinary people. The vast majority of men and women are condemned to the daily struggle for livelihood, to a humdrum existence built on routine and mechanical activity, they are thrown into the dark deep abyss of poverty, ignorance and disease, and thus are deprived of any real chance to develop or even to discover their mental, emotional or physical capabilities, to become conscious even of the eternal gift that all people possess, that of a spontaneous, inborn artistic creativity which is so evident in popular culture.

The human being is artistic and creative by nature. He or she is capable of finding solutions to new problems, and does it all the time. This is the essence of creativity, which is a universal human gift, and not a distinction confined to any specific group. He or she is engaged in a constant struggle to improve life and make it more beautiful. The folkloric songs, legends, dances, arts and crafts handed down through the ages indicate that the most beautiful artistic expression can be the work of thousands or even millions of ordinary men and women.

Whenever I have sat writing in my closed room, despite the four walls that hemmed me in and isolated me from other people, and despite the nature of the writing process, which is a purely individual form of action, I have always felt that I was deriving my thoughts, or drawing what we call inspiration, from the creative imaginations of the men, women and children among whom I had lived, or was still living. Even if I rebel against many of the traditions and customs that govern their lives they remain the rich and lasting source of inspiration for my thoughts and feelings. I have come to realize that my literary or scientific creativity can only develop and flourish if fed through the multiple network of relations and links that I have established over the years with the people of my city Cairo and my village Kafr Tahla. These links are also the support and the protection that have spared me the sorrow of loneliness and the alienation of excessive individualism. My desire to nurture my art and to preserve my individual identity, my pressing need to be alone, away from people, so that I can meditate and contemplate are accompanied by an equally pressing need to be in contact with people, not because I want to write about them, but because I must live with them and touch with my hands the fibre of their support.

Creativity, imagination and reality

The processes related to reflection, meditation and contemplation of the past enhance the sensitivity of the individual, like a tool refined and sharpened by practice, or a fine wire made taut by stretching its limits. Thus it is that he or she is brought step by step to a discovery of the new in the old, the particular in the general, the astounding in the ordinary, the contradictory in the harmonious, and the harmonious in the contradictory. The creative process can only unfold itself in conjunction with this process of contemplation and reflection, which permits the individual to live through reality once more, yet in a way that is different, which permits the individual to experience a reality that although real, is not the exact replica of the reality known before. In him or her is developed a new capability: that of being able to visualize reality, to see it and experience it in the imagination. For ideas, thoughts, and concepts are not born outside reality but within it, inspired by it, born of its matter, its energy, its dynamic forces. What grows out of the creative process is in fact reality, but it never is – and never should be – a mirror image, or a photographic copy. The creative process is more difficult than mere copying, more complex than an exercise in imagination. It is the capacity to restructure reality, to endow it with a different content and form, so that it appears as a new reality.

As the years passed, my own creative freedom expanded and developed to the degree that I became increasingly capable of grasping the details of reality, visualizing its multiple aspects, seeing its different faces, probing its varying depths in time and space, and thus capable also of depicting it in a more human or less pain-provoking manner. I also began to understand that the practice of artistic creation leads to the development of a new language and a new culture in the art of expressing reality, so that out of it is born, or can be born, a better and more beautiful reality. Then it was as though an inner voice was constantly whispering to me, telling me that my mind was capable of creating pictures other than those expressing the pain that is reality. My hand would reach for the pen and almost instinctively begin to trace the images and ideas that flooded my mind. At such moments, expression became as imperative and as necessary as breathing, and I existed only in order to convey my thoughts beyond myself to others.

In the early years of my life my outlook was idealistic and I believed in an absolute truth. Crossing over the stage of certainty to the stage of doubt I reached a more mature and human understanding of things in which it was no longer important whether an absolute perfection existed or not. Now what mattered was the constant striving to attain that which is more perfect, to move higher, to progress. What counted now was to be sincere, to be engaged in an unending creative effort directed to humanity and life, to move along a road which would never end with success or failure, with imprisonment or even death. A road that carries with it the agony that is an integral part of creative life, but also the exaltation and happiness that transcend all suffering.

What does creativity seek to attain?

I have never really known why I pick up my pen to write. Writing to me has been a response to the need for expression of my thoughts, which is vital to my life as a human being. I was not involved by the debate on whether art should be for art's sake or goal-oriented. In my opinion authentic art, built on a sincere quest for truth, serves the cause of art, and with it that of life and society. Creative work or action reflects an individual's opinions in life, and his or her attitude towards the system prevailing in society, in a spontaneous, almost unintentional manner, as though the creative process carries within itself the seeds and consequently the birth of these opinions and attitudes. It is as though a creative work is transformed from something to which life has been given, into something capable of giving birth to life, from something created into a creative force. Hence it becomes capable of evoking new ideas and feelings in the hearts and minds of others. And this is the aim of creativity or innovation. It leads to the development of new ideas and feelings which help people to attain a more complete understanding of themselves, of what constitutes the essence of the human being, of what is most powerful and noble and dynamic in human nature, so that their hopes and determination in the struggle for freedom and justice, their anger and rebellion against all forms of oppression and injustice, and their capacity to perceive the new ways in which beauty and love can manifest themselves are strengthened. Creative thought and action help people to become stronger, more confident, and richer internally, less prone to impose their authority, more given to treat others in a simple, gentle and helpful way.

But in all this the basic prerequisite that ensures the attainment of these goals remains a sincere quest for truth. For without this quest, creativity is transformed into an empty, sterile shell. Without truth, there is no creativity.

Society and truth

The patriarchal class system prevailing in our society is based on the dominance of the man in the family and on the dominance of the classes that possess wealth, and authority, in society. This system can only thrive and grow on the basis of many different forms of oppression and tyranny; these range from the denial of the freedom of the child to discover his own body organs, discrimination between boys and girls within the family, and racial discrimination, to exploitation, the old colonial and the new colonial order, multinational capitalist companies, and world imperialism. Under such an oppressive system, freedom, justice and truth become difficult to attain, and the path leading to them is fraught with dangers that can lead the individual even to madness or death. And yet there is no other path, no easy path that leads to the burial of a system based on oppression and tyranny.

The hazards and risks involved are even greater for women and for those who lack the weapons of money and authority. The whole patriarchal class system, with its sciences, its arts and its religions, has in fact been built on their sacrifices, their deprivation and suffering, their sweat and blood.

That is why women's physical, mental and psychological capacities so often deteriorate between childhood and the end of life. The woman who is able to break the grip of the all-powerful system that surrounds her inside and outside the home, on the street, on the factory floor and in the bedroom is indeed a rarity.

Men, if they belong to the class of landowners and rulers, still have the opportunity to safeguard and develop their creative abilities. Men of the poor class, who like women strive day and night to earn their living, only have limited or rare opportunities. A woman of the land-owning or ruling class may have a better opportunity to realize her creative intellectual abilities. But she still wavers between two considerations: first, her intellectual capacities, and second, the fact that she is female. This wavering is only natural since she has been taught since childhood, from the very first lesson in religion, that intellect is for the man – who is God's image on earth – and that Eve is only a desecrated and headless body.

Lucky is the woman who is able to learn how to read and write and is not fully taken up with a constant striving for her livelihood and with endless household work in the service of family, husband and children. She can at least give the time and effort necessary to become aware of the manifestations of oppression and tyranny. This fortunate woman represents a small minority in Arab countries and among the peoples of the Third World, where the vast majority of men, women and children are left crushed and breathless in the continuous struggle for life. Such a woman is capable of developing her creative abilities if she can overcome the sense of guilt and perversion arising from the fact that she is a woman with a mind capable of creativity just like she has a womb capable of childbearing.

The creative woman occasionally allows herself to step back and forget her true self, her reality; she practises what men practise, uses their weapons to compete with them, to achieve what they refer to as glory, fame, success, genius, and all the other dazzling terms that blind her eyes to her own reality and to her creative striving towards truth. If a creative woman slides down into this quagmire, she is assimilated by the patriarchal class system and becomes a part of it, she loses her identity, even though she may continue to work and produce. Her creative work declines steadily, even though her bank account and her fame might be mounting rapidly.

But she is sometimes saved from this state of futility by a distressing incident in her public or private life, or a tragedy that sets her on a collision course with the system within the home or in society. It is then that she realizes her fundamental, deep-seated rejection of its injustice and renews her struggle against it. Circumstances might drag her down to the company of the sick, the poor, the rejected, the prisoners, the divorcees or the prostitutes, thus allowing her to get acquainted with the ugly face of this system and to realize that she is not part of it. She begins to struggle to recover her self and her truthfulness, and recovers creative ability side by side with those whose life she is now partly sharing. Her creative work rings with the authenticity that comes with truth and has a greater impact on the minds and hearts of people.

The power of creative action

The basic power of creative action, in my opinion, is the ability to penetrate and influence the minds and hearts of people. This ability is only translated into creative action when the person involved really lives the life of the people, and shares their sorrows and aspirations. When she keeps in close contact with people and reality, a creative action makes the creative woman capable of recording the minutest details related to time, location, and the incidents and personalities constituting the essence of reality. This record may permit her to immortalize the fleeting moments involved in the rape of a girl, the beating of a prisoner, the death of a child from hunger: immortalize them because thousands and even millions of minds and hearts are gripped by such moments. They relive them through a narrative, a play or a film. The incident that was a part of the past, and might have died and been buried with it, is revived by creative action and resurrected to become a living part of the present, of the minds and hearts of people in different ages and places. It disturbs the placid waters of resignation, evoking new thoughts and feelings in people's minds and hearts. They seem to acquire new minds and hearts, are transformed into individuals with stronger character and a greater determination to rebel against oppression.

The power of creative action thus lies in its ability to implant the seeds of revolution in the minds and hearts of oppressed men, women and children. This revolution might not materialize in the form of a popular movement capable of changing the system within their age or lifetime, but at least the seeds will have been sown and as surely as the sun rises from the east, they will ultimately flourish. Revolution is the natural result of creative action and freedom is the daughter of the revolution. Revolution and freedom together constitute the form and content of any creative action.

The power of creative action protects the individual involved from the oppression of authority, strengthens her in the face of crises, and lifts her above personal ambitions, ideological struggles, and religious, sectarian, tribal and sexual prejudices. The creative women becomes identified with the people deprived of freedom and revolution in all ages and places. This universal identification with humanity is not that of a starry-eyed romanticist, neither does it stem from a head-in-the-clouds attitude. It is the capacity to lift your sights high, to scan universal horizons and yet to remain firmly anchored to a specific reality.

Originality and universalism are two sides of the coin of creativity, like objectivity and subjectivity. Subjectivity endows creativity with a genuine individual identity, with a special, local flavour, whereas objectivity provides the components for a true vision of the human experiment. Perhaps this explains my constant attachment to my country, land, people and Arabic language. No matter how far and wide I travel, I must always return to where I belong.

Some problems encountered by creative women

The relationship between science and art   Human society, whether in the West or the East, still suffers from an arbitrary separation between science and art, thought and emotion, mind and body. For many reasons, women in particular are the victims of this dichotomy; above all because historically it was conceived as a weapon in the service of the slave system, private property, the division of society into classes, and the patrilinear family system. It was enveloped in a religious mystique, provided with sacred trappings according to which Eve became symbolic of the body and Adam of the mind.

It is probably true that this manner of conceiving things played a role in the development of civilization, science, and technology, the fruits of which we enjoy today, but there is no doubt also that it simultaneously served another purpose by creating and reinforcing the patriarchal class system, with all the injustice that dominates within it up to the present day. And through the splitting of the human being into two distinct parts, mind and body, mind was elevated to the throne of God, science, the man, religion and authority, whereas the body was relegated to the lowest level: that of the woman, the devil, shame, heresy and submission.

The creative woman, with her exceptional mental and psychological capacity to break through traditional values and ideas, is quick to realize that the splitting of the human being into mind and body, thought and emotion, is a concept that conflicts with nature, a concept imposed on society by the force of arms, of authority and law. She is also able to understand that it gave birth to the idea that science is a product of the mind, whereas art is the product of emotion and feeling. Creative people, whether women or men, cut through all artificial partitions, all the walls that divide life into watertight compartments, and reconstitute the essential unity that makes of the human being a whole composed of body, mind, emotions and feelings.

Perhaps one of the first contradictions I was obliged to face in practical life was that created between science and art, between medicine and literature. As a medical doctor and a writer, wherever I went I was pursued by the question 'How do you manage to combine medicine and literature?' The question was always asked in a tone denoting disapproval, and suggesting a dire need for me to choose one profession, which of course could only be medicine, and specifically gynaecology, so that I could spare women from being handled by a male doctor. My insistence on pursuing both my medical and my literary activities surrounded me with an aura of strangeness, especially as no one else in my society had followed a similar course. The few male doctors (about three or four) who had opted for a literary career abandoned the medical profession at quite an early stage, and subsequently devoted themselves to their literary activities or else worked as journalists. So how was it possible for a woman to combine two professions which even the men were incapable of practising at the same time?

I myself did not perceive any fundamental contradiction between my medical and literary activity. On the contrary they nourished one another. My knowledge of the medical sciences, my work in rural areas, my relations with male and female patients, fed my writings with a deep and rich experience, and with human and artistic material characterized by its reflection of the reality I was living and the wealth of details related to it. In the same way my passion for writing, my love of art, and my contemplation of life as it flowed past permitted me to see human beings in all their depth, helped me in my work as a medical doctor, and made me realize the imperfections of my profession, and its inability to cope with the main problems related to society and people.

Medicine provided me with facts, knowledge and living experience, whereas art gave me vision, clarity, courage to express my views, a love of freedom and justice, and a hatred for human bondage and oppression. However the simultaneous practice of medicine and art sometimes made me feel the difficulty of the path I was following, a lonely path over which I moved as a solitary figure. But then, progressing along it I was discovering new ideas and feelings – ideas and feelings that had their source in the interlinkages between science and art, body and mind, male and female, God and human beings. Out of this mutual interaction was coming to life a new, wonderful creature, encompassing within itself qualities that were both human and godly, a new science of knowledge in which were combined the qualities of both science and art, and a new courage which I felt coursing through my mind and body, crossing over the frontiers between them to face the greatest dangers, to face even death, with firmness and determination.

Conflict with authority and the dominant powers in society One of the most difficult problems that confront a creative woman is the inevitable conflict that breaks out sooner or later between her and authority, between her and the system dominant in society, because this system is built on patriarchal class relations. The intensity of this conflict is proportionate to the effectiveness of the action undertaken by the creative woman. The methods and weapons used against her differ according to the type of society, and the surroundings in which she lives. The war waged against her increases in ferocity if she is felt to be dangerous to the prevailing system, its laws and values. There are many factors that permit the system to succeed in overcoming her resistance in most cases. Foremost among these is the fact that it possesses a whole range of oppressive instruments such as censorship, police forces, prisons, newspapers and mass media as well as religious and cultural institutions. It is therefore always capable of breaking any individual or individuals who try to rebel against it, except if these individuals succeed in building up a people's political organization capable of standing up to the powerful forces that will be unleashed against it. This task is an extremely difficult one in societies where liberty and freedom are no more than words devoid of any real content, where a single individual commands the destiny of a nation, and where any form of criticism or difference in opinion is outlawed. In such situations creative people, and especially creative women, feel themselves surrounded, cornered, threatened by obvious and obscure dangers every moment of their lives.

I myself have had this sensation of being encircled by enemy forces at different stages of my life. I could feel the silent struggle going on between me and these forces, a struggle that increased in intensity as time passed and I became more mature, and as my activities grew in extent and depth whether in the medical or the literary field. Now the struggle was no longer hidden or silent but open and declared, character-ized by the variety of weapons used, ranging from neglect, disapproval, criticism and vilification to warnings and threats which ended in my being deprived of a job during the period 1972–78, and in a total censorship of all my writings so that I was obliged to publish my books outside Egypt (in Beirut). This situation prevailed until I was able to obtain a job in the Economic Commission for Africa as an adviser on women's programmes for Africa, and later in the Economic Commission for Western Asia as senior programme officer in charge of the Women's

Voluntary Fund. My work in the field of women's programmes, and my choice of the United Nations in particular, was an attempt to break through the siege that was meant to close in upon me and throttle whatever efforts I was making. But to my great disappointment I discovered after two years of work in the United Nations that things had been no different there, because once again I was trapped in the logic and the rigid chains of a bureaucratic establishment built on patriarchal class relations and the balance or struggle between international and national forces. A man or woman who enters the ranks of this establishment is not evaluated on the basis of his or her work and creative ability, but rather according to a capacity for adapting to the traditions and norms that prevail within it, for submissive obedience to those in command, for cleverness in maintaining or creating relations with influential circles and people. The UN establishment, to my mind, resembles a cemetery in which the tombs are carved out of smooth, expensive marble surrounded by decorated walls and rich heavy curtains, furnished with luxurious leather armchairs and thick soft carpets and run by soft-spoken men who move and speak with studied care in return for high salaries, a comfortable life and security. It is a cemetery because despite the beautiful trappings and outwardly efficient appearance, within its precincts any attempt at original creative work is buried and suffocates deep down under the smooth marble.

Problems of the creative woman arising from her sex Society is not yet accustomed to the creative endeavour of women or to their original thinking in any field of activity. In consequence a creative woman must be extremely productive, and expend much greater efforts than her male colleagues, in order to obtain recognition as a creative individual.

In many societies, certain subjects are considered so sensitive that they are placed out of bounds for discussion. Such subjects include sex, and matters of a religious nature. They take on explosive proportions if dealt with by a woman. There are also certain forms of struggle that the ruling authorities refuse to recognize, or to bring into the open, because they consider them a danger to the system. The class struggle is one of them. Yet is it not true that no original creative thinker, whether man or woman, can give free rein to intellect, and produce works that are of value, while at the same time avoiding the three subjects of sex, religion and the class struggle? A woman who dares to touch upon them runs much greater risks than a man, because of the double moral standards prevalent in our societies.

In general a man enjoys a much greater degree of freedom in the areas of sex, moral and social behaviour, and thought than does a woman. The mere fact of being female carries with it a whole range of constraints; a woman is therefore obliged to pay a much greater price if she wishes to express herself freely in both thought and action.

Marriage remains the only legitimate channel through which woman can satisfy her need for love, sex and motherhood. This is particularly true in the Arab countries, where marriage is still governed by rules and traditions that make the man a guardian and keeper of his wife's body, of her thought, and of her social, economic, and political activities. A creative woman inevitably lives through an acute conflict between her need for love, sex and motherhood and her refusal to accept the tutelage of the man, and the rigid mould of a traditional marriage. Another problem for the creative woman is that the duties of a wife and mother in serving her children, family and husband still remain sacred in the eyes of society, since they are the duties she has been born to fulfil. Any other activities are considered secondary, of little importance or even harmful, since they can divert her from carrying out the tasks related to husband, children and family.

At certain stages of my life the care I was obliged to give first to my daughter and then, later, to my son, and the efforts entailed in providing this care were the cause of much loss of time, and of a fatigue that often reached the point of severe nervous and physical exhaustion, just so that I could be sure that they would obtain the minimum of food, rest, cleanliness and affection which was their due. My feelings of motherhood were deep and strong, and it was often so difficult to think of my medical or literary work when, for one reason or another, I might be worried about my children.

Loneliness and the political vacuum At all stages of my life, I experienced a need to cooperate with my female colleagues in order to overcome loneliness and gain the necessary strength with which to confront those who were in authority. Even within our small family I tried to cooperate with my sisters so that we could obtain more rights. I did the same in school and later at the university, after I graduated. That is why at one stage for example, I tried to establish an association for Egyptian women writers registered in the Ministry of Social Affairs. This association was active for some time but was quickly smothered by the influential circles in the literary movement. I attempted for several years to work through the Medical Association and reach my female colleagues working in urban and rural areas, but once again the reactionary pillars of the medical profession cut down my efforts, although at that time I had already lost my job in the Ministry of Health. In addition I was instrumental in the establishment of an association for health information and education, which published a monthly magazine of which I was the editor-in-chief for several years. This time we were forced to close down by a financial boycott orchestrated by the then Minister of Health, who issued instructions preventing companies from advertising in our magazine.

More recently I have been travelling in the Arab region and this has permitted me to make contacts in different Arab countries with women I have come to know over the years, and to promote the constitution of groups which I hope will grow into an Arab women's movement. These groups are now meeting to discuss their objectives and programmes of action, but who knows whether they will be left to grow and develop, or whether they will be quickly strangled by the forces of reaction?

No doubt my contacts with people and the outer world depend essentially on my writings. But experience has brought me to the realization that thought and writing, no matter how essential, are not capable alone of bringing about the necessary social and political changes. In addition creative women are in dire need of organized popular support if they are to resist with success the numerous attacks and pitfalls to which they are increasingly exposed.

In Arab countries there are a number of progressive parties and organizations. Yet despite their self-styled 'revolutionary' orientation, they have so far proved incapable of reflecting the problems of women and of mobilizing women to tackle these problems. Quite often they consider this area to be of secondary importance. In addition party politics are often built on a kind of rigid loyalty and obedience that precludes discussion and original thought. Perhaps this is one of the reasons why I have never belonged to any political party. In the mid-1970s I made an appeal for the constitution of a women's party, though the idea was opposed bitterly right from the start. For despite the fact that I know full well how complex the cause of women's liberation is, and how it can never be served outside the framework of the struggle for a comprehensive radical change in the structure of society as a whole, yet I believe that the creation of a women's organization makes an extremely important contribution to the total revolutionary effort. Such an organization must grow and mature so that it can fuse its efforts with other organizations in the struggle to overcome the patriarchal class structure of our present society, and its numerous ramifications within our institutions including those of marriage, the family and the relations between the sexes.

Motherhood as a creative endeavour

The female of all living beings is capable of creating life anew through child-bearing, but the woman is the only being who is able, through her mental ability, to transform child-bearing from a semi-mechanical biological process into physically, mentally, and emotionally creative work.

The patriarchal class system has robbed the woman of her most precious possession, namely her mind, and has replaced it with the hymen (an Arab proverb says that a girl's virginity is her most precious possession). The woman has been deprived of her capacity for mental, psychological and even physical creativity. Her capacity for child-bearing and her creative human motherhood have been transformed into bonds, burdens and agony, all of which exhaust and weaken her, rather than strengthen or develop her abilities.

The woman who is not fully taken up with never-ending struggle to make a livelihood and never-ending household work can find some time or energy to become aware of her creative powers. This fortunate woman represents a small minority in Arab countries. Though rich in resources, the Arab world is poor because of continuous external and internal exploitation. However, this fortunate woman cannot, in most cases, overcome a sense of guilt. She continuously wavers between two facts: that she is a woman, and that she is creative.

The ancient female goddess was the creator, but since the emergence of the patriarchal class system all gods have been males, while Eve became a desecrated, headless body. Mental and sexual oppression did not help women to develop their physical, mental or emotional powers. Women are also oppressed politically, economically, socially, culturally and morally. Consequently their creative capacities deteriorate steadily.

Creative women within the professions

Because of the prevailing system few women become professional, and those who become creative are even fewer. Certain professions are more traditional than others. The medical profession, to my mind, is more traditional than writing. Being a medical doctor and a writer I noticed that women doctors tend to be more traditional and less creative than women writers.

I think creative women or men can change the ethics and attitudes of their profession if they represent the majority or mobilize others towards this change. Traditional women cannot change the prevailing ethics and attitudes. Sometimes they safeguard them. However, the mere presence of women in a profession, even if they are veiled, creates a new working atmosphere, and new social relationships between themselves and their colleagues. Out of these, new ethics and attitudes may develop.

A female physician may be treated as a nurse, especially in rural areas. This is considered degrading, since the nursing profession is looked upon by the patriarchal class system as lower. What we need is equality between professions as well as equality between female and male colleagues.

I did not pay much attention to whether I was treated as a physician or not. Sometimes I preferred not to belong to the medical profession. I noticed how sick people were exploited by doctors, especially in rural areas. Most of my friends were not doctors. However I did not like to be treated as a nurse either. I came to realize over the years that the creative doctor finds her real self among the sick more than she does among doctors. I also reached the point where I preferred reading the letters of readers rather than the comments of professional critics, which no longer gripped my attention as they had done in the past. Most of these critics are men who intentionally attack creative women writers or ignore them.

Especially within her profession, a creative woman may be exposed to men or women who manifest a form of hate or envy towards her. Women might appear to be more hostile to, and jealous of, the creative woman than men. My experience in life, however, has taught me that the envy and hostility of men towards creative women is deeper and more intense, but they are more capable than women of masking their feelings because they have become well-versed, under the existing system, in disguising their real feelings generally. Men, moreover, are more sympathetic to the patriarchal system since they are men and fathers. The creative woman poses a constant threat to the man, not simply because he is a man, but also because she is a threat to the whole system that has made him this kind of man.

This kind of man could be a colleague of the creative woman at her work, her boss, her husband, her father, her brother or any other man who crosses her path, within the home or without. She might have to engage in a struggle with him in order to move him out of her way. Her most effective weapon in such a struggle is her creative work, the umbilical cord that links her to the people and is the source of her strength. Therefore she should not abandon her creative work for any man, or for any other reason. How well I remember the day when my second husband threatened me, 'You must choose between me or your writing.' I said, 'My writing.'

Strategies for psychological and economic survival, and for coping under stress

The situation and problems of women in our contemporary societies are born of developments in history that made one class rule over another, and men dominate over women. The creative woman cannot expect praise or acceptance. This understanding can alleviate the impact of the attacks to which she might be exposed. Moreover, the expectation of the infliction of harm makes her ready, and this readiness equips her to confront her enemies, helping her to win, or at least to sustain as little loss as possible. Even though victory is a pleasant experience for any human being, defeat can also be a useful experience. The transformation of defeat into experience requires that the woman should have no regrets and that she should press ahead steadily, with courage, confidence and freedom.

The freedom of human beings is restricted by their essential economic needs, or by nonessential needs that become essential under the influence of exploitative consumerism and advertisements. Moreover, the ruling classes can threaten creative women by depriving them of certain economic needs. Consequently, the creative woman must learn to restrict her economic needs to the realm of necessities. This increases her economic independence, and so increases her freedom. The same holds true for her psychological needs. She must learn to become psychologically and socially independent, able to live alone under any conditions. It also applies to her physical needs.

Under the prevailing system, stress is inevitable and the creative woman may be called upon to pay a heavy price in her private or public life.

The basic power of creative woman, in my opinion, is the ability to penetrate and influence the minds and hearts of people. This ability is only translated into creative action when she really lives the life of the people, sharing their agonies, sorrows and aspirations. The real support for the creative woman is organized collective action, both national and international. Such organized networks can also be a vehicle for communication between large numbers of women in the same country and outside.

No creative person (man or woman) can live without love and true, close friendships. Only the men and women who have maintained their real selves, or in other words have retained a capacity for creative work, are capable of such human relationships. How fortunate is the woman who meets such people during her lifetime. They are admittedly few, but they exist and I think they are increasing in number as we proceed along the path of progress, revolution and freedom. My joy at meeting such a man or woman has no parallel in anything else. I can still remember my joy at meeting Sherif, my present husband. Over the years we have been able to live a creative, innovative life, which has been emotionally and intellectually rich. With our daughter Mona and our son Atef, we have also managed to build a new type of family – based on understanding, cooperation and love.

Conclusion

It is undoubtedly difficult for the creative woman to safeguard and develop her capacities under the prevailing system of society. She is often called upon to pay a heavy price in her private or public life. She may divorce (I was divorced twice) or be expelled from her job (as I was, more than once). She might have to face harsh circumstances which pose a threat to her reputation, or to her economic, psychological and even physical stability (sometimes I have been threatened with bodily harm or death by bigoted fanatical individuals, groups, or in-stitutions). The creative woman must realize that she is struggling against established, well-equipped powers, whose weapons include not only awesome facilities, but deeply rooted values. She must mobilize all her powers in this struggle and depend on the real forces that can support and protect her, namely the force of those men, women, young people and children whose hearts and minds she touches through her creative production. I believe that were it not for the hundreds and thousands of readers who sincerely and enthusiastically support my writings, buy my books and attend the lectures I give, I would not have been able to maintain my activity and keep on writing. The forces of authority in my country and in other Arab countries would have been able to crush me completely.

[Presented to a United Nations Institute for Training and Research (UNITAR) seminar, Oslo, 9–13 July 1980]

CHAPTER 19

Prosecutive Journalism

On 3 March 1990 Ahmed Bahgat, an Egyptian journalist who contributes a daily column to the official newspaper *Al-Ahram*, wrote an article entitled 'A new Salman Rushdie in Egypt'. In this article he accused a hitherto unknown writer named Ala'a Hamed of insulting the prophets, of heresy and of atheism in his novel published in Arabic under the title *A Space in the Mind of a Man*. The journalist demanded that the author be prosecuted and tried.

I was very angry when I read this article. I did not know the novelist, nor had I read his novel. I expected that many of our writers and journalists would express their indignation at what Ahmed Bahgat had written. But apart from a very minor comment in one of the opposition papers, I read nothing. So I sent an answer to *Al-Ahram* in which I said the role of a journalist should be to express what he thought and not to serve as an arm of the prosecuting authorities.

But of course the newspaper did not publish my article. *Al-Ahram*, like all other newspapers in Egypt, has consistently refused to publish any criticism of journalists who occupy important positions in the official press and who have of course reached these positions through government intervention.

A few weeks after this incident I received a summons from the prosecutor's office attached to the State Emergency Security Court in the district of old Cairo requesting me to be a witness in the case taken by the authorities against the writer Ala'a Hamed for what he had expressed in his novel.

Before I went to the prosecutor's office, the author sent me a copy of his novel which I read through carefully. The book contained a criticism of some of the ideas and myths contained in the sacred writings handed down in the three monotheistic religions. In my view it was not a well-written novel.

I responded to the summons. I defended the author's right to express freely whatever views he held, and pointed out that no one should attempt to restrict freedom of expression by punitive measures. I added that literary works should not be judged by moral or religious values. I insisted that the religious institution of Al-Azhar had no right to play the role of judge or critic where artistic or literary creation is concerned. Two years passed during which I heard nothing more about the case. Then, suddenly, at the very end of 1991 there was an uproar. Ala'a Hamed, the printer of the book, and the distributor Madbouli, who is a prominent figure in Egyptian life, had been condemned to eight years' imprisonment. Now there were leading articles on the issue in all the newspapers. The journalists who wrote them were clamouring in defence of freedom of expression. I could not understand this sudden enthusiasm.

Next day, however, I found out the reason. A friend of mine telephoned me and as we were talking she asked, 'Did you hear the news about Ala'a Hamed's case on the BBC a couple of days ago?' So the problem now facing the authorities was what is called here 'the image of Egypt'. It was not freedom of expression that was at stake. 'The image of Egypt' is a concept that permits things to happen on condition that international opinion does not find out. So now the official journalists and writers in Egypt have become champions of freedom, while heaping insult after insult on the head of Ala'a Hamed who is being depicted as a scurrilous rascal, or an opportunist.

Now they are asking Mubarak to intervene and abrogate the judgement of the Emergency Security Court. This he can do in agreement with the prime minister who, according to the emergency or martial law that has been in operation for as long as I can remember, has the power to revoke court decisions taken under the system of Emergency Security Courts.

When I think of these things, when I think that the real defenders of freedom are marginalized all the time so that the official spokesmen can strut on the stage freely, when I see what is going on here in Egypt and in other Arab countries, I am not surprised that religious fundamentalism is capturing one stronghold after another.

Moreover, the double game that is being played all the time in the Egyptian press, where fundamentalism is criticized and cajoled and glorified alternately, is proving to be dangerous; it is paving the way to a fundamentalist takeover. I have in mind what happened in the decree dissolving the Arab Women's Solidarity Association and handing over its property and money to an association called Women of Islam. The court case that will decide whether this decree is legal or not has been postponed again to 20 February 1992.

[First published in Arabic in *Al-Ahali* (Cairo), 8 January 1992. Translated by the author]

CHAPTER 20

Seeking the True Colour of Things

I was born in a wondrous age in which one is herded into prison because one is born with a thinking mind and a heart that beats for truth and justice, because one writes poetry, short stories or novels, or publishes a scientific or literary study or an article calling for freedom, or because one has philosophical leanings.

Since I was born in this era, it was not at all strange that I should go to prison, for I have committed all the crimes: I have written short stories, novels, and poetry; I have published literary and scientific studies and articles calling for freedom; and I have philosophical leanings.

The greatest crime, however, is that I am a free woman in an age that desires only servants and slaves. I was born with a mind that thinks in a time when they are trying to eradicate the mind.

My father was free, and my mother was free. From my childhood, freedom has run in my veins along with the blood. I have seen my mother rebelling, refusing to accept the martial authority of her father and revolting against her husband if he raised his voice at home. I have seen my father angry, revolting against the government, the king and the British. I have heard my grandmother, a poor peasant, singing out against oppression and poverty, and the accumulated grief of many years.

My brother was bigger than I: when he lifted his hand to slap me I raised mine higher and struck him. He did not attempt it again. When my first husband wanted to negate my existence, I erased his presence from my life. When my second husband shouted, 'Me or your writing!' I replied, 'My writing.' We separated. When the Minister of Health, shaking with anger, raged, 'Obedience or dismissal,' I said, 'Dismissal.' And I lost my job. When Sadat said, 'The banners of freedom are fluttering, and so are those of justice, prosperity and peace,' I said, 'Where is freedom when people are bound in chains and censorship hangs like a sword over their thoughts and minds? Where is justice, or prosperity, when the poor are getting poorer and the rich are growing richer, reaping their millions? Where is peace, as the arms deals multiply and the war in Lebanon grows ever more ferocious?'

Never in my life have I entered the game of politics, political parties, journalism, elections, or women's groups chaired by the wives of the rulers. I have even abandoned the profession of medicine. I have seen doctors buying country estates and erecting apartment blocks with the blood of poor patients. People contract illnesses as a result of poverty, hunger and oppression – diseases for which medicine has no cure.

My only remaining weapon is the pen, with which I defend myself, my freedom and that of people everywhere. I have only the pen with which to express my thoughts on the tragedy of the poor, of women and of all those enslaved, and to tell others that I loathe tyranny and love justice, that I respect human beings and refuse to bow down before authority whatever the circumstances may be. Nor do I participate in plebiscites, or listen to rumours and absurdities. I lock my door to those employed in the courts of power. I do not make offerings to show my fealty. I obey only my mind, I write only my opinion, I do not march in celebratory processions or have a clique or attend galas. I do not deck myself out like the consort or wash my hair with American shampoo or drink Israeli beer. Newspapers give me nausea.

Perhaps all this explains why they broke down my door by force and led me off to prison. I was not particularly surprised: truth cannot lead an unfettered existence in an age of lying. I wasn't frightened, but I *was* angry, and I refused to open my door to them.

I refused to disappear in the night noiselessly, I refused to be led off silently without creating an uproar. I would not go to jail, or to my death, without showing my anger and expressing my rebellion. I felt no embarrassment about this. Rather, I was self-assured, even arrogant: why shouldn't I be? A police state with all of its trappings and afraid of me! Of one unarmed woman whose fingers grip a pen, never a trigger. Do my words on paper frighten them to this extent?

In that case, I will go on writing. I will keep on writing even if they bury me in a grave. I will go on writing even if they take away my pen and paper. I will write on the wall, on the surface of the earth, on the disc of the sun and the face of the moon.

There is nothing called 'impossible' in my life.

When the prison official bellowed, 'If I find a pistol in your possession you'll get off easier than if I detect a pen and paper,' I decided that before the end of the day I would have both pen and paper in my hands. How? I had no idea. But I yearned for a pen and some paper with every atom of my being. Throughout my life, whenever I have wanted something that much I have managed to obtain it. And before the *shawisha* – the prison official serving as our doorwoman and guard – had locked the door upon us that day, exactly at 4 p.m., I had a pen and some paper in my possession. It was only toilet paper, but I could read what I had written.

When both the State Security Police officer and the *shawisha* had disappeared and night had advanced, I arose and sat on the base of an inverted jerrycan, under the yellow light of the electric lamp. Resting my back against the wall, I wrote my first words in prison:

> Because democracy is a lie, the person who composes poetry or a love story can enter prison. A sincere love story may be more dangerous than a case of explosives or time bombs, for it reveals the cores and pits of corruption in the society. Those who tell lies in bedrooms are the same people who lie in the corridors of parliament, seats of state, or newspaper pages. One cannot tell lies by night and then be truthful by day, or have a body that lies and a truthful mind. And as for those who combine falsehood with truth – they are damaged in appearance and mind.

But there is a supreme historical tragedy in this: these damaged individuals are the ones who attain the seats of power and harvest the wealth. As their riches and possessions grow, so does their parched yearning for more, like an ailing stomach that thirsts for more water the more it is given to drink.

Thus the world's wars know no end, while the number of damaged individuals increases. You'll see them taking interest solely in the events of war and in matters of politics.

While still a child, I came to loathe politics, and as a young woman I detested politics. And I detested war. Political matters did not occupy me. No front page or headline could stir me up. I was engrossed in art and literature, but I discovered that art and literature have no existence without truth, which cannot live without freedom, which does not exist without revolution. For the sake of freedom, the artist finds herself or himself in the arena of politics. For the sake of freedom, she or he cannot separate art from political activity. Freedom is revolution: the freedom of all individuals in the society, men and women. For if women are denied freedom there can be no revolution. Can revolution run its course in a society when half of its people are shackled?

The road to freedom that lies ahead of us remains a long one. Politics consists of hypocrisy and lying. Men of politics are of a certain characteristic sort. So are those of journalism. The most dangerous journalists and politicians are those who survive in every era: they ascend the thrones of journalism and politics, art and literature and medicine, and remain in place as firmly as the sun sits in its sphere. I can see their persistent immovability revolving, round and round, on a capacity to lie that is unparalleled. Their skin alone changes, but they do not.

I am a woman. Yes. From the moment of my birth until the day I entered prison, my life has been difficult. In spite of that, my heart has not changed. I cannot feel suspicious of anyone for, in my view of the world, people are innocent and the gods are guilty. Humankind was not created evil and human natures do not tend that way. From the very first moment, I trusted the *shawisha* who kept watch over me and bore the keys to my cell. I have an awesome power of intuition by which I have lived since childhood. It has grown with me and continues to expand, and I fear that it will grow to the point where I will see more than society can endure – and after putting me in prison, what more can they do with me?

But I am still dissatisfied with my writings. I am not writing in an unfettered manner, with the freedom I desire. I have lived in a world that gives preference to lying in every sphere – politics, society, morals, art, scientific knowledge. This has given rise to a set of people who own books but don't read, while those among them who do read don't use their own minds, but rely on the minds of others. Such a person rejoices in claiming to be the ruler's friend, or relates that the ruler said to her or him 'such-and-such'. I have not come across a single member of this group who belongs to herself or himself. What such people cannot accomplish in the open they do in hiding, and they write what they do not live. When I observe or hear such people, a feeling of alienation comes over me.

I write what I live. I am a human being who has decided what she wants and has lived what she desires. I have come to own myself – and people too. I have come to have a piece of the sky because I can dream.

In prison I did not lose my capacity to dream and hope, or my ability to rage should I wish. One day, I threatened to burn down the cell and the whole prison with a match.

At times, my sense of hope may slide down an abyss to the lowest possible point – into the earth's depths – but then it drags itself out and takes off obstinately towards the tree branches to soar into the sky like a bird. How can my hope be so strong? How can one find hope, really feel it? I cannot sleep when I realize that a bomb will strike inevitably in a nearby spot. I cannot sleep and dream that I am happy for twenty-four hours without the sound of a bullet cutting that dream short.

Struggles outside and inside the country – and inside myself too, clashing, compelling me to utter things that I have experienced in a crazed fashion. I say these things now, in words that appear small and meaningless to me, but despite all this, I do fall asleep and awaken and dream of revolution. The pistol fires a bullet; what do words on paper let loose?

Prison is a stagnant place, but the one imprisoned there is not sluggish or stagnant. In jail, one learns the true colour of all things, discovers the most gorgeous hues and the most beautiful people as well as the ugliest ones. Yet one thing sweeps away all the gradations of colour: the hope of breaking down the doors, the bars and the locks, the hope of taking off into the air carolling like a bird.

Hope is the revolution and the bird's free warbling.

But I remain dissatisfied with myself, as I still do not possess my freedom. I have not yet written the book of which I dream, or the novel that lives with me. I have not lived the life for which I was born, and I was not born in the right era. There are still many men and women in our country who believe that the face of a woman is one of her private parts, to be treated with shame. And there are those who think also that revolution is like a woman's face, requiring the conceal- ment of veiling. There are those who speak daily of the revolution – how numerous are the revolutions of which we have heard, that are said to have taken place in our country! Revolution after revolution, one correcting another. From the abundance of revolutions we have come to dream of a life devoid of revolution. The word has lost its meaning, as have all words. 'Protective detainment in a secure place' is to be put in prison. 'Revolution' becomes the nonrevolution, or the abortion of the revolution. 'Food security' means food poisoning. I told myself I would stop writing until I could come across new words, words that have not become hackneyed with use.

Can revolution carry the meaning of still more poverty, submission, and dependence? Is it possible for revolution to mean that the people whose country this is have come to have less worth and dignity in their own land than the foreigner?

Can it be possible that the revolution means imprisoning warbling birds in cages and setting free crows, hawks, eagles and all clawed creatures who are able to snipe and snatch?

[Introduction to the Arabic edition of the author's prison memoir, *Mozakerati fi-Sign al-Nissa*, published by Dar Al-Mustaqbal Al-'Arabi, Cairo, 1982, and translated by Marilyn Booth. Published in English as *Memoirs from the Women's Prison*, Women's Press, London, 1983]

PART SIX

Women Organizing for Change

CHAPTER 21

Arab Women and Politics

The marginality of women in politics

The Arab national movement has developed as a progressive movement directed against foreign imperialism and aiming at establishing Arab unity in the political, economic and cultural fields. Nevertheless, it has remained a man's movement and reflects the dominant economic, social and cultural relations in Arab society. Prominent among these relationships are those that have arisen between men and women. Change in this area has been very slow and they differ little from the old relationships that existed between master and slave, despite variations in their external form, or internally in the degree of subjection imposed on the woman, or in the degree of domination exercised by the man. As a result, Arab women in general have been unable to assume the responsibilities of a complete human being who can exercise initiative and take positive action. They have tended to remain mere objects that react to events, the extent of their reaction varying from one situation to another. Very often they have been incapable even of reaction and have remained no more than passive objects.

As a result, Arab women so far have failed to play an active role in the national movement. They have remained marginal and largely ineffective, limiting themselves to varying degrees of response according to the situations that have arisen, or to the acuity of the economic, social and military crises to which their countries have been exposed. The roles they take, the functions that are assigned to them, may vary, but the substance of their relationships with the movement and with the men participating in its ranks have remained almost unchanged. This relationship is mainly that of slave to master, of a follower to the leader, of an object to the subject, and manifests itself in all areas of life, whether within the home or outside in the wider fields of life.

This statement is true not only within the boundaries of the progressive movement, but also to varying degrees in all social and political movements and parties including those that profess socialist principles and platforms. Communist parties are no exception. For despite the progressive content of their programmes which aim at abolishing imperialist domination and all forms of exploitation, whether external or internal, including the exploitation of one nation by another, or one class by another, and the establishment of equality between all human beings irrespective of race, religion, creed, sex or class, nevertheless the exploitation of women by men (woman is not yet considered to be included in the category 'human being') has remained outside the theory and practice of such movements and parties, and is still a topic exiled from the main arenas of social struggle.

Revolution, crisis, and the satisfaction of participation

The main area of social struggle is that of politics, of political thought and action. This area is monopolized by men. Their organized political force, political parties and collective movements permit them to exercise complete control, and to prevent women from organizing their own forces, constituting their own parties, or engaging in any form of effective and independent collective action. This monopoly also ensures that, when required, a woman can be allowed or made to participate in political struggles, but always as an individual, whose force is necessarily weak and dispersed, and always under the control of a man, who dominates her as father or husband in the home, as supervisor or boss at work, etcetera, and as political leader in the political movements.

History shows that during periods of acute crises accompanied by popular rebellions, uprisings, coups or revolutions, men have been impelled to use women in the political and military struggles and revolutionary movements as instruments or fuel with which to feed the flames of popular action. Women have died in these struggles, been burned to ashes, or lived through them, but once the crisis is over they return to the home, the field, the factory or the office to become an instrument of another kind. Their functions thus change according to the economic and social needs of men. But no matter how much they vary, the initial and main female function remains unchanged, namely that of serving the man in his home as well as his family and children.

The political, social, economic and military crises to which the Arab countries have been exposed possess both positive and negative aspects. The most important positive aspect is that they lay the ground for revolution. Revolution itself has both positive and negative aspects. The most important positive aspect of revolution, apart from the overcoming of imperialist domination, or the overthrow of a corrupt and exploitative ruler or ruling class, is that it breaks through traditions, habit and custom. This breakthrough is impelled by a need to use all the available human and material forces, including not only manifest but also hidden and potential resources. It provides a rare opportunity to all the oppressed groups, classes, and categories in society, including women, to break through the chains and limitations that remain intact during periods of calm.

The problem always faced by the groups or classes of men in power at the head of the state during periods of calm, or at the head of the revolution in periods of crisis, is that the movement of human forces within society, and the movement of human history cannot be held back or controlled by an individual, a group, or a class no matter how strong the monopoly they exercise over power. This is because the history of society and human development is a vast social phenomenon in which individuals, groups and classes participate actively including the oppressors and the oppressed, the masters and the slaves, the women, the children, the young and the old. And this is also because the history of society is the result of many social, economic and cultural factors which play a manifest or hidden role.

At different periods, this characteristic of historical development has contributed to the liberation of exploited classes or groups, for example of slaves during the transition to feudalism, when the desire of the masters had been to increase the exploitation of the slaves. Women also have been able to benefit from this situation. For example, husbands have encouraged women to work in factories so as to alleviate the effects of the economic crises they face. The income earned by the woman is in fact of help to the man, but when he acts in this way the man forgets that a woman is a human being who once she has experienced the satisfaction of even the slightest degree of independence, or of participation in an area hitherto forbidden, will refuse any attempt to reduce her to her previous situation.

This phenomenon reproduces itself in political movements and revolutions. The men who occupy the controlling positions encourage women to take part and thus contribute to the solution of the political or military crises faced by them. Sometimes they succeed in overcoming these crises with the help of the women, and of other poor and exploited classes or groups, but they forget that once the crisis is over, women who have experienced the satisfaction of participation and effective action will refuse to go back to their previous situation and to be subjected to the same forms of domination, even if the price will be their lives.

During periods of crisis or revolution, therefore, Arab women have been able to resist attempts to push them back to their initial situation, and have been successful in achieving minor successes and winning over new positions in the struggle for liberation. However, these changes have not been fundamental; they have not led to a radical change in women's situation. Nevertheless, in addition to gaining new positions in the home and in society as a whole, women have been able to improve the mobilization and the organization of their forces. This was the case in Egypt after the national revolution of 1919. In 1923, the Federation of Egyptian Women was established. Another example is Algeria, where women expanded their role during the national revolution, and formed the Union of Algerian Women after the French colonialists were obliged to withdraw. Similar changes took place in other Arab countries.

It was natural that these organizations of women should reflect the prevalent social structure, and the social forces that were predominant at the time. As a result, the Federation of Egyptian Women was largely composed of the wives and sisters of the feudal pashas, and of the new ruling classes that shared political power with the British after the revolution of 1919, or who gained new positions in the economic development of the country. When changes took place as a result of a military coup, the women who took over the controlling positions in the associations or groups very often belonged to the families of high-ranking officers. In most Arab countries there are examples of these types of women's organizations or groups, which are essentially appendages to the political organizations and ruling classes that control the government and state apparatus. They can be considered mainly as administrative bodies affiliated to the ministries of social affairs, and their activities are confined to the area of voluntary social services. Sometimes they may be allowed to engage in limited political activities; then, specific directives will be sent from the higher levels and put into effect with the help of the lower levels of women members. This system also applies to other mass organizations which group workers, peasants, youth and students, as well as to professional associations and trade unions; it is characteristic of political activities in the various Arab countries where democracy remains largely formal.

Exclusion, isolation and alienation

We cannot deny the fact that Arab women, throughout the years, have carried on a patient and long struggle against their inferior position in the home and in society. They have fought enduringly during periods of peace and war, crisis and revolution; perhaps one of the signs of the success they have attained is the fact that Arab nationalist thought is now obliged to discuss issues related to the political movement of women. This is an indication of the continuously increasing strength of the political force of women. The main problem remains, however, that the women's movement has not attained an appropriate level of strength, its development has been slow, and it has only succeeded in imposing itself on Arab political thought as an idea in panels, lectures and discussion forums. In short, it has tended to remain an idea to be studied and talked about, rather than being transformed into concrete action raised to the level and role it deserves within the Arab political movement.

In my view, the crucial problem remains the policy of exclusion and limitation practised against the forces of Arab women. It is thus that men hope to maintain their domination over the women's movement, and to imprison it within the confines of social work (in the same way as individual women have been confined to domestic and family service within the home). These limitations have prevented women from growing into an effective organized collective force, taking collective decisions that will serve their interests, or participating in political movements as an independent political movement for women capable of engaging in political struggles and using its power to extract the rights which are women's due.

Hence Arab women have continued to join the different political movements as isolated individuals rather than as a collective force. In addition, women active in the political arena have remained a very small minority compared with the total number of women. Arab women have therefore largely been unable to exert an influence on any Arab political movement and as a small minority have tended to suffer from the alienation and psychological disorders that affect such minorities. They feel the gap that exists between the reality imposed upon them and that to which they aspire, and realize that the political movement in no way represents them or expresses the problems they face every day in the family, in the workplace, and within society as a whole. Arab women are deprived of the right to reflect their situation, and the difficulties which they face. The reason given to explain this neglect is that a number of other important problems should be given priority. That is why most women tend to escape into silence or suffer from a sense of guilt which makes them ashamed of raising the issues which concern them. For the same reasons, the majority of conscious or revolutionary Arab women tend to refrain from joining the various Arab political movements or participating in their activities, and end up in a state of isolation or passivity. They are unable to render their creative thought fertile through its combination with practical action.

The few women who form the Arab political movements and

become members find themselves surrounded by an atmosphere that leads them to adopt the ideas and way of thinking followed by the men in control of these movements. They tend to repeat the same ideas and slogans, and deny the existence of what we may call the problem of Arab women. Even if the existence of this problem is recognized, it is considered of secondary importance, or relegated to the category of issues that can be dealt with at a later date, since the time has not yet come when they should be faced and solved effectively, or it is treated as a matter that will find a spontaneous solution as soon as imperialist and class domination have been abolished.

The opposition to an independent Arab women's movement

It was the struggle between master and slaves that gave birth in society to the activity called politics. Politics is the attempt to find solutions to the struggle between the oppressors and the oppressed, to overcome these struggles by peaceful or violent means. Since politics was a domain forbidden to women, the struggles related to their situation and life remained dormant. Politics were monopolized by men, and therefore their struggles alone received attention. Politics was also forbidden to slaves and continued in one way or another to be outside the purview of all exploited groups and classes. Class struggle did not take the form of an open political struggle until relatively recent times when the organized social force of the oppressed masses had become stronger and more effective. In the same way the national struggle may become active or may die down depending on the relative strength or weakness of the oppressed nations facing the oppressor nations.

At no time in history have the oppressors allowed the oppressed to practise politics, or permitted the various classes and groups into which they are divided to constitute strong, organized political movements. Such rights are never granted. The various phenomena related to oppression have arisen precisely because the oppressed masses are denied these rights. Otherwise they would have become a very powerful force on the political scene capable of leading events in the direction they wished.

The factors mentioned above explain why the creation of an independent Arab women's movement that would draw its strength directly from the millions of Arab women has so far met with fierce opposition. This opposition bases its stand on a series of arguments. One of the main points put forward is that no conflict exists or should exist between men and women, that the struggle between the sexes has no roots in reality, that men and women are partners in the family and in society, and that women are neither exploited nor oppressed by men. This insistence on the absence of conflict between men and women is made possible by the fact that women have no organized political force. Arab women should not wait until men permit them to establish their independent political movement.

Another argument often used to deny women their right to independent political action is that women do not constitute a social class and therefore they cannot constitute a political party. According to this concept a political party is solely an instrument of class struggle. This means that the proponents of this idea consider class struggle to be the only form of politics. Some men may agree intellectually on the existence of a sex conflict between men and women, and therefore on the need for a women's movement, but only on condition that it does not constitute itself into a political party, but develops as a popular social women's movement.

The national movement considers that the national struggle is the most crucial struggle. The socialist movement places class struggle at the centre of its preoccupations. The sex conflicts between women and men will remain an absent, neglected or even forbidden issue if not imposed by the political force of Arab women. The national struggle itself remained dormant or absent and was prevented from coming out into the open by the forces of feudalism and imperialist domination until it was able to express itself as a political force, namely the Arab national movement. The class struggle in turn remained absent or dormant, and was prevented from coming out into the open and even from being spoken of until the appearance of an organized Arab socialist political movement. Similarly, the struggle between the sexes will remain absent or dormant, or will be prevented from surfacing in the form of ideas or action until women become organized in the form of an Arab women's political movement.

The progressive nature of the appeal for the creation of an Arab women's political movement

The progressive nature of the appeal for the creation of an Arab women's political movement and its revolutionary content are embodied in the fact that the appeal is a response to genuine democratic principles, authentic Arab nationalism and true socialism. It is also a response to accepted human values. This is because it gives voice to the needs and rights of half the society, and is a response to the severest forms of open and hidden oppression exercised by half against the other half, that is, by men against women. Its progressive nature is also due to the fact that it is a response to class, group, and professional oppression – since the vast majority of Arab women are peasants, workers or poor toilers – and it is also a response to national oppression – since Arab women are a part of the Arab nation, which is subjected to exploitation by international capitalism and Zionism.

It is the above characteristics that render the women's movement of particular significance, a significance that arises from the triple oppression to which women are subjected. The roots of this oppression go way back thousands of years into history, and penetrate into the home, the bedroom, and the bodies of women. The roots of this oppression rise up and expand to englobe the nations and states, and the alliances built up between them all over the world, in a total structure through which the forces of oppression exercise their effect. It is this progressive significance of the women's movement that explains the unrelenting attempts made to forbid it and prevent it from coming into existence. Efforts are made at all levels, from the very bottom to the top, internally and externally, to kill the movement before it is born.

There is no doubt that the Arab national movement is progressive in nature since it is a struggle against the forces of international capitalism, imperialism and the multinationals that control the world market. Its area of struggle is, however, confined to national limits. Similarly, the Arab socialist movement is also progressive in nature since it is mobilizing resistance to international capitalism, imperialism, and class oppression, whether exercised by internal or external forces. Nevertheless, its arena is limited to the class struggle. The feminist movement, however, in consequence of its specific nature and the triple oppression exercised on women, qualifies as the most progressive and revolutionary of all movements since it includes the struggle against national, class, and sex oppression.

Capitalism, religion and solidarity

In recent times international capitalism has developed new forms of global economic exploitation, reinforced by cultural and psychological oppression, which cross over the frontiers between nations. International capitalism is driven to raise the slogan of 'universalism' as a cover for the multinational nature of its investments and exploitation, and as a means to break down trade barriers on the world market when this is required. International capitalism accepts and encourages 'universalism' or 'solidarity' between the exploiting nations in order that it may be better able to oppress and exploit the smaller or weaker nations of the world. But any appeal for solidarity or 'universalism' amongst the smaller, weaker or oppressed nations is considered a breach of the international economic order. In its continued attempt to open up the markets of the more backward nations which have been maintained in their state of dependency and backwardness by years of colonialist and neocolonialist exploitation, international capitalism must also export its values and culture and reinforce what it considers to be a world culture at the expense of the specific national cultures of individual nations. Cultural frontiers are thus broken down just as economic frontiers have been destroyed, so that cultural goods may be 'sold' simultaneously with consumer goods. In order to render these activities convincing, capitalism conceals its real intentions by talking of 'humanity' as a whole, the 'oneness' that groups the whole human race, the 'unity of culture' and the 'universality' of religion and its principles whether Christianity, Islam or Judaism. This appeal for unity is immediately discarded and replaced by an opposing position, however, if the Arab nations raise the slogans of economic, political and cultural unity between one another. Any appeal for unity between the individual national movements of the exploited countries meets with fierce resistance.

This situation is the breeding ground for many of the contradictions that can be observed in our countries, and that weigh most heavily on Arab women since they constitute the weakest and most exploited sections of the population, both politically and socially, as a result of the triple oppression to which they are exposed. One of the notable contradictions that may be observed in recent times is the fact that the influential capitalist circles of the West have launched a campaign for unity between the religions of the world. However, when their interests necessitate a change of position this slogan is dropped, and in the Arab region they encourage divisions based on religion and creed as a means to oppose the establishment of Arab unity. Religion is thus transformed into a dangerous weapon in the hands of international capitalism and the ruling classes linked to it in the dependent countries of the world. We are faced with the strange spectacle of Western encouragement to Islamic movements in many Arab countries, as a means to build up barriers against the progressive forces, to strengthen retrograde structures and to divide the national movements within the region on the basis of religion and creed. The major capitalist countries resist Islam where it is an instrument of progress and unity, and encourage it whenever it serves to divide and weaken. Here lies one of the sources of severe contradiction in the lives and struggles of Arab women.

The struggle against imperialism in the Arab region sometimes takes on a nationalist content and form, and at other times bases itself on religious concepts and principles. Islam in certain situations is capable of playing a progressive and unifying role in the national movement, if it draws inspiration from the principles of justice, freedom and equality between people irrespective of colour, class or sex on which it is based. The real problem, however, arises from the fact that the ruling capitalist and feudal circles all over the world, in order to serve their own interests and use religion for their own purposes, discard its essence and concentrate on the formal textual teachings, without relating them to one another, or to time and circumstances. They extract isolated quotations, which are often contradictory; and bend them to serve specific and changing interests. The interpretations put forward tend to ensure that oppression and exploitation of dependent nations, and of the lower masses of the world, are maintained. Religion thus becomes a means for the exploitation of the poor, the toilers and women.

All over the world, however, the poor working masses are wrestling their rights from the classes that have so far decided the destinies of the world, and are moving forward to a more humane, rational and egalitarian concept of society. To do this they are simultaneously exposing this 'double dealings' game with religion, and realizing at the same time that religion can be put either to retrograde or to progressive purposes.

Women in particular tend to be the most numerous victims sacrificed at the altar of religion, or more precisely at the altar of retrograde interpretations of religions. They are therefore forced to become a progressive social force that ardently desires to cooperate with other progressive forces in emphasizing an enlightened interpretation of religion and using it to liberate women. The Arab feminist movement therefore has no intention of repeating the mistake made by other progressive movements, namely of falling into the trap of opposing religion, a trap that imperialist and reactionary circles continue to lay with cunning and care, hoping that the quarry will fall. For it is not religion that is the enemy, but rather these same imperialist circles and the reactionary classes or groups allied to them. The Arab feminist movement will remember these lessons, and exhibit a greater degree of understanding and consciousness. It will be a popular movement drawing its ideology and practice from the broad masses of women, rather than from isolated groups living in a theoretical world of their own. This fundamental orientation will protect it from falling into the trap of not seeing its real enemies.

Religion is an integral part of society, and a product of the social and human structure of which society is made, in both its theological and its practical aspects. It results from the interaction of different social factors, and exercises an effect on the conscious and subconscious areas of social and individual human existence, but historically it is not, and never has been, the original reason why man has dominated woman and exploited her.

The need for a rereading of Arab women's history

What, essentially, is the factor or factors that leads to the domination of man over woman? To answer this question the Arab feminist movement must undertake a new but necessary task, which is to discover the real reasons why in history man was enabled to dominate over woman, and more specifically why Arab man was able to dominate Arab woman. An error in the diagnosis of any situation or malady inevitably leads to an error in treatment. We therefore cannot afford to make any mistake in our analysis. This is what renders the rereading and reinterpretation of human history in general and of Arab history in particular so necessary for women. Arab women will never be able to change their situation unless they understand how it arose and developed historically.

History has never been, nor can it be, a neutral science, a totally objective science that exposes the complete truth. Many of the true facts concerning the lives and struggles of the popular masses over the years have been buried, or erased, or distorted, or misinterpreted to serve the aims of particular forces in society. This applies to world history as well as to the history of the Arab peoples. There is nothing unusual or mystifying about this situation, for he who writes history does so from his own point of view, and in order to serve specific purposes or interests. In general, therefore, history has tended to express the viewpoints and interests of the dominant forces or classes in society. That is why history has tended to be changed from era to era, or to be rewritten whenever a new political force came on to the scene.

The Arab national movement therefore is carrying out its own study of history to extract those facts, ideas and explanations that were hidden or distorted in order to mask or weaken the roots and origins of the Arab national movement and its subsequent development. The Arab national movement is seeking those elements and interpretations of its history that will serve to reinforce, consolidate and clarify its forward movement, rather than weaken its forces and push them back. A rereading of Arab history shows that the Arab national movement has powerful roots in the past, and that its origin differs from the birth of the national movements in Europe or in general from the origin of the bourgeois nationalist movements in developed countries. The Arab national movement arose not simply as a capitalist development against feudalism, but much earlier as a long process of struggle against foreign invasion of the Arab countries, a process that dates back fourteen centuries. It is not the nationalism of capitalist monopolist interests, but the movement of an Arab nation linked by language, religion, history, geographical interconnections, civilization and the promise of a common future and destiny.

The socialist movement in its turn has attempted to reread history and to view the historical movement as an interaction of economic, social, political and cultural factors, in which the various component groups and classes engage in a struggle that is the dynamic force of change. This takes the form of antagonism between the feudal landlords and peasants, the capitalists and workers, and so on. Some Arab socialist thinkers have tried to investigate the Arab Islamic civilization anew on the basis of their historical methodology and concepts. Studies of Islamic religion have been published in which a new analysis and interpretation of events constitutes the main contribution. For example, Islamic theology and practice have been visualized as being composed of two main currents broadly considered to be 'progressive' and 'traditionalist', left and right. The left wing has been traced back to the early stages of Islam with the resistance initiated by Abu Thar Al-Ghafari against the successors of Muhammad and the influential power groups that surrounded them and engaged in the accumulation of riches at the expense of the masses of the poor. It has then been traced down the ages as a progressive militant wing of Islam, embodied at various stages in movements like that of the Mu'tazila, the Karmathians and others reaching down to the present period.

A rereading of Arab history and of the Arab Islamic civilization is essential for any Arab national or socialist movement (including the Arab feminist movement). It will permit such movements to build themselves on a firm base, to discover their roots, it will ensure their continuity and thus embody a past, a present, and a future for the Arab nation and its toiling masses. Without this process of historical identification such movements will remain without character or specificity, without originality, and no more than a pale imitation of what has happened elsewhere. In the absence of an original historical analysis they will continue to be dependent on the outside. On the other hand authenticity, based on the facts of history and past experience, will permit them to analyse the present more correctly, envisage the future more clearly, and strengthen their links with the broad masses of the people.

From this understanding arises the need for a reinvestigation of history by the Arab feminist movement in order that women should discover that their struggle against national, class and sexual oppression was not born in the present, but goes back deep into the past. The Arab feminist movement will then acquire substance and flesh, develop its own contours, feed on its own roots, and rise from the soil of Arab lands, rather than become another copy of feminist movements in the West. It will find itself in the history of the Arab civilization and of the fourteen centuries of Islam, from the days when the early Muslim women protested against Muhammad when he limited himself in the Qur'an to addressing men and used the masculine pronouns alone. History has registered this famous protest to Muslim men in the words the women used: 'We have become believers in Islam, like you, and we have done what you did, and yet you are mentioned in the Qur'an and we are not.'¹ As a result Allah responded with a change which from then onwards ensured that both men and women were addressed equally. 'Al Muslimina, wal Muslimat, wal Mu'minina wal-Mu'minat.'²

The struggle of women against male domination was not limited to words, or to changes in the Qur'an, nor did it manifest itself only in the relations between ordinary men and women; it rose even to the level of the Prophet as man and husband. 'Aisha, the wife of the Prophet, often disagreed with him, or criticized what he did, or gave vent to her anger when he married another woman. There were times when she or his other wives would rebel against him. 'Aisha was even capable of objecting in her own way to certain verses of the Qur'an. An example was the occasion on which the Qur'an gave Muhammad permission to marry any number of wives. 'Aisha expressed her disapproval as follows: 'Indeed, Allah responds to your desires without delay.'³

The struggle of Arab women has been a long and arduous one, and has extended throughout the ages. It has weakened or grown in strength at different periods of time. Its fluctuations being linked to the changes in the struggles of the Arab peoples. Women have put up resistance not only in the area of sexual discrimination and male domination, but also against national or class oppression. Arab women have taken part in political struggles, in war, in economic activity and in literary or scientific endeavours. They have taken up the sword and fought with slaves and serfs for liberation, and in resisting internal exploitation or foreign invasion. At other times, the struggles of women have tended to shrink and almost die out.

Modern Arab women will find difficulty in achieving an original independent Arab and human identity built on understanding and a high level of consciousness unless a certain harmony is created between the historical struggle of women and the historical struggle of the other exploited and oppressed groups and classes of society. The feminist movement will thus strike back into the past and extend through the present to the future. It will be an original and creative enrichment to the historical Arab movement in the economic, social and cultural fields, and add its contribution to the store of human knowledge and Arab thought. Its critical content will throw new light on the development of history and submit it to the critical analysis that is a reflection of the new content that a feminist movement must mentally bring to the arena of social and political theory and action. Women will no longer be objects of history, but active subjects of change.

The original contribution of the feminist movement to historical development will result from the fact that an integral analysis covering the root causes of sexual, class and national oppression will be made since the missing female or sex link will now be included. The efforts made by women throughout Arab history will come to light, and they will therefore achieve a new dynamism which will serve to transform them into active makers of events rather than passive objects. Women will become makers of history, and critical analysts of the society in which they live, thus lifting themselves up to new levels, able to see clearly and to avoid the confusion so often caused by male conceit and flattery, which often tend to hide the true nature of developments, and make out of history either a long and magnificent procession of events, devoid of failings and impunities, or a long dark night, full of failures and disappointments, through which no ray of light seems to arrive.

The remoulding of our cultural heritage, of the Arab civilization, from the point of view of the half of society that is composed of women, and of the dispossessed and exploited popular Arab masses, is a vital and urgent task. It is essential if our ideological and cultural heritage is to contribute positively both in thought and in action to the total liberation of the Arab peoples, and if it is to ensure that science and rationality rather than myths and superstition, become the basis for dialectical exchange, theory and practice.

Rational and scientific thinking has deep roots that strike back to the early beginnings of Arab history. It is not an invention we have adopted from the West. Even materialist philosophy has been developed and analysed in the writings of Arab thinkers and philosophers, for example by Ibn Khaldun, Ibn Rushd, Ibn Sina and Al-Razi. Arab thought was not always idealistic or metaphysical in content. There were Arab scientists who did not believe that history is engendered by supernatural powers, or by shadowy forces existing outside the limits of the universe and society. On the contrary, they considered that historical development was the result of a range of social factors and forces which took on different forms at different times and interacted or struggled with one another. To them, riches and poverty were not a product of divine law, but rather the result of social developments and laws that had led to the domination of a privileged minority. To them, the division of property likewise was not to be considered as a heavenly precept or another divine law but again as a product of a specific social development which had made man the owner of land, of slaves, and of women, and consolidated all his property within the framework of the family. The word *familia* in Roman times meant the sum total of the property owned by the head of the household composed of the cattle, the slaves and the women. The philosophical and political concepts prevalent at that time refused the right of freedom to both slaves and women, and therefore refused their equality with masters, landowners and men. Plato and Aristotle, both prominent philosophers of ancient Greece, considered slavery a natural and just system to be maintained for all those who possessed nothing, and the domination of men over women as something arising from human nature itself. In Roman law, whatever existed in society was divided into two main categories, namely people and things. People were men who possessed land, and things were cattle, slaves and women.

A rereading of our history and the discovery of whatever positive aspects or elements have existed at various stages do not mean a refusal to enrich it with the knowledge, science and culture of other countries, nor do they imply any neglect of the efforts made by thinkers of both sexes in other countries and at various stages of human development. This common heritage of humanity has been instrumental in developing progressive thought in sciences and humanities. Similarly, it is necessary that we follow closely the political thought and experiences of other countries, and submit them to critical study so as to ensure that we know what is happening in the rest of the world, its impact on our own development, and how it can serve to clarify our own thought and action to the advantage of the Arab peoples in particular, and the peoples of all countries in general.

This is an important element in the development of the feminist movement. In many countries of the world today, and particularly in the Western capitalist countries, feminist movements are developing, and beginning to impose themselves more and more openly on the social scene. These feminist movements are publishing a growing number of studies with different social and ideological orientations, and have accumulated practical experience over the years. This store of theoretical and practical knowledge needs to be studied and understood by Arab women in a positive and critical way, to ensure that their own knowledge is enriched and to permit fruitful exchange with the feminist movements in these countries.

Limitations forced upon women but not men

Among the most important factors that prevent the participation of the vast majority of Arab women in the Arab national movement or in other political organizations aiming at the liberation of the Arab region are the bonds that surround her body, mind and self under the present family system built on the domination of the father, the grandfather, the husband, the brother or any other male member of the family. These bonds vary in strength and in character from one family to another, and from one class to another. They may be legal, or moral, or religious, or psychological, and therefore invisible. They may be visible to the eye or palpable to the hand like walls, or closed windows and doors. They may even take the form of iron chains that surround the woman's body and legs and prevent her from moving.[4]

The use of chains on women's bodies is a product of the patriarchal family to which they are historically linked. The patriarchal family has bestowed upon the father and the husband certain rights over women including the right to punish them if they are not obedient. The patriarchal family came into being simultaneously with the division of society into masters and slaves and the establishment of private property systems. It was at this stage that the *familia* was born. The form and size of the family changed over the ages through the various historical stages of slave society, feudalism, capitalism and socialism. Nevertheless, to this very day, even in socialist societies, the family remains as an institution headed by the father or husband who gives his name to the children. Socialist systems have succeeded in abolishing classes to various degrees, but the system of patriarchy still prevails in all the socialist countries despite some changes in its form and content. Women and children largely remain the property of the father. Truly socialist countries have sometimes abolished private ownership of the land, factories, dwellings or banks, but not private ownership of women or children. In capitalist countries private property in all things is the rule, including women and children as a result of the patriarchal class system. The Arab countries have strongly entrenched patriarchal class systems where elements of tribal, feudal, capitalist and sometimes even socialist relations intermingle to various degrees. The position of women is way down the social and human scale. The man possesses his women and children totally in both body and mind. He has the full right to punish them and the degree of punishment may vary from verbal blame to blows, abandonment and divorce. Under certain circumstances a man is even allowed to kill his wife, daughter or sister in order to defend his honour. In these cases tradition, custom and law will consider him a 'real man', since he has fulfilled his duty in preserving the family honour.

To this day Egyptian law does not consider the assassination of a woman in defence of the family honour as a crime similar to that of killing in another context. Capital punishment is not applied in these cases and usually the culprit will escape with a relatively short prison sentence, the duration of which will depend on the degree of sympathy evinced by the judge for the man whose sole fault is seen as a legitimate sense of honour. In such cases, the honour that is considered to have been sullied is always that of the man; the woman is merely the object through which his honour has been blemished. The woman is not a human being with honour, but rather a thing that can cause dishonour or shame. This is a source of some of the manifestations of a double standard in the moral, social and legal areas of Arab society. Honour is the sole possession of the man, and this total ownership gives him the power and the right over the being who possesses no honour, namely the woman. Nevertheless, the woman is solely responsible for maintaining this honour. She bears total and complete responsibility for it.

This double standard has arisen as a result of the separation between property and responsibility, or between power and responsibility. For man derives his power from his property (from the ownership he exercises over land, money, religion, science and state power). None the less, he is not responsible since the responsibility devolves on someone else (the woman, or the slaves, serfs and wage earners, or the people). The result is that in our countries a ruler is not accountable for his actions, and a man may have relations with any number of women either openly or secretly but remain honourable. The woman alone is responsible and therefore liable to punishment. The subject is not to be punished, but the object is. This is the essence of the oppression and the injustices that have arisen in human society since the birth of class society: namely, the separation between power and responsibility, and the transformation of women into objects or things that take over the full burden of sin and punishment from the 'doer', just as Eve bore the responsibility of Adam's sin.

Transforming woman from an object to a human being

One of the most important areas of struggle for the Arab feminist movement is that related to the necessary transformation of Arab women from mere things or objects into total human beings enjoying a complete range of rights including the right to do or act. This signifies that women must become subjects of action instead of objects being acted upon. The word subject or doer here means a person who has not only the theoretical right to act but also the capacity and the circumstances that make such action possible, who can choose what action to take and assume its responsibility, and who as an end result will gain the fruits of action whether they be sweet or bitter.

The feminist movement must comprehend this interpretation of action or work if it is to rightfully raise the right of women to leave their homes and seek work. For such a demand can be confusing and even misplaced if we forget that at the present moment in fact millions of women do leave their homes daily and go into the fields to labour but their efforts are not really considered to be work since they are not paid. Similarly the vast majority of women toil increasingly in their homes to serve their husbands and children but receive no pay. Their labour here too is not considered work. The millions of women who work on the land or in shops as part of family or household enterprises are not remunerated for their work, the proceeds of which go to the man. Putting forward the demand 'work for women' within a system that treats women as objects owned by the man inevitably leads to a double form of exploitation. For in addition to being a work instrument within the precincts of the home, the woman also becomes a work instrument outside the home to the greater benefit of the men in the family. This is exactly what has occurred to the majority of educated and professional women from the middle and higher middle classes who have gone out to work in the Arab countries during the past period. Of course it is undeniable that a small minority of these women have been enabled through working for a wage to be liberated from the domination of a man. However, this freedom remains only partial and does not extend to other social, psychological, moral and cultural aspects of their lives.

When the woman comes to be considered a complete human being instead of a 'thing' or an instrument of work she will be accorded her full human rights and achieve both freedom and true equality. As part of her freedom she must enjoy the right to choose the work or profession she desires, and the man she wishes to marry; she must also have the right to receive the full remuneration for any work she may do just as is the case with men. In this way no specific job of work or profession should be forced on a woman simply because of her sex. Specific functions within the home or outside it should not be considered as specifically reserved for women. All work irrespective of its nature, including housework and the rearing of children, should receive appropriate and fair payment. This must be the case with all human effort. This will end the division of labour on the basis of sex, or inheritance. All professions and types of work will be left open for women and men to choose according to their abilities; all forms of education and training will be open to children irrespective of sex or class. The full range of health services and of complete nourishment, whether physical or mental, will be provided to all children without restrictions or conditions.

The division of labour on the basis of class has continued to be vigorously condemned in socialist thought and opposed more and more vigorously with the growing political strength of the working classes. But the division of labour on the basis of sex has not received the same attention in the Arab socialist movement. This is natural since it is not logical to expect that a movement controlled by men will fight against a situation which if changed will lead to the men themselves being deprived of some of the rights and privileges they had inherited over the ages.

[Paper presented to a conference on Arab women held in Beirut, Lebanon, September 1981. The author was not able to present the paper in person as planned because she was arrested and imprisoned. Subsequently this paper was published in Arabic as a booklet of the Arab Women's Solidarity Association and adopted as the organization's philosophy.]

Notes

1. Muhammad Ibn Sa'ad, *Al-Tabakat Al-Kubra*, Dar El Tahrir, Cairo, 1970, Part 8, p. 45.

2. Sura al-Ahzab, Qur'an aya 35.

3. Muhammad Ibn Sa'ad, *Al-Tabakat Al-Kubra*, Dar El Tahrir, Cairo, 1970, Part 8, pp. 140–41.

4. During a visit to Damascus in 1980, I saw a television series about Syrian women and young girls who had been clapped into iron chains and imprisoned in one of the rooms of the house or in the bathroom or toilet by the father, or husband or another of the male members of the family. In Egypt there are fathers who fetter their daughters in iron chains. *Al-Ahram* reported one such

incident, which resulted in the woman's death, in its issue dated 21 March 1981 (page 13), under the following title: 'A father chained his daughter in iron fetters to prevent her from visiting her mother.' This incident raises a question about the rights a father has to punish his daughter. The strange aspect of this incident is that the magistrate in the court of South Cairo, a man named Mohamed Kamal Hassan, derived support from a judgment from the Court of Appeal permitting fathers to put their daughters in chains as a form of punishment. His objection was directed against the fact that the chains used by this particular father had prevented the daughter from moving. He considered that the father had every right to use this form of punishment, but that he had overstepped his paternal prerogatives by using chains that limited her movement severely, hurt her body and left abrasions on her wrists, all of which observations had been registered in the coroner's report. Of course his honour the magistrate appeared to know nothing about the mental and psychological trauma that can be caused to a human being by such a procedure.

CHAPTER 22

Women in Resistance: The Arab world

The Arab peoples, including Egyptians, whether women or men, have continued to resist the forces which deprive them of their right to a human and peaceful existence. Time and again they have risen up in revolt to overthrow reactionary rulers or have fought to expel foreign invaders.

Over the years Egypt has remained the heart of the Arab world due to its strategic position, the size of its population, and its long history of resistance against colonialism and imperialism.

Egyptian and Arab women participated right from the beginning in the struggle for liberation of themselves and their countries. Since the evolution of the patriarchal class system, women in Egypt and other Arab countries fought against slavery and oppression.

Women in ancient civilizations (in Egypt, Iraq, Palestine and others) enjoyed respect and high status, in all domains of life; political, religious, social and cultural. In Egypt we had our goddesses Isis and Ma'at. They were symbols of knowledge, wisdom and justice. But with the beginning of the patriarchal class system women started to lose their position in relation to men. This change was found to correspond with the appearance of private property, feudalistic systems and foreign invasion. Since then, the vast uprisings and rebellions which swept the Egyptian people, including women and slaves, never stopped.

The same happened in different Arab countries. Women were dethroned from their position as head of tribes and clans, deprived of their right to name the children born of their own wombs, and transformed into unpaid slaves in the marriage code.

The forces of colonialism that hurled themselves in successive waves on Egypt and Arab countries were able to plunder many of their economic and cultural riches, to conceal many historical facts and ignore the role of women in resistance and women's resistance against oppression and injustices.

However, throughout the second half of the nineteenth century, the resistance of the people in our region – men and women – to foreign and local domination mounted steadily. Strengthening resistance was accompanied by a vigorous reawakening and enlightenment in the areas of political thought, literature and knowledge. The Egyptian and Arab women's liberation movement was part of this struggle. Among the women pioneers were 'Aisha El-Gaymouria, Zeinab Fawaz, Malak Hefni Nassef and May Ziada. They fought with their pens against all types of oppression including the oppression of women by their men inside the family.

They paid the price of their courage. One of them, May Ziada, was rewarded for her brave writings by loneliness, accusations of madness and an early death. While still a young woman she was put in a mental hospital called Asfouria in Lebanon. As she stepped over the threshold, she looked around her and said, 'Could they not find a more dignified prison for me than this one?' She begged the hospital authorities to let her leave, and went on hunger strike time and again. This situation continued for several months until a committee of eminent doctors was commissioned to examine her. The report affirmed that she was completely free of illness. But the hospital authorities still refused to discharge her.[1]

Resistance by poor working women

In Egypt and Arab countries the poor classes represent the vast majority of the people. The patriarchal class system, whether tribal, feudal, capitalist or socialist, has exploited the poor and offered them the most arduous and inferior of jobs for the lowest pay. Women, of course, have had the worst of the bargain. They have had to work both outside and inside the home.

In Egypt the first census of women participating in the wage-earning labour force was taken in 1914. They were only 20,000 at the time, that is, 5 per cent of the total number of employees. In those days girls and women from poor families sought jobs in large numbers in the factories and ginning mills. The working day exceeded fourteen hours, and the daily pay was around 3 piastres, but sometimes dropped to 18 millimes (= 2 cents). As a result of inhuman working conditions, long hours, exhaustion and undernutrition, a woman could stand the pace at a factory for no more than four or five years; after that she was no longer fit for anything. The owner of the factory would discharge her just as he would get rid of a wornout part.

These poor unhappy women, exhausted in body and in soul, were the first women to rebel in twentieth-century Egypt, the first to strike and to occupy factory premises, the first to demonstrate in the streets and demand that their human dignity be respected, that the hours of work be shortened and determined by law, and that maternity leave be accorded for pregnancy and childbirth. In those days no maternity leave whatsoever was allowed, and a working woman who had given birth to a child would hasten to the factory on the following morning lest she lose her job. Women who were looking for jobs would never mention that they were married, for unmarried girls were always preferred by managements. If a woman happened to become pregnant she would do everything to hide the signs, as though she had committed some crime, or was bearing an illegitimate child. In most cases she would try some unhealthy method of abortion. This very often ended in her dying of haemorrhage or infection.

The first women's organization

During the same period women of the upper classes in Egypt started to form the first women's organization in 1923. However class barriers meant that they knew nothing about the conditions of the poor working women. One of the demonstrations organized by working women in factories ended in a gathering at the premises of the new Women's Federation, but the aristocratic leaders who were responsible for its activities paid no attention to the grievances of these poor women.

Women's role in the revolution of 1919

Toiling women in the industrial areas and rural villages of Egypt constituted the female force that participated vigorously in the national revolution of 1919. It was from the ranks of those women that the female martyrs of the 1919 revolution came. They were killed by British troops when they went out on to the roads cutting telephone wires and disrupting railway lines in order to paralyse the movement of British troops. Some of those women martyrs are known; they include Shafika Mohammed, who was killed by the British on 14 March 1919, Hamida Khalil from Kafr El Zaghari Gamalia and others.[2] But hundreds of poor women lost their lives without anybody being able to trace their names.

Those poor women played an outstanding role in resistance and liberation but history and historians ignored them, and concentrated the limelight on the men leaders, and a few women from the upper classes who made a contribution to the national uprising of 1919 but did not lose their lives as had the poor women.

The beginnings of the women's liberation movement

Hoda Shaarawi is recognized by historians as the first leader of the women's liberation movement in Egypt. She founded the first Women's Federation in 1923 with Cesa Nabarawi, Nabaweya Mousa and some other women from the upper and middle classes. They fought to abolish the veil, to raise the age of marriage for girls (to sixteen years), to prevent polygamy, to diminish the absolute right of men to divorce, and to give women the right to vote.

In spite of their efforts they could not change the marriage and divorce law, but they succeeded in raising the age of marriage for girls to sixteen years. They failed to win for women the right to vote.

They also fought to increase the chances of women to obtain higher education and professional work. Nabaweya Mousa was one of the leaders who encouraged girls and women to be educated and gain jobs in a range of professions. She was the head of the secondary school for girls in Abbasseya in Cairo called Banat El-Ashraf Girls School. I became a pupil at this school in 1944 after graduating from the primary school in my village. I had to put on a black suit and thick black long stockings. She was very strict with the girls, but encouraged them to study and look forward to a career. I left the school after one year to go to Saneya secondary school for girls.

Nabaweya Mousa was also a writer and one of her important works is a book called *Women and Work*. In this book she criticized the old traditions that prevent women from obtaining education and professional work. She wrote:

We neglect the education of Egyptian women so that they become un-qualified for work. But we encourage foreign women to enter our homes and look after our vital needs. Egypt's capital is lost for the benefit of those foreign women and foreign interests. If we educate our women they can replace those foreign women. We are fighting for our political independence – why are we so slow in fighting for our economic independence?[3]

Hoda Shaarawi and her organization worked hard to bring women's rights to the forefront as part of the national struggle for liberation. Women started to be aware of the fact that they have to fight a double battle: not only against the British and foreign exploitation, but also against male domination or patriarchy in the family and in society. The new constitution adopted in Egypt on 19 April 1923 stated that all Egyptians are equal in front of the Law. But women were not given the right to vote. The Law of Election issued on 30 April 1923 stated that the right to vote was only for males. It was after this that Egyptian women started their fight to gain their political rights, and to combine women's liberation with national liberation.

Doreya Shafik was a very brave fighter for women's rights. She was the first woman to organize a political party for women in Egypt, in 1953, which was called Hizb Bin Al-Nil. Two years earlier, she had led a demonstration to the parliament demanding the right of women to vote. She wrote thirteen books in the course of her life, including studies on women, poetry and fiction.[4] In spite of her efforts with her women colleagues to change the situation of women, she came to feel that she had failed, and she ended her life by jumping from her sixth-floor apartment in Cairo in 1975.

As regards the vote, Egyptian women did not gain this right until the constitution of 1956 was promulgated following the 1952 revolution.

Arab women resisting colonialism and neocolonialism

Women all over the Arab world participated in the struggle for national liberation and women's liberation. Despite the severe curtailment of democratic liberties, and the constraints put on all political activity, especially women's political activity, at different periods women in almost all the Arab countries, including Algeria, Palestine, Lebanon, Syria, Iraq, Sudan, Yemen and Tunisia, have organized their struggle on various fronts of activity whether military, political, economic, social or cultural.

The Palestinian women fought against foreign occupation of their land by the Israeli army. They gave a long list of martyrs. They are still fighting and dying in the Intifada side by side with their children and men. They have organized a strong resistance against the military and administrative authorities, and participated in their hundreds and thousands to raise the banner of civil disobedience and to demonstrate in the cities and towns of Jerusalem, Nablus, Al-Jalil, Ghaza and others.

Every day women and young girls volunteer to join the ranks of the Intifada and the Palestine Liberation Organization. They are aware that liberation of their country is not separate from liberation of themselves. They know the link between imperialism and Zionism internationally, and the patriarchal and class systems locally.

The women's liberation movement in Egypt and Arab countries is aware of the link between the international and the national forces of exploitation and oppression. The neocolonial powers have developed an arsenal of divisive weapons which it directs against the forces of resistance in our region. In addition to using military and brute force (the massacres of Palestinians and civil war in Lebanon) discord and division can be sown by exaggerating tribal and national differences or by encouraging unhealthy racial or chauvinistic tendencies as well as religious fanaticism.

The neocolonial powers propagate notions of modernization and liberalization linked to consumerism, sex tourism, pornography, naked bodies of women in advertisements, etcetera, in so far as these encourage commercial activities and increase the profits of the multinationals. But at the same time they provide encouragement and assistance to fundamentalist movements either directly or through intermediaries.

Women in our region are the first victims of this double game. As consumers and sex objects they are called upon to become more liberal and more modern. This is what we witness amongst women of the urban elite, women professionals, women working in branches or affiliates of multinational corporations in Egypt and Arab countries, upper-middle-class or rich housewives, women in tourism hotels and night clubs. But the mass of Egyptian and Arab women in rural and urban areas are told to stay at home rather than go out to paid work, to wear the veil, to be overworked, exhausted by their double workload and several roles inside and outside the home, and to hold more firmly to traditionalist religious practice.

The end result is to divide women on a class basis, isolate the elites and subjugate them to the world market, while turning the majority into an instrument of reactionary forces and a nonproductive force in a market stricken with economic crisis and widespread unemployment.

In order to back up an increasingly difficult and unjust situation for the vast majority of women (and men) in our region, it is necessary for the authorities to control their minds so that they do not resist or rebel. Thus a combination of Western acculturation and religious indoctrination has become the daily mental nutrition of women, children and men in our countries, through the television and mass media.

This renders resistance more difficult: when the chains enter the mind and souls of women they become invisible. They also mean that the woman can become her own jailer, and that in order to change, in order to resist, she has to fight forces within herself.

The Arab Women's Solidarity Association

Women and men in Egypt and other Arab countries are aware of the importance of unity and unified power in the face of the unified powers of neocolonialism, Zionism and imperialism. Arab unity is a goal and Arab women's unity and solidarity are important weapons in fighting for the liberation of women and of our land and economy.

We started the Arab Women's Solidarity Association in 1982 following in the footsteps of the previous pioneers in the women's liberation movement.⁵ We fight for our freedom and human rights inside the family, as well as nationally and internationally.

If the neocolonial system is global, then resistance to it must be global. If the patriarchal class system is global then resistance to it must be global. This global women's resistance requires political and organizational efforts to unite women all over the world.

Only minds liberated from their chains can make resistance and revolution a fact. Revolution can be attained step by step from within the system if women build up their own political organizations.

We need political power to continue our struggle. We need the power of knowledge and awareness. We need solidarity within our countries and internationally.

[1990. Translated by Sherif Hetata]

Notes

1. Taher Al-Tanahi, *Al-Sa'at Al-Akhira*, (The Last Moments), pp. 111–12, and Nawal El Saadawi, *The Hidden Face of Eve*, Zed Books, London, 1980, p. 173.

2. Abdel Rahman Al-Rafi'i, *Fi-A'qab Al-Thawra Al-Misria*, Vol. 1, Maktabat El Nahda Al-Misria, Cairo 1959, p. 211; Nawal El Saadawi, *The Hidden Face of Eve*, Zed Books, London 1980, p. 176.

3. Extract published in *Noon*, No. 4, February 1990, p. 17. *Noon* was the magazine of the Arab Women's Solidarity Association.

4. See *Noon*, Nos. 2 and 3, 1989.

5. *Women in the Arab World: The Coming Challenge* (papers of the First International Conference of the Arab Women's Solidarity Association, Cairo, 1986), Zed Books, London, 1988, pp. 2–6.

CHAPTER 23

Women and Politics in Britain

Greenham Common

I can still remember that day, still remember there was no sun, and that the black clouds crept over the sky from the north in a slow, heavy movement. An icy shiver went through me as I sat on an ancient tree trunk, which lay there as though it had been cut down centuries ago.

She squatted on the ground as old, as wizened, and as powerful as the treetrunk. Her face looked out at me from under the tent: stone white with a bluish tinge of cold, its lines deeply curved as though with a knife, her chapped lips almost bloodless under the strong nose. Her voice resounded with an inner strength hidden somewhere in the tired body: 'Their cruise will have to cross over our bodies.'

A circle of eyes looked at me through the open door of the tent, gleaming in the semidarkness with a strange light: the young eyes of girls under twenty, the old eyes of women over seventy. When I lifted my head to examine the tent's surroundings, through the steel wire mesh I could see an endless space of ground covered by trucks and machines of various kinds. Further away there were houses for the families of the Americans occupying the base, with schools and gardens. I could imagine children playing in the grey morning. I could see them but could not hear their voices. There was something terrible in this vision of silent children, on the playground of nuclear war.

All I could hear was the heavy pacing of the Sentinel tanks and armoured vehicles behind the wire fence and the occasional click of metal on metal. Through the wires the soldiers' eyes looked out at us like coloured glass, and under the helmets the skins were white and sometimes black. Now and then I glimpsed the occasional fullness of a female breast.

The women had erected their tents outside the wire. Every group of tents was designated by a different colour, so there were 'the yellow tents' and 'the blue tents' and 'the green tents'. The old woman had dug a small pit in the ground and filled it with dry wood from the tree. Now she lit a fire. A young woman was scraping the mushrooms she had collected with a small knife and throwing them into the cauldron. A dark-haired girl wearing a long, full dress went off into the neighbouring forest to collect wood, and came back carrying some in her skirt. A third woman who had been warming her big, rough hands at the fire stood up, went into the tent, came out with a plastic jerry can, and disappeared somewhere to look for water. Close to the fire a number of women collected for the weekly meeting of delegates from the various groups of tents.

My eyes followed what was going on around me in some bewilderment, but each time they would return to the woman sitting in front of me, who was like the trunk of a powerful tree.

'My name is Mary,' she said.

I followed the deep lines in her face, wondered at the vitality in her voice and eyes and thought, the soul inside has defied the passing of time.

'At night we listen carefully for the sound of wheels. They try to get the cruise in when they think we cannot see them,' she said.

'But how can you stop them?' I asked.

'With our bodies. As soon as we hear the wheels, we lie down on the ground. Their rockets will have to pass over us if they want to get in. I prefer to die here rather than alone in my room. Then at least there will be some meaning to my death. Maybe my grandson will be proud of me. I have lived for seventy years but no one has ever been proud of anything I have done.'

Her voice still echoes in my ears, and her wrinkles speak to me at different times, in buses, and planes, or when the night is silent. I remember now her body was thin, without flesh, and around her shoulders she had wrapped a dirty yellow shawl. When I looked down I could see her feet swollen in their grey stockings, and wet with the rain and the mud of the forest.

I shivered with cold, but I felt the warm blood flow under my ribs. She brought her feet close to the fire: 'The first winter here, in 1981, was really bad, but in 1982 things were easier. This is the third winter we have been here and you can see ... ' She broke off, closed her lips tightly, and stared at a big metal sign on the other side of the iron gate leading into the military base. I followed her glance and read the black letters: 'WE HAVE ORDERS TO SHOOT' ...

She brought her head close to the fire and blew into it until the embers flared up again. She chuckled like a child. 'During the night we crawled up to the gate and dismantled it. They were obliged to use the other gate, and there we made a rampart with our bodies.'

She leaned over a hole in the ground. It contained a number of huge iron scissor-like cutters. She pulled one of them out, put it in my hand, and gave me a piece of steel wire. 'Try and cut it,' she said.

I put the wire between the two edges of the wire cutters and pressed down with all my might. Immediately it broke into two. I heard her chuckle again: 'That's what we do at night. Yesterday they saw four of us cutting the wire and put them in jail. But next Saturday we will assemble five thousand men and women to cut the whole fence. Do you know,' she added, 'that in England now there are one hundred and two military bases. We have become an occupied land. If we want to be free these must be closed down.'

'Which part of England do you come from, Mary?' I asked.

I heard her swallow with difficulty. She paused for a moment before answering: 'I was born in South Africa of an English mother and father. I used to see my father beat my mother at home, then go out to work where he would beat the blacks on the farm. My mother killed herself in front of my eyes. And so I learned to hate my father and to hate those who colonize others. Then I married.' She paused for a moment. 'My husband taught me to hate marriage, to hate any form of oppression. As the years went by I realized you can't separate different kinds of oppression, that imperialism, colonial, racial and sexual oppression are all linked together in one way or another.'

And so in Greenham Common some of the things my life had led me to realize were confirmed.[1] Before the winter of 1983 I had been to London several times, but that was the first time I visited the women at Greenham Common. From that winter onwards each time I came to London I returned to the peace camp, to the women I had seen before on the common, to Mary and Karen and Liz and Sue and tens of others. I wanted to look into their eyes once again, to feel their strength and their will, and to watch their common effort. I wanted to listen to the things the media never spoke of.

'We lived through two world wars. We're here determined there'll never be a third.'

'In the past our men left home to go to war, now we women are leaving home for peace.'

Year after year, winter and summer, they laid their bodies down on this patch of Berkshire scrubland. Step after step they built up a new force against nuclear war, resisted police harassment, trials, periods in jail. Month after month they grew from a small movement into a vast protest which grouped tens of thousands of people, mainly women. The initial group was constituted under the name Women for Life on Earth. They carried out a 110-mile march which started from Cardiff and ended in Greenham Common where the Women's Peace Camp was established. This peace camp later became the spark that inspired many of the recent peace movements in Britain, Europe and the United States.

The women of Greenham Common were the reason I chose to write about women and politics in Britain. For I felt that they represented something totally new, that they were a novel political movement of women full of a great human potential, a movement destined to develop and to grow even if it did not survive in the initial form. I realized that women in Britain would continue to play an increasing role, become a catalyst and a driving force which would contribute to a vast movement of all the oppressed, whether they be oppressed by class, or race, or sex, or for any of the other reasons that make the oppressed of this earth oppressed. For in their camps and tents the Greenham Common women stood up and resisted the most powerful and the most dangerous forces the world has ever known, the forces trying to build up and prepare a nuclear war.

For months and years these women stood the hardship of this primitive life on Greenham Common. Through months and years of effort they succeeded in mobilizing the 50,000 women who surrounded the nuclear war base on 11 December 1983, who formed a human barrier around the nine-mile fence and with their sheer weight made substantial parts of it collapse. They suffered rough handling by the police who carried many hundreds of these women off to jail. And although they failed to stop the installation of cruise missiles at the base, the result of their action has been the development of a peace movement in Britain that today groups more than 400,000 men and women.[2]

Women occupy the hospital

Again it was winter, this time two years later during February 1985. There was no sun, but no black clouds either, just an icy cold. It was a world where everything seemed to be made of lead except the buses and the young faces of the people who hurried along the pavements, or rode bicycles swiftly through the streets. My companion this time was an English young woman of Turkish origin, her name Algin, her occupation unemployed for the last year. She is one of the 12 per cent looking for work, one of the 4 million people in the reserve army of labour who serve as a threat to those who have a job.

'Which are the most active feminist groups these days?' I asked Algin.

'The lesbians,' she answered with a smile.

'I meant active politically,' I hastened to clarify.

'Lesbian activities are political activities.'

'I heard that a group of women has occupied one of the hospitals and is running it, and that another group has occupied a church.'

'Yes, that's true. You probably mean the South London Women's Hospital. The women took it over last summer and it's still in their hands. As regards taking over the church that goes back to the spring of 1982.'

'I'd like to see them,' I said.

So we took the underground to South Clapham. As we approached the hospital I caught sight of the banners hanging on the walls. They said a lot to me. As I walked up, my feet were light, rapid, eager over the steps. 'South London Hospital – Women Will Not Close', 'No Cuts of National Health Services', 'Stop This Racist Attack on Women', 'Fight Back – We Can Win', 'Women Need the South London Hospital', 'Centralized Hospitals Treat People Like Sardines', 'Building Medical Empires' – that's what the banners said.

In the entrance hall I saw women sitting on the floor. Some of the faces I had seen before, maybe in Greenham Common or elsewhere. But most of them were new. To the left of the entrance was a room with a glass panel facing the hall. Behind it were men wearing blue helmets. Below the helmets their eyes watched us through the glass panel as we walked in. One of the men held a telephone receiver in his hand, and we could hear him informing the district health authority about the situation in the hospital.

In one of the rooms I found a group of women sitting on cushions arranged neatly on the floor. As soon as I walked in one of the women stood up and warmly shook hands with me. I recognized Mary, my friend from Greenham Common. There was something motherly in the way she embraced me, in the touch of her arm on my shoulder, in her voice so soft and yet so strong.

'I was at Greenham Common when we heard that an order had been issued to close the hospital. We held a meeting composed of delegates from the groups and decided to occupy the hospital and run it on our own so that the patients could continue to get the care they needed. Many of the members of the staff – women doctors and nurses – decided to continue working. One of the nurses, called Ruth, was at the head of this movement and when the authorities tried to transfer her she resigned from her job and decided to stay on with us.

'We have been running the hospital for the last seven and a half months, since June 1984. We're beginning to feel the strain. There's so much to do. We have to clean this huge hospital ourselves. We are against the closure of this hospital because it serves the women in this district. Most of them are immigrant women belonging to racial minorities from Africa and Asia including Muslim women whose husbands refuse to allow them to go to male doctors. The decree to close the hospital down is not only against women. It is racist and it's directed against the poorer classes: working women and housewives married to working men.'

Another of the women I met there was Jane, a dark English woman born in India. She was carrying a magazine called *Mokti* which is published by a group of Asian women mainly from the Indian subcontinent.

'I live in this district of south London. My four children were born in this hospital and have been taken care of ever since by the doctors and nurses who work here. There is no other place where I can go for medical services.'

In answer to my questions, Jane told me, 'Yes, I am a feminist and I carry on political activities together with other Asian women who live in England. We issue a magazine and participate in marches and demonstrations. We lived for some time at Greenham Common with the women, and we joined the miners' wives in their activities to support the miners' strike.'

Lying on her back in one of the corners was a woman whose body was covered with a grey blanket. She wore an old black shawl.

'If they want to close this hospital they will have to move in over our bodies.' I remembered the women at Greenham Common. She spoke the same words, and she had the same look on her face. It was the face of someone who is being driven beyond fear.

Caroline was standing near us, her greying hair lying over her shoulders, her eyes gazing straight ahead with a strange absorption. 'We expect them to expel us next month,' she said. 'They want to sell the hospital and found a company that will make huge profits. Now we know that sooner or later we will be evicted. It took us some time to realize that they are stronger. That's what happened too at Greenham Common. But we are learning, and as time passes, when we get over the setbacks, resistance will grow.'

I spent two nights in the hospital talking to women of different professions and races, to whites and blacks, Asians, West Indians and Africans. Names and faces crowd in on my memory: Vicky, Viv, Ruth, Caroline, Mary, Karen, Suzy, Sue and many others. We gathered around as though seeking warmth in the cold night. A young English woman of Pakistani origin made us some strong tea. The heating in the hospital was not functioning, but as the night went on exhaustion got the better of us, and the women dropped off to sleep one after another in rooms that had been emptied of everything except a few medical appliances. But I was unable to sleep. I walked along a deserted corridor looking for the kitchen. I was thirsty and needed a glass of water. Coming back I lost my way and ran into a young black woman sitting with her back to the wall. A young white woman huddled up close to her. The black woman said her head was spinning, and that her hands and feet were icy cold. Her words and her weak voice served to remind me that I was a medical doctor. I dropped down on my knees and felt her pulse. It was distant, hardly to be felt, and her lips were almost blue. Then I heard her say, 'I came from Greenham Common this morning and have had nothing to eat for two days.' Together with her friend I helped her to walk down the corridor. We lifted her on to an empty bed, and wrapped her in a shawl, then covered her with three blankets. Two cups of tea and coramine drops gradually brought some warmth back to her body. I looked in my bag and found a bar of chocolate. As she munched into it we started talking.

'I've been out of a job for over two years. When I'm hungry I go to the market and steal food, and when I want to read I go to a bookshop or a stall and steal books.

'I come from a working-class family in Kent. My mother wanted me to have an education. But my father was a hard man and treated both my mother and myself very badly. So I ran away at the age of seventeen and worked as a secretary. Then I fell in love with a man and we lived together. But he was just like my father, and the day came when I could stand it no longer. I left and never went back. This time I got to know women in the feminist movement and joined the Women's Health Group. I fell in love with a girl and realized I was a lesbian. Now I live on my unemployment benefit which is twenty-eight pounds a week, and at the same time I work here in the hospital as a cleaner. I work more than the others because I am younger and have no higher education and because I'm black.'

During this time the white girl who sat with us had said nothing, but now she joined in. 'My life is no better than hers. My real mother was a Catholic. My father and mother lived together without marrying and as soon as she became pregnant he left her. After I was born my mother left me in a home, and there I remained until my adoptive mother and father came along. They made me work in the house like a servant, so I ran away at the age of twelve. After a short while I started to live with a friend, but he left me as soon as I became pregnant. It was after this that I became friendly with some members of the feminist movement. They came to my rescue and helped me to get an abortion.'

As we sat chatting around the bed a dark girl called Helen came into the ward and sat down beside us. I wondered for a moment where she had suddenly sprung from. She was very slight, with short hair and big, childlike eyes. It did not take long before she started to tell her story. She had been born in Cyprus of a Turkish Muslim mother and English father. When she came to England with her father she was only eleven. He married her off to an Indian businessman from Bengal. She bore him two sons, but after four years of marriage he divorced her. She joined the feminist movement and started to work in a shop in order to bring up her children. Now, at the end of each day's work, she comes back to the hospital to spend the night with the other women.

Suzanne was a woman who had given birth to her child during the period when the women took over the running of the hospital. She had named her daughter Scarlet, and the child was now five months old. The mother was only twenty years old and had been born in Canada. She worked as a nurse in the hospital and was struggling with the other women in their attempt to keep it open.

As the night went on our group kept growing. Marion told us she was born in Jamaica and had five children by an English man. But he had abandoned his family and left them on their own. She lived with the children in a small room close to the hospital and was dependent on her unemployment benefit. She stared at me with her big eyes, which were big enough to carry all the sadness of these lives. Yet in her voice there was something like joy when she described the political action she was undertaking with the other women. She was black, she was poor, unemployed, abandoned first by her father as a child then by her husband. Yet her eyes carried a message of pride as she sat there between her women friends.

A woman's demonstration in King's Cross

The mornings had not changed: still grey, still icy, infusing energy into my body accustomed to the warmth of subtropical sunshine. Now as I walked there was ice under my rubber shoes; it crunched with a sound like desert sand, taking me back for a moment to those I had left behind.

Two days ago in the *Observer* I had read an item of news. A mother and her child had died of cold. The mother, Helen Smith, was found dead in her south London flat. Near her lay Natasha, eleven years old. The boy Michael, just turned thirteen, was in an advanced state of hypothermia.[3]

I felt suffocated in the underground, felt I was breathing in stagnant air already breathed out by thousands of men and women who had breathed it in from others before. I was in a never-ending vicious circle of intoxication, of queues, and crowds, and sallow unhealthy faces, faces with the sallowness that shows through white and black, and brown and yellow skins. Exhaustion looked out from the faces yet the feet moved quickly over the stairs and along the passages underground.

I had put on my woollen coat and wrapped my neck in my woollen shawl, but my feet were cold. I walked as fast as I could, rising from the tube into the fresh air, breathing in oxygen again, chasing the fumes from my head. I was going to the King's Cross Women's Centre, and as I approached I could see crowds of men and women closely packed around it carrying banners and singing in chorus:

'Arise you prisoners of starvation.
Arise you wretched of the earth.'

I asked one of the women: 'Why the demonstration?'

'We're picketing the Ferndale Hotel. The people of the National Front have made it into a headquarters for themselves, and it's close to our women's centre. During the past months, on several occasions they have attacked individuals and organizations in the area including our centre. Police and councillors have said that the Ferndale Hotel is a base for Nazis.'

The demonstration advanced, a slow-moving human river surrounded by lines of policemen, then came to a halt in front of the Ferndale Hotel. I heard hundreds of voices clamour in one breath, 'Sweep out the Nazis. Smash the National Front.'

The police pressed in more thickly around the demonstrators. Over their heads I could see the banners flapping in the wind: 'Youth in Unity', 'Women against Apartheid', 'King's Cross Women's Centre', 'Black Women for Wages for Housework', 'South London Women's Hospital', 'Arab Women's Group', 'Miners' Support Committee Hackney', 'English Collective of Prostitutes', 'Women Against Violence', 'Students' Union', 'Irish Women's Group', and 'Federation of Bangladeshi Youth Organizations'. There were many others. As I looked round I caught the same pallor showing through the skin of the faces. The same tired features. The same old threadbare coats. Blacks and whites, women and men, youth and children, housewives, women teachers, women with jobs and women without, prostitutes, lonely mothers and divorced wives, women living with men and women living without, women living with other women, Asian women, African women, Arab women, Irish women and American blacks. Women of all ages and colours and professions but all from the poorer ranks.

As I had come to see women in Britain and to know more about them, next morning I was back at the King's Cross Women's Centre before their clock had struck nine. The room was neither big nor small. The windows were covered in faded curtains and the legs of the chairs swayed slightly when anybody sat down on them. A group of women had gathered there, most of them immigrant blacks or Asians; a few were white. On the dark walls they had hung posters and photographs. My eyes were attracted to a big photograph hanging on the wall in front of my seat: it was of a group of women wearing black masks. Underneath was a caption in block letters:

OCCUPATION OF THE HOLY CROSS CHURCH BY THE ENGLISH COL-
LECTIVE OF PROSTITUTES AND SUPPORTERS TO PROTEST AGAINST
POLICE ILLEGALITY AND RACISM IN KING'S CROSS. THEY OCCUPIED
THE CHURCH FOR TWELVE DAYS AND NIGHTS (FROM 12 TO 29
NOVEMBER 1982).

I asked why they were wearing black masks and the women next to me said, 'So that the police should not be able to distinguish between those who are prostitutes and those who are not and so be able to arrest the prostitutes.'

On the same wall was a poster bearing words of Virginia Woolf:

To sell a brain is worse than to sell a body, for when the body seller has sold her momentary pleasure, she takes good care that the matter shall end there. But when a brain seller has sold her brain, its anaemic, vicious and diseased progeny are let loose upon the world to infect and corrupt and sow the seed of disease in others.

I turned back to the group. A dark-faced woman was speaking in a low but clear voice: 'Feminists who belong to the middle class do not understand the problems of women like us who have to live under the very different conditions, imposed on people from the working class who have immigrated from other countries. We are faced with poverty, unemployment, racism, with police brutality, the threat of deportation and with racist immigration laws. They think that their enemy is the man. They are against prostitutes because women who practise the profession have sexual relations with men. They are against porno-graphy because it leads to rape, and rape in their view is in the nature of men. Can you imagine that in A Women's Place they do not allow boys over the age of twelve to enter the centre?'

At the head of this group are two women, Selma James and Wilm-ette Brown. Selma is an American Jew but is against Zionism and considers that it is a racist movement just like apartheid in South Africa. 'That's why the relationship between the two is so close,' she said. Wilmette is a black American born in a New York ghetto. She lives in London and is active in the black feminist movement in Britain. 'Racism makes black women the poorest, and the most deprived.' She punctuated her words with a sweeping movement of her long, beautifully chiselled hands. 'Many of us have been forced to migrate by the international arms trade, the arms race, NATO, and foreign aid in support of military dictatorships. It's the poorest classes in the United States who pay the price for these policies, and when we fought back they tried to make life impossible for us. So we came to Britain as migrants and refugees. The struggles in our home countries are contributing to the defeat of the war machine here and there. Our struggle against police powers in Britain has opened a way for the peace movement's challenge to the nuclear state. For us black women, sexism reinforces the racism that upholds and is upheld by nuclear weapons. Apartheid in South Africa is inseparable from the US–British military industrial complex. Struggle against racism is also struggle against the mining of uranium in Namibia for Trident nuclear submarines.

'Women and men, black and white in our countries do owe something to women and men in the so-called Third World. Not only do the multitude of daily struggles for survival and liberation there confront the issues that are crucial for survival and liberation elsewhere, but they give power to us here by challenging the military industrial complex that rules us both, and which is based on plundering the Third World in our names.'

I sat there taking notes as the discussion went on. Selma took over and started to summarize what in her view were the differences between their group and some of the groups of what she called 'white feminists'. 'We fight politically side by side with other oppressed people like black women, immigrants, black men, the mine workers and their wives. We struggle against racism, class oppression and sexual oppression. We do not postpone our fight in any of these three areas. And our enemy is never the man, as the white feminists seem to think. That is the first difference between us and these other groups.'

'What are your other differences?' I asked.

'Our second difference,' she replied, 'is that we demand wages for housework. Sheila Rowbotham is one of the first women who drew attention to this question in her article entitled "Women's Liberation and the New Politics" published in 1969.[4] In our group we are struggling so that women should be paid, as of right, a living wage for physical and emotional housework, and this money is to come from the military budget of the government. We working-class women have worked enough. Every time they have let us in, it was to find for us some traditionally male enclave, some new level of exploitation. Here we can make a parallel between underdevelopment in the Third World and underdevelopment in our countries. Capitalist planning proposes to the Third World that it develop, that in addition to its present agonies, it too should suffer the agony of an industrial counterrevolution. We women here have been offered the same so-called aid. But those of us who have gone out of our homes to work have warned the rest: inflation has riveted us to the bloody typing pool or to the assembly line and in that there is no solution. We refuse the development they are offering us. But the struggle of the working woman is not to return to the isolation of the home, any more than the housewife's struggle is to exchange being imprisoned in a house for being tied to desks or machines. The challenge is to find modes of struggle that, while helping us to liberate ourselves from the home, at the same time avoid a double slavery and another degree of capitalist control and regimentation. This is the dividing line between reformism and revolutionary politics within the women's movement.'

The miners' wives

It was 24 February 1985. The sky was a deep blue and the sun shone down on London most of the time. Now and then, a white billowing cloud hid the sun, turning the bright green expanses of grass a dark olive, almost metallic colour. I stood enjoying the sunshine and the feeling of being and yet not being a part of the ocean that had flowed down into Hyde Park. They had come from different parts of England, Scotland and Wales: miners, members of the National Union of Mine workers, from villages, cities and towns, workers from industrial districts all over the country, representatives of the trade unions and their federations, of the political parties, of different people's organizations, of women from the feminist groups, and of the miners' wives.

The miners' wives. They had been anonymous women at one time, like millions of other women who go about the hard daily job of looking after the house, and the children, and the man, on a working wage. But in the Britain of 1985, irrespective of what else had happened in the year-long miners' strike, they had carved a place for themselves in the history of the miners' movement, in politics, and most likely in the shaping of future events.

That day they had come from many parts of the UK carrying their banners. One of the wives was carrying a huge poster depicting a working man and a working woman holding hands and marching together. At the bottom of the poster were the words: 'Miners' Wives Action Group.' My eyes quickly ran over some of the banners: 'Card-awan Women's Support Group', 'Barnsley Women Against Pit Closures', 'Miners' Wives – Kent Area'.

The demonstrators marched along. Column after column of men, women, youth and children filed past. On the coats and jackets, sweaters, blouses and dresses were yellow badges printed with black and red letters: 'COAL NOT DOLE', 'SUPPORT THE NUM', 'KEEP FIGHT-ING', 'STOP PIT CLOSURES'.

Lines of policemen, mounted or on foot, hemmed them in on either side, trying to control the unending human tide of marchers. Thousands of voices shouted in unison in support of the miners and against the British prime minister, Margaret Thatcher: 'The workers united will never be defeated. Maggie out. Maggie, Maggie out out. Maggie Maggie Maggie, out out out.' Trade union leaders, politicians, workers followed one another onto the rostrum. I could hear the voice of one of them soaring over the wide open spaces above the clamour of voices. Tony Benn, the labour leader was followed after a while by Dennis Skinner, another member of Parliament and a one-time worker himself. Then there was a roar and the thunder of clapping hands.

I saw a column of women approaching under their banner, which floated high above their heads. Their eyes lit up as a white cloud fled across the sky, letting the sun through again. One of them, a tall blonde woman full of vitality, which showed in the way she moved and talked and shook her head, was Margaret Holmes. She spoke to me of many things, and I confined myself to taking notes.

'I started as an agricultural worker and became active in a trade union in the Kent area. I was the only woman in the regional committee for general transport workers. Agricultural workers are not politically aware and the employers discriminate against women. They push them into low-wage work, or into working fewer than thirty hours a week to deprive them of many legal rights. I have been married to a miner called Joe Holmes for the last twenty years. We have four children. Miners' wives depend on their husbands' jobs since there is no work for them in the mines. After the strike started, we formed a miners' wives' group to support our husbands, then later we formed our Kent area committee. I am the vice-chair of this committee. At the national level we have constituted the committee known as Women Against Pit Closures. Ann Lillburn is its president. Our strength comes from the local communities. If we are defeated, it's going to be very bad not only for us here in Britain but for the whole of Europe, and for the working class all over the world. We are looked upon as a leading force.

'I was born in 1942. I have no college education, only a technical secondary school education. I participated in workers' demonstrations in 1972, 1974 and 1984. What is new in the miners' strike is that women, for the first time perhaps, are in the front ranks. We formed our own women's committees, and these activities helped us to gain a new awareness of our rights as members of the working class, but also as women. Most of us have joined local union organizations and are now active in the trade union movement. This has broken down barriers between us and other women and helped us to find out more about their problems. We began to understand the meaning of women's solidarity, and built up relations of mutual help and cooperation with the feminist groups. On the eighth of March we are going to Germany and Denmark to celebrate International Women's Day.

'We women in mining communities have realized that the destruction of the trade union movement is a part of government plans to dismantle the public sector. Thatcher is using every possible device to defeat the miners. The closure of what are called uneconomic pits is a device to hide the truth. The introduction of automation in the centralized coalfields will cut down manpower in those areas by 50 per cent in the short term. Pits that were considered uneconomic a year ago have now become economic. As the pound falls, the price of imported coal goes up. Thatcher's monetarist policies are in disarray. Unemployment is increasing daily. Last month alone it rose by one hundred thousand. Thatcher's attempt to starve the miners back to work pushed up the trade deficit with the rest of the world by £52,750 million, and fuel oil imports rocketed by 73 per cent in 1983, reaching a new level of £4,010 million.

'For many of us women it started in the kitchen,' she went on. 'But instead of catering for our families we were catering for hundreds. We left our homes, organized women, raised money, spoke at meetings and demonstrations, and travelled in this country and abroad. When our husbands were arrested we went on picket lines with the men. We risked imprisonment ourselves. But through all these activities we united women and whole communities against pit closures and Thatcher's policies.'

After she had finished speaking to me I talked to a number of miners' wives as we walked along in the demonstration, which led us from Hyde Park to Trafalgar Square. One of the most interesting women to whom I talked was a miner's wife named Anne Marie Norris. Very white-skinned and rather large, she nevertheless did everything with a

smooth quickness. Together with one of her colleagues she was carrying a banner. She managed at the same time to carry on a lively
discussion with me as we walked. Her friend said to me, 'Anne collected
money for the miners' families in a very novel way.' In answer to my
question she continued, 'She made a bet that she would reduce her
weight by one kilogram every week if the person paid her fifty pounds.
She succeeded in reducing her weight by twenty kilos in twenty weeks
and collected one thousand pounds this way.' Anne smiled and said, 'I
still have eighty kilos that are worth four thousand pounds.'

The women laughed merrily. They reminded me of my relatives in
the village of Kafr Tahla on the banks of the Nile. For the voices of
village women, or of those who live away from the big cities, have
much in common. They are not cultured voices, nor do they pronounce
words in a sophisticated way. But they are voices full of life. They ring
true and they carry with them that good humour and readiness to fight
that make certain moments in life beautiful.

It was the miners' wives who forced the strike to survive for almost
a year. It was these laughing, almost childlike voices that lived through
the harsh struggles and rarely weakened. But a minute later they were
drowned out by the sound of galloping police horses closing the way
to Trafalgar Square.

When it was time to leave we sat for a few moments on the kerb of
a pavement. Anne looked at me in her smiling way and said, 'If the
miners' union declares the strike at an end this will not mean that we
have failed. We will continue to fight by other means until we win.'

Feminism and socialism

'Look,' Hilary said to me. 'Look how some people sleep in London
during the winter months.' I followed the angry gesture of her hand as
she pointed to the human bodies, to the men and women and children
sleeping in cardboard boxes in the shelter of the Royal Festival Hall. My
eyes strayed to the beautiful concert hall lit up in the night, to the
opulence that still lingers over the rich quarters of London, to the waters
of the nearby Thames, then back to these people lying on the ground.
I felt my heart held in a vice.

'A few days ago,' Hilary went on, 'the *Daily Express* published an item
about a woman called Hadow who died recently. In her will she donated
one and three-quarter million pounds which was all she possessed, to the
care of animals.[5] I'm not against being kind to animals, but I'm against
a system that permits animals to inherit millions of pounds and obliges
human beings to sleep on the ground during the icy winter nights.'

Hilary is a professor in Oxford. She describes herself as a socialist feminist and as not belonging to Oxford society. 'Oxford University,' she says, 'is one of the most conservative British universities, and this makes me very proud of the fact that last week the Oxford authorities refused to bestow an honorary doctor's degree on Margaret Thatcher.'

My first meeting with Hilary had taken place in Oxford at the house of a woman named Troth. She is the daughter of a rich family, and her father is a member of the Conservative Party. In Oxford she started to read about socialism and became interested. She joined the Labour Party and married a Marxist. 'One of the problems we have,' she said to me, 'is that I have become a vegetarian, whereas my husband loves meat and tries to provoke me by filling the freezer up with quantities of choice cuts which I have to cook for him.'

'Why doesn't he cook them himself?'

She shrugged her shoulders. 'He's really too busy to be able to cook, you know. Politics takes up a lot of his time.'

We sat near the fire chatting. Troth said, 'I don't think women can be liberated under a capitalist system. Socialism for me is not only a question of class struggle. Women must struggle not only against class oppression, but against patriarchy also. We concentrate essentially on fighting the oppression exercised against women, and I think that the women's liberation movement has made important contributions to some of the sciences and helped to change many concepts that at one time were considered fundamental. This is true not only of the medical sciences but also of other areas such as biology, psychology, philosophy, history and the social sciences. Now in many universities there are departments of women's studies.' She went off to the kitchen and came back with a tray of tea things.

Meanwhile Hilary was speaking. 'In more progressive universities like Essex, Kent, Warwick and Sussex, departments of women's studies have been established. But in the more conservative universities such as Oxford they do not exist, and most of those in charge are resisting such a step.'

Troth picked up from where she had left off. 'We started our activities by establishing a Natural Childbirth Trust.'

'What does that mean?' I asked.

She went to get the teapot and sugar, then came back with them in her hands. She answered my questions as she filled up our cups. 'It means having a baby without medical intervention and training women to do it themselves.' She laughed in a ringing voice, then went on. 'In the Victorian era doctors refused to use anaesthetics during labour because the Bible says that women would give birth to their children in sorrow and pain. But later on, Queen Victoria issued directives permitting the use of anaesthetics.' Now her laughter rang out again. 'We have discovered that a woman can give birth to a child without either pain or anaesthetics or sorrow.'

That day a number of other women were present at a gathering in Troth's house. Five of them lived in a village called Cholsey fifteen miles from Oxford: Ginny, Caroline and three other women, all of whom were housewives. They had started a group called National Housewives Register for Lively Minded Women. Working together had helped their ideas to develop further, and had led them to join first the Labour Party and later the women's peace movement. Some of them had been arrested during the demonstrations of March 1982 directed against the installation of cruise missile bases in Britain.

One of the members of this group, Marlene, was a Communist. She had been born in Cholsey and both her parents had been members of the Communist Party. Eventually her father had left it to join the Labour Party, but her mother had stayed on as a member.

'In 1968,' Marlene said, 'there was a split in the Communist Party and we formed the Communist Party of Britain. The main area of disagreement with the orthodox party is on the issue of what we call the "British road to socialism". We believe that this road will necessarily be extraparliamentary. Although I work with the group of women we have been talking about, I also share in the activities of the Committee for Women within our party.'

Marlene's words launched a long discussion about the relationship between the women's movement and socialist parties. During the rally in support of the miners' strike held in Hyde Park I had met a woman named Bea Campbell who was one of the leaders of the Communist Party, and I now remembered the views she had expressed on this subject. To her, being a party member and being involved in the activities of the women's wing within the party were very important for whatever work she undertook in the women's movement in general. There was no contradiction between the two. On the contrary they were mutually supportive. She said that problems of class, sex and race were interlinked. 'Yet we cannot give the same emphasis to all three at all times. There are moments when one of the three is a priority and race or sex are pushed into the background. At other moments race or sex could come into the foreground.' My contention to her had been that left-wing movements tended to push sex to the background at all times, in other words neglected it, avoided giving it a rightful place. The fear among left-wing movements was that problems related to women's status and women's role could militate against the development of the class struggle and confuse its issues. It was a matter both of understanding and of practice. The women at the Oxford meeting considered socialist feminism as a movement that refused to postpone or tone down the struggle for women's liberation in order to give emphasis to the class struggle. They believed that both had to go hand in hand.

Later on, when I met Joan Ruddock, chairwoman of CND (the Campaign for Nuclear Disarmament), she expressed the same views. We had lunch together in a small restaurant opposite her office in Reading. 'Yes,' she said. 'I am a socialist feminist. But I am also active in the peace movement and in the struggle against nuclear war. I am a member of the Labour Party and intend to stand for Parliament. Political activity in the area of women's movements should be undertaken through Parliament and also by extraparliamentary means.'

I found the same concepts reflected again in my discussion with Glenys Kinnock, wife of the then Labour Party leader Neil Kinnock. I felt she was a woman who had made her way in the political movement as an independent personality and through many years of effort. She is active in the women's movement as well as in the peace movement and has done a lot in support of the miners' wives. She invited me to her house in South Ealing and we had a long talk over tea and biscuits. 'I am a wife and a mother but I am not dependent on my husband in any way. I became a member of the Labour Party at the age of sixteen long before I married. My father was an active member of the Labour Party and played a role in my anti-colonialist position. In 1956 when the British invaded Egypt I heard my father say angrily, "It's their canal."' I asked about her job and she told me that she was a teacher but had not gone to work because the teachers were on strike. 'The government has reduced the wages of teachers by thirty per cent,' Glenys said. 'Thatcher can hit out at the miners' strike because coal can be imported from Poland or the United States. But she can't import teachers from abroad.'

Valerie Wise was chairwoman of the Women's Committee of the Greater London Council (GLC). She was a tall, blonde woman, twenty-nine years old. Her mother, Audrey Wise, was an active member of Parliament, and Valerie was brought up in a family where politics was part of daily life. As a results she joined the Labour Party at the age of fifteen.

I met Valerie in her big office at the GLC's huge offices at County Hall. We had lunch together in the cafeteria. She too calls herself a socialist feminist, and for further precision she added, 'I am anti-sexist, anti-racist, anti-imperialist, anti-Zionist. But I'm also against hetero-sexism.' She added with a laugh, 'Meaning that I'm not opposed to lesbian groups. Through the Women's Committee we give financial support to more than six hundred women's groups. But the government wants to abolish the GLC. I am therefore engaged in the campaign that has been launched against the abolition of the GLC. I believe in political action through parliament and by other means.'

Many women in Britain belong to the movement that calls itself socialist feminist. And most women writers in the country seem to be favourable to the ideas of socialist feminism. That is what I was given to understand by Michèle Roberts, who is herself a writer and whom I met in a café near Piccadilly. She sat opposite me on the other side of the small table, tranquil and yet as nervous as a butterfly. She said in a quiet voice, 'But the problem that faces most feminist women thinkers and writers is not the choice between capitalism and socialism. We know that women can never be liberated under capitalism. But socialist women need a new consciousness, or, to put it differently, a new unconsciousness. We have to shift from raising feminist consciousness to raising feminist unconsciousness.'

The following evening I met a group of women writers at dinner in a Covent Garden restaurant. Present were Germaine Greer, Marilyn French, Debbie Taylor and myself. Marilyn French was very much in favour of the idea that feminists need to shift from raising 'consciousness' to raising 'unconsciousness'. But Germaine Greer saw things differently. 'We have to shift from the First World to the Third World.' 'To do what?' asked Debbie Taylor with the disarming charm she brought to everything. And thus we found ourselves launched on one of the discussions I had heard whenever an international conference brought women from the so-called First World and the so-called Third World together.

This ongoing discussion is undoubtedly important, but it is too complex an issue to be dealt with in a few lines here. It is perhaps necessary to consider one point, though. Nobody can deny that, starting from the sixties, feminist writers, and in particular socialist feminist writers like Sheila Rowbotham in England, have played an important role in developing feminist thought not only in their own countries but also in other parts of the world. Many of them believe, however, that feminist struggles in the practical and ideological fields are limited to the Western capitalist world, and that women's liberation movements in other countries owe their impulsion and their ideas exclusively to what has been done, said or written by feminists of the First World. For example, Sheila Rowbotham herself writes: 'Demands like monogamy, birth control, education, the right to organize were borrowed from Western capitalism.'[6] But this is not correct. Methods of birth control were known and used by women in Egypt, as well as in other Arab and African countries, many centuries ago. Similarly the struggle for monogamy and against other patriarchal customs and values has a very long history in our countries.

In a later passage, Sheila goes on to say: 'In the 1920s an incipient feminism emerged in developing countries which resembled the early "equal rights" feminism of middle-class women in capitalist countries.'[7] But Victoria Brittain, who is a journalist on the *Guardian* newspaper and a friend of mine, does not agree. Over a glass of wine in the living room of her house she told me, 'Such sweeping statements are liable to lead us astray for two reasons. Firstly, ideas and their practices take different forms according to the societies in which we live. The struggle of women in the Third World countries took forms that are perhaps not recognizable by the criteria that Western feminists use. Second, the Third World is not a homogeneous bloc, and to reach such a conclusion without making a concrete study of the historical movement of women in each country is rather a hasty way of dealing with social movements.'

Women's reproductive rights

Tindle Manor Building in London is a huge modern construction with many corridors and many rooms, where groups of women were meeting, or talking, or moving around, were doing things all the time.

After a while I felt that I was visiting a feminist hive. But these feminists were very different from the ones I had met before, although all had in common their position against the Conservative (Tory) government and against policies that had come to be known as Thatcherism.

The groups I had spoken to previously, whether socialist feminists, miners' wives, or immigrants, were opposed to what they called the 'monetarist' policies of Thatcher. The groups I met in Tindle Manor Building, however, were opposed to another category of policies implemented by the Thatcher government, namely what they called 'moralist' policies.

We were sitting round a table in one of the numerous rooms, a group of about twenty women of different ages, some still very young while others were in their middle years or older. Nicky, a short blonde woman, explained to me what they meant by 'moralist' policies: 'The revival of Victorian values that the Tories are fostering means that women are left holding the baby while the men go off to war.'

One of the women around the table intervened: 'Doesn't this remind you of Hitler?' Then she added, 'Perhaps we should tell you a little about the groups in this building.'

I soon discovered that my earlier impression of a 'feminist hive' was correct. For Tindle Manor houses a large number of feminist groups including Rights of Women (ROW), the Women's Aid Federation, Women's Aid Refuges, a rape crisis centre, a battered women's group, a prostitution group, a lesbian group, a health and therapy centre, a legal advice group, Women Against Pornography, Women Against Rape, Women's Reproduction Rights group and others.

I spent several hours in the building moving from one group to another. Each one of them was involved in one form or another of activity aimed at providing services to women and helping to solve many of the problems they face. Such groups have spread rapidly not only in Britain but in many countries of Europe, and in the United States. Amongst the most recent is a group constituted in England under the name Women's Reproductive Rights. When I asked what was meant by 'women's biological rights', a phrase that often came up during the discussion, the woman who seemed to be in charge of the group said, 'We women have the right to determine our own sexuality, the right to decide if and when to have children. We must also have the right to comprehensive national health services. They are necessary in enabling us to back up our decisions, whatever these decisions may be, and irrespective of whether we are married or not, black or white, poor or rich, heterosexual or lesbians.'

When these women used the word 'lesbian', it came naturally into their conversation, without a hint of reservation, just like anything else that was an integral part of daily life. As I moved from room to room, one of the groups I met was Lesbian Mothers' Rights. It had been constituted with the aim of defending the rights of lesbian women and particularly those who had children. Among the main issues was custody of the children and these women's rights as mothers to bring up children, but there were a whole range of other matters, including defending lesbians against discrimination in legal matters, education, social services and social security.

A long discussion about lesbianism and lesbians ensued. I noticed that the lesbians were divided into two main groups. One group considered that lesbianism is the way to women's liberation and that the political and sexual future of women lies in lesbianism. The second group considered lesbianism as a transitional stage the aim of which was to rid women of their need for men and replace this by an alternative. To them this alternative was not only sexual but also emotional, social and familial. I found that there were a growing number of families that can be considered 'new female families', in which two female partners rear the children together. The central idea in the thinking of this second group is that the absence of an alternative to the 'male' makes men authoritarian and 'irredeemable' (meaning recalcitrant to any change or improvement).

I asked them, 'And now are men any better than before?' One of the young women present, a tall, blonde girl, laughed before she replied, 'Not at all. Now the men are bypassing their need for women by building relations with one another. That's why the gay movement is growing and gay families and clubs are spreading all over the country.' Another young woman intervened. 'I was lesbian but I discovered that in a lesbian relationship, too, inequality exists. One partner tries to dominate the other. That's why I have become bisexual. This gives a woman more freedom.'

I also attended a meeting with the Women Against Rape group. The women present were exchanging ideas about the causes of violence and rape, and I noticed a tendency to consider aggression as being a male characteristic. When I asked, 'Aren't women sometimes violent and aggressive too?', a white-skinned woman with short grey hair answered, 'Of course, but it's always a reaction to the aggression of men. Violence in men is an intrinsic part of their nature, it's biological instinct. Men love war but women love peace. That's why the peace movement is mainly composed of women.'

I said that I found it difficult to accept such statements. If we did so we would find ourselves prisoners of Freud's concept that 'Anatomy is destiny'.

A tall slender girl who had been silent all the time now intervened. 'I agree with you completely, Nawal. And I must tell you that there is a split in the women's movement around this issue. One sector of the movement considers that violence is a male characteristic and that man is therefore the enemy. A spokeswoman of this group maintains that the movement of the women of Greenham Common and the political movement against nuclear war have diluted the feminist movement because women have diverted their attention and efforts to so-called superior issues. According to her, nuclear war was only one of the symptoms of male supremacist culture, and women should not put their energies into attacking the symptom, instead of attacking the fundamental cause, which is perhaps too dangerous to confront, namely the man next door.'[8]

The young woman continued, 'But I and many other women do not believe that violence is a male biological characteristic and peace and gentleness are female qualities. If so, it would be difficult to explain Thatcher.' She smiled.

There was silence in the room; perhaps many felt that peace and war *are* linked to issues of social justice rather than to our hormones. I moved on to another group sitting around a long table. One of the pamphlets I picked up was entitled, *Surrogate Motherhood*, and when I asked if this was a new 'biological right' a young woman sitting by my side said, 'Not yet. But we try to protect surrogates from any form of exploitation which could be exercised against them by private profit-making organizations. Poor women can be used for reproductive purposes, as wombs for producing babies, and a black-market situation could then be created. This is especially so since under current British law any woman who undergoes a pregnancy is legally the mother of the resulting child, no matter whose egg is used.'

One of the women asked me, 'Have you followed the discussion going on on the television about embryo research?'

I nodded, so she added, 'What do you think about it?'

'I think it's a false issue although I support research that gives women more freedom.'

'I agree with you. They only talk about the right to life when they discuss embryos and foetuses. They have never made a fuss about the thousands of black people who are killed and maimed in South Africa.'

A woman sitting at the other end of the table commented, 'Defending the rights of the unborn means denying the rights of women. All the issues related to this question are being raised to deprive women of some rights such as abortion.'

'Yes,' said the young girl by my side. 'But the problem is that reproductive technology such as artificial wombs, sperm banks, embryo freezing, trans-species fertilization, cloning of embryos etcetera – all these can be useful to some women if properly directed. But scientific research is male-dominated and is usually directed to serve men and not women.'

The woman sitting at the head of the table made a final remark: 'Anyhow, unless some clear justification is found and has clear public approval, we see no reason to spend money on cloning of embryos in a country that cannot afford to provide adequate health care out of the national purse.'

Flying thoughts

I rested my head against the back of my seat, and left my body to enjoy the deep feeling of relaxation which comes after effort, the gentle lift of the plane rising higher into the sky, the sensation of abandoning myself to the care of other people. I stretched my legs over my handbag swollen with books and magazines from feminist bookshops, from Silver

Moon, Sisterwrite and others. Feminist bookshops and publishing houses had multiplied in Britain during the seventies and eighties, a reflection of the growing interest in feminist ideas. Feminist magazines such as *Spare Rib*, *Out Write* and others had played a role in reflecting different aspects of the women's movement for liberation both in Britain and in some of the developing countries of Africa, Asia and Latin America.[9] Feminist films and organizations such as Cinema of Women (COW) had succeeded in breaking the monopoly of men where the visual arts are concerned. I had seen a film called *A Free Country*, which deals with the subjugation of Irish women and the efforts they were making to liberate themselves and their country from British oppression.

Through my mind flashed the many faces I had seen, and the many things I had heard during the previous two weeks. I had seen so many women, heard so many voices, watched the play of feelings on their faces. But one thing I had perhaps known before I arrived, and now it had impressed itself indelibly on my heart and mind. Here I had been in a country where the head of state and the prime minister were both women. And yet the rights of British women were more in jeopardy than they had ever been in recent times. This confirmed what I had learned from my own experience in Egypt. What really mattered were the economics and the politics of the system under which women lived. What mattered were the interests of the class or classes that held sway over the system. What mattered was the political awareness of women, the strength of their organizations and their ability to fight.

I also knew, better than before, from my visit that the feminist movement in Britain as a whole was a progressive and liberating force, which continued to enrich the political and social life of the country with new ideas and new forms of struggle, and was also contributing to the development of the feminist movement in other countries through its experiences, through its successes and its failures, through the painful birth of new concepts, of new ways of seeing the problems of women and men and of solving them.

Parts of the British feminist movement might show a tendency to adopt extremist positions either in the area of conceptualization, or in the daily political and social struggle, or in both. But this is natural, especially for a movement that has a relatively short history and is involved in a very complex and difficult struggle. With time, and by dint of effort, even though setbacks are inevitable, issues will become clearer, and forms of action will be more effective.

Revolution and change are a break from all that is usual, customary and known. They are necessarily accompanied by anger against all forms of oppression and by great enthusiasm for justice and freedom. At all moments of my visit I felt myself involved both mentally and emotionally with what was happening in the feminist movement in Britain, even though I disagreed with some of the views expressed to me. It made me more optimistic, more confident, happy to feel that we women of Egypt and the Arab countries were not alone, and that we have friends in Britain and in many other countries of the world.

As the airplane crossed over the Mediterranean shores of Egypt the sun shone brightly and the sea was azure. I was happy to be home. I was happy to have lived this rich experience with my feminist sisters in Britain, and looked forward to the future which I knew was full of hope.

[Edited version of an essay first published in English in 1985. Translated from the Arabic by Sherif Hetata]

Notes

1. Greenham Common in Berkshire was one of the military bases chosen to hold the UK's 160 cruise missiles. See Barbara Harford and Sarah Hopkins, *Greenham Common: Women at the Wire*, Women's Press, London, 1984.

2. Since this essay was written, the cruise missiles have been removed from the base, the ultimate testament to the women's camp's success.

3. *Observer*, 17 February 1985, p. 1.

4. Sheila Rowbotham, 'Women's Liberation and the New Politics', in *Dreams and Dilemmas: Collected Writings of Sheila Rowbotham*, Virago, London, 1983, p. 20.

5. *Daily Express*, 14 February 1985, p. 1.

6. Sheila Rowbotham, *Women, Resistance and Revolution*, Allen Lane at the Penguin Press, 1972, p. 202.

7. Ibid., p. 203.

8. See *Breaching the Peace*, a collection of radical feminist papers, published by Only Women Press, London, 1983, pp. 18–21.

9. Since this was written, the Sisterwrite bookshop, and *Spare Rib* and *Out Write* magazines have all closed down.

Index